LLEWELLYN'S

2012

Magical Almanac

Featuring

Elizabeth Barrette, Deborah Blake, Blake Octavio Blair,
Boudica, Tabitha Bradley, Calantirniel,
Dallas Jennifer Cobb, Autumn Damiana,
Raven Digitalis, Ellen Dugan, Denise Dumars,
Emyme, Sybil Fogg, Ember Grant, Magenta Griffith,
James Kambos, Melanie Marquis, Graham Miller,
Mickie Mueller, Diana Rajchel, Janina Renée,
Suzanne Ress, Laurel Reufner, Harmony Usher,
Peggy Wheeler, Tess Whitehurst, and Abby Willowroot

Llewellyn's 2012 Magical Almanac

Editor/Designer: Ed Day

Cover Illustration: © Tammy Shane

Calendar Pages Design: Andrea Neff and Michael Fallon

Calendar Pages Illustrations: © Fiona King

Interior Illustrations © Meraylah Allwood: pages 21, 24, 95, 102, 253, 256, 293, 296, 335, 338; © Neil Brigham: pages 47, 51, 76, 82, 151, 153, 311, 314; © Carol Coogan: pages 13, 53, 54, 57, 85, 133, 135, 137, 229, 246, 249, 282, 286, 288, 291; © Chris Down: pages 68, 71, 74, 105, 109, 155, 157, 160, 349, 353; © Kathleen Edwards: pages 35, 39, 42, 127, 130, 274, 279, 319, 322, 340; © Paul Hoffman: pages 62, 66, 119, 239, 242, 270, 273, 308; © Wen Hsu: pages 27, 31, 114, 230, 235, 258, 263, 266, 328, 331; © Mickie Mueller: pages 15, 17, 87, 91, 139, 145, 147, 298, 303, 304.

Illustration pages 78, 81, 341–343, 345 by Llewellyn Art Department.

Clip Art Illustrations: Dover Publications

Special thanks to Amber Wolfe for the use of daily color and incense correspondences. For more detailed information, please see *Personal Alchemy* by Amber Wolfe.

You can order Llewellyn annuals and books from *New Worlds,* Llewellyn's catalog. To request a free copy of the catalog, call toll-free 1-877-NEW-WRLD or visit our website: www.llewellyn.com

Astrological data compiled and programmed by Rique Pottenger. Based on the earlier work of Neil F. Michelsen.

Llewellyn Worldwide Ltd.
2143 Wooddale Drive
Woodbury, MN 55125

About the Authors

ELIZABETH BARRETTE has been involved with the Pagan community for more than twenty years. She served as managing editor of *PanGaia* and Dean of Studies at the Grey School of Wizardry. Her *Composing Magic* explains how to write spells, rituals, and other Pagan material. She lives in central Illinois and enjoys magical crafts and gardening for wildlife. She has done much networking with Pagans in her area, including coffeehouse meetings and open sabbats. Other writing fields include speculative fiction and gender studies. http://ysabetwordsmith.livejournal.com/ http://gaiatribe.geekuniversalis.com http://reviewarchive.iblog.my.

DEBORAH BLAKE is a Wiccan High Priestess who has been leading Blue Moon Circle for many years. She is the author of *Circle, Coven and Grove, Everyday Witch A to Z, The Goddess is in the Details,* and *The Everyday Witch A to Z Spellbook,* all from Llewellyn. Deborah was a finalist in the Pagan Fiction Award Contest and her short story, "Dead and (Mostly) Gone," is included in *The Pagan Anthology of Short Fiction.* She is also working on a number of novels, most of them featuring a Witch, of course. When not writing, Deborah runs The Artisans' Guild and works as a jewelry maker, a tarot reader, an ordained minister, and an Intuitive Energy Healer. She lives in a hundred-year-old farmhouse in rural upstate New York with five cats who supervise all her activities, both magickal and mundane.

BLAKE OCTAVIAN BLAIR (Carrboro, N.C.) is an Eclectic IndoPagan Witch, psychic, tarot reader, freelance writer, energy worker, and a devotee of Lord Ganesha. He holds a degree in English and Religion from the University of Florida. Blake lives in the Piedmont Region of North Carolina with his beloved husband, an aquarium full of fish, and an indoor jungle of houseplants. Visit him at www.blakeoctavianblair.com or write to blake@blakeoctavianblair.com.

BOUDICA is reviews editor and co-owner of *The Wiccan/Pagan Times* and owner of *The Zodiac Bistro*, both online publications. A former New Yorker, she now resides with her husband and eight cats in Ohio.

Arizona author **TABITHA BRADLEY** is the author of eight books including *The Misadventures of Alex T'Kayn, Treasure Hunter,* and *Peacekeeper* as well as several articles for Llewellyn's *Witches' Datebook* and *Witches' Calendar.* In addition to writing, Tabitha is also a freelance book editor and professional digital artist. Her artistic work has been featured on the covers of her Dirandan Chronicles series for Renaissance as well as other books from the same publisher. She maintains a full gallery of her work on her blog, Diranda Studios. Tabitha lives in Bullhead City, Arizona, with her husband and two children.

LISA ALLEN/CALANTIRNIEL has been published in many Llewellyn annuals and has practiced many forms of natural spirituality since the early 1990s. She currently lives in western Montana with her husband, teenage daughter, and three young cats, while her older son is in college. She is a professional astrologer, tarot card reader, dowser, flower essence creator and practitioner, a ULC Reverend, Usui Reiki II, and a certified Master Herbalist. She has an organic garden, crochets professionally, and is co-creating Tië eldaliéva, "the Elven Path," a spiritual practice based on J. R. R. Tolkien's Middle-Earth stories. www.myspace.com/aartiana.

AUTUMN DAMIANA is a writer, artist, crafter, and amateur photographer, and has been a mostly solitary eclectic Witch for about fourteen years. She is passionate about eco-friendly living, and writes about this and her day-to-day walk on the Pagan path in her blog, "Sacred Survival in a Mundane World" at http://autumndamiana.blogspot.com/. When not writing or making art, you can find her outside enjoying nature or investigating local history in

her hometown of San Jose, California. Contact her at autumnda-miana@gmail.com.

RAVEN DIGITALIS (Montana) is the author of *Planetary Spells & Rituals*, *Shadow Magick Compendium*, and *Goth Craft*, all from Llewellyn. He is a Neopagan Priest, cofounder of the "disciplined eclectic" tradition and training coven Opus Aima Obscuræ, and is a DJ. Also trained in Georgian Witchcraft and Buddhist philosophy, Raven is a Witch, Priest, and Empath. He holds a degree in anthropology and is also an animal rights activist, photographic artist, Tarot reader, and the co-owner of Twigs & Brews Herbs. www.ravendigitalis.com www.myspace.com/oakraven.

ELLEN DUGAN, the "Garden Witch," is an award-winning author and psychic-clairvoyant. A practicing Witch for more than twenty-seven years, she is the author of many Llewellyn books; her newest are *A Garden Witch's Herbal* and *Book of Witchery*. Ellen encourages folks to personalize their spellcraft, to go outside and get their hands dirty, so they can discover the wonder and magick of the natural world. Ellen and her family live in Missouri. www.ellendugan.com.

REV. DENISE "DION-ISIS" DUMARS, M.A. serves Thoth as a writer, a professor of writing, and a writer's representative. She is a founder of the Iseum of Isis Paedusis, which was chartered by the Fellowship of Isis in 2001. She and the other Iseum Adepti hold seasonal rituals at Pacific Unitarian Church in beautiful Rancho Palos Verdes, California. She hopes to visit Egypt some day, but in the meantime she volunteers for the American Cinematheque at Grauman's Egyptian Theatre on Hollywood Boulevard.

EMYME is a solitary practitioner who resides in a multigenerational, multicat household in southern New Jersey. Hobbies that renew her are: gardening, sewing and crafts, and home care and repair. Emyme has self-published a children's book about mending families after divorce and remarriage. She is an avid diarist; dabbles in

poetry; creates her own blessings, incantations, and spells; and is currently writing a series of fantasy fiction stories set in the twenty-fifth century. Her personal mantra is summed up in four words: Curiosity, Objectivity, Quality, Integrity. catsmeow24@verizon.net.

SYBIL FOGG, also known as Sybil Wilen, has been a practicing Witch for more than twenty years. She chose to use her mother's maiden name in Pagan circles to honor her grandparents. She's also a wife, mother, writer, teacher, and belly dancer. She lives in Portland, Maine, with her husband and their plethora of children. www.sybilwilen.com.

EMBER GRANT is a poet and freelance writer and has been contributing to the Llewellyn Annuals for ten years. Her first book from Llewellyn, *Magical Candle Crafting*, was published in March 2011.

MAGENTA GRIFFITH has been a Witch for more than thirty years and a High Priestess for more than twenty. She is a founding member of the coven Prodea, which has been celebrating rituals since 1980, as well as being a member of various Pagan organizations such as Covenant of the Goddess. She presents classes and workshops at a variety of events around the Midwest. She shares her home with a small black cat and a large collection of books.

JAMES KAMBOS is a regular contributor to Llewellyn's annuals. Born and raised in Appalachia, his magical traditions have been influenced by the folk magic ways of Appalachia and by his Greek heritage. When not writing, he enjoys painting and cooking. He currently lives in the beautiful hill country of southeastern Ohio.

MELANIE MARQUIS is a full-time Witch and writer. She's the founder of United Witches global coven, and she also organizes a Pagan group in Denver. She's written for many New Age and Pagan publications. A nondenominational Witch, she specializes in practical spellwork, tarot, and spirit communication, teaching a personalized approach to the magickal arts. Her first book with

Llewellyn, *The Witch's Bag of Tricks: Personalize your Magic & Kickstart Your Craft*, was released in July 2011. injoyart@yahoo.com.

GRAHAM MILLER is a practicing solo eclectic Pagan. He is the author of *The Busy Pagan* and two novels: *The Loch* and *The Madman's Guide to Britain*. He is also a professional tarot and Rune reader. In his spare time, Graham gardens, makes jewelry, carves stone, and casts statues from melted aluminium cans. He has a fascination for stone circles and prehistory. Graham lives in a small village in rural Kent in the southeast of the United Kingdom with his wife and three children.

MICKIE MUELLER is an award-winning and critically acclaimed Pagan spiritual artist. She is Co-High Priestess of Coven of the Greenwood, an ordained Pagan Minister. She is also a Reiki healing master/teacher in the Usui Shiki Royoho tradition. Mickie is the illustrator of *The Well Worn Path* and *The Hidden Path* and the illustrator/writer of *The Voice of the Trees: A Celtic Ogham Oracle*. She is a regular article contributor to Llewellyn's publications, and her art is published internationally. www.mickiemuellerart.com.

Jacci Sutton, simply known as Owl or **PANITEOWL** in the Pagan community, lives in the foothills of the Appalachians. She and her husband have acres of natural woodland and are developing a private retreat for spiritual awareness and host two annual events on Owl Mountain. She is founder and Elder High Priestess of the Mystic Wicca Tradition. Jacci has given workshops at Pagan events on the East Coast and in Canada. Her articles and poetry have been published in various Pagan periodicals and websites, as well as in Llewellyn's annual publications. Look for her on Facebook!

DIANA RAJCHEL lives in Minneapolis, where she engages with the city spirit daily. A full-time writer, artist, and priestess, she enjoys the world around her and connects to the spiritual through her creative efforts. http://dianarajchel.com.

JANINA RENÉE is a scholar of folklore, psychology, medical anthropology, the material culture of magic, ritual studies, history, and literature. She has written *Tarot Spells, Playful Magic, Tarot: Your Everyday Guide, Tarot for a New Generation,* and *By Candlelight.* Janina continues to work on multiple books, including ongoing research projects into the ways folk magic and medicinal techniques relate to medical hypnosis, as well as the modulation of Asperger syndrome and other sensory processing problems. http://TarotMagicAdventures.blogspot.com.

LAUREL REUFNER's mother can verify that she grew up a "wild child" in farming country. She's been a polytheist for nearly twenty years. Ten of those years have been spent writing for Llewellyn's almanacs, which has been wonderful. Laurel really enjoys writing about topics that grab her attention, such as history and mythology. She currently calls southeast Ohio home, where she lives with her wonderful husband, two wild children, and her best friend. One can find her blog at oaknolive.blogspot.com.

SUZANNE RESS has been writing nonfiction and fiction for more than twenty-five years. She is an accomplished self-taught gardener, beekeeper, silversmith, and mosaicist. She lives in the woods at the foot of the Alps in northern Italy with her husband, daughter, two dogs, three horses, and an elusive red stag.

HARMONY USHER is a freelance writer, researcher, and social worker in small-town Ontario. She shares her world with two creative, dynamic teenagers and is blessed to celebrate life, love, and the phases of the Moon with a fantastic circle of like-spirited women.

PEGGY WHEELER has been writing for over thirty-five years. Her work includes magazine articles, technical writing, a book about an oracle she invented, and an ongoing column for an online spirituality column. Peggy's poetry has appeared in national anthologies

and magazines, won first prize in the *Evergreen Women's Press* poetry contest, received honorable mentions from both The Academy of American Poets and the L.A. Poetry Festival contests; and has been nominated for a Rhysling award. Peggy was chosen as one of only twelve UCLA students to study with Robert Pinsky, former United States Poet Laureate. Her master's degree is in creative writing.

TESS WHITEHURST is an advocate of self-love, self-expression, and personal freedom. She's a Llewellyn author, columnist for *NewWitch* magazine, intuitive counselor, and feng shui practitioner. Her website and e-newsletter *Good Energy* include simple rituals, meditations, and musings for everyday magical living. Tess lives in Venice Beach, California, with two magical cats, one musical boyfriend, and a constant stream of visiting hummingbirds. www.tesswhitehurst.com.

ABBY WILLOWROOT is an artist, writer, metalsmith, and Priestess and Goddess. Her online goddess temple is the Spiral Goddess Grove. Serving the metaphysicacl community since 1967, Abby's work reflects many diverse cultural and artistic influences. Abby has nine pieces in the Smithsonian's permanent collection. Creator of the Spiral Goddess, Abby's Goddess Art and Willowroot Wands have been featured in books and museum shows. Llewellyn regularly publishes articles by Ms. Willowroot.

GAIL WOOD has been a Witch, Priestess, and Tarot Reader for nearly thirty years. She is a High Priestess and Elder in the Raven-Myst Circle, a tradition of American Wicca. She is the author of four books and numerous articles on Pagan and Wiccan themes. www.rowdygoddess.com or darkmoonwitch@earthlink.net.

Table of Contents

Earth Magic

The Green Man:
Spirit of Abundance

by Mickie Mueller

The woods were dense with leaves and the air thick with the heady scent of pine needles and leaves warm on the forest floor. Sunlight filtered through the leaves, backlit overhead. The great trunks stood like brown rustic pillars among the vast green as their branches arched above like the buttresses of some great, ancient cathedral. From time to time the breeze would pick up a bit, rustling the trees above and causing them to sing in a voice that could only be understood by some arcane magic. It was there in the woods that I met the Green Man.

When I say met, I don't mean that he walked right up, tipped a leafy green hat, and introduced himself. He existed there in the woods as part of it, a spiritual entity, and the spirit of the green, growing wilderness. Anyone can find him in the woods; he is the essence of life, growth, and abundance. You'll find him in other places, too. He snickers as the leafy plant breaks through the concrete sidewalk. He snoozes in the lawn beneath the trees on a summer afternoon. He roars with pride as a long-abandoned residence is overtaken by vines, weeds, and saplings.

The Green Man is commonly seen as garden ornaments and architectural detail throughout the ages. His leafy countenance is a recurring theme in medieval art and decoration. The origins of Green Man are very deep and far-reaching. He is a representation of the spirit of nature, of the forest, and of the growing seasons. Green Man is the joyous and laughing God of growth and woods. He is an excellent spirit to call upon for assistance when you are looking for prosperity and abundance. He also represents renewal and the endless ability for life to find a way.

A Green Man State of Mind

One of the most well-known and widespread Pagan god images is the Green Man, also known as Jack-in-the-Green or The Man in the Oak. Let's talk about ways to bring the spirit of Green Man into your life to help enhance growth, prosperity, and abundance.

Deep down, I think humans understand that our personal abundance and prosperity depends on the fruitfulness of the earth. Even these days when we've covered half the earth with concrete, this truth still holds true. That must be why the foliate Green Man has been so prevalent through time as an ornament and even was carried over into church décor in medieval churches—because deep down, we know we need him, no matter what.

Green Man is a generous spirit. When working with him, showing generosity of your own will get his atten-

tion and bring his spirit into your life. Obviously, Green Man also is more likely to be joyous to share energy with people who care for the environment; he's about growth, renewal, and life. If you're going to be working magic with Green Man, don't be chucking your fast-food trash out your car window. Anything that you can do for the environment—even something small—will help to show the spirit of Green Man that you're genuine and will help get your energies aligned with the energies of the green earth. Get a stainless steel water bottle to replace your bottled water. How about offering your favorite tree some fertilizer? Respect for all living things is another great way to connect with this leafy spirit—catch a spider and release it outside instead of squashing it. While at the garden center, if you see a potted plant knocked over, pick it up and scoop the soil back into the pot. Try donating your old clothes instead of throwing them away. You get the idea. Generosity toward others and the environment are the kinds of things that Green Man smiles upon.

Now you are working in alignment with Green Man energy, and you're ready to start working with him magically to bring prosperity, abundance, and renewal into your life. Here are some spells you can use, and perhaps they will inspire you to create some of your own.

Green Man Prosperity Magnet Spell

Purchase a Green Man magnet or acquire a copyright-free image of Green Man and make your own. The Green Man is such an old figure that there are many cool, classic images of him in the public domain available for you. You can put a picture of Green Man on a printable magnet available from any office supply store, or glue a round magnet on the back of a wooden disk and paint or glue a Green Man on the front. In a small envelope, place a one-dollar bill, a sprinkle of basil, and a leaf from your favorite tree, and then seal the envelope. Using the magnet, stick

the envelope to your fridge. Empower it with the following charm:

> *Draw to me the mighty green*
> *Prosperity shall come to me.*
> *Open my opportunities*
> *Drawing forth magnetically.*

Green Man Better Business Spell

Whether you are a salesperson working for commission for a big company or you sell on Etsy or eBay, who doesn't want to increase business? You'll need a box with an environmental motif. (It can be green, wooden, or have an image of a tree, leaves, or Green Man on it.) On a piece of paper, write a list of business goals. These should be written in the present tense, as if they are already true. Instead of, "I'm hoping to sell five items every week," write "I sell five items every week." You can also write plans to promote your business, reorganize, or offer new products. In the box, place a cinnamon stick, an acorn or nut of some kind, and the contents of one tea bag of chamomile tea. You can burn incense with a woodsy or pine scent and light a green candle. Now summon up the aid of the Green Man, by reciting aloud:

> *By leaf, bark and seed, and flower,*
> *I hereby summon up the power,*
> *Mighty Green Man I do implore,*
> *Bring more business through my door.*

Now read the list that you made to the Green Man. Then fold the paper three times (toward you), and put it in the box.

Let the candle and incense burn out. Work on completing your ideas for promoting and reorganization tactics, and drop a penny in the box every time you do.

Never-Give-Up Green Man Spell

If the Green Man is one thing, he's tenacious. He never gives up. He is after all, the spirit of life and, as they say, life finds a way. We all get to a point where we feel like we want to give up, or give in. Whether you're trying to save money for something special, find a job, or get a promotion, sometimes it feels like you just can't get ahead and you might want to throw in the towel. But that's when you never should—because something great might be just around the corner if you can just hang in there. When you feel hopeless, call upon the friendly leafy spirit to nurture your dreams and help you power through. You can do it!

You'll need a piece of jewelry either with a Green Man face or leaves/flowers, a gold candle, a green candle, and olive oil. Anoint both candles with olive oil, and rub what's left on your fingers on your piece of jewelry. Place the jewelry piece between the candles, green on the left, gold on the right. Light both candles and empower your piece of jewelry with the following charm:

> *I carry Green Man within my heart*
> *My dreams coming true shall be at this start,*
> *Teach me to grow, thrive, and be strong,*
> *I'll carry your teachings all the day long.*

Then pick up your jewelry and, holding it, have a heart-to-heart with Green Man—tell him what you wish to accomplish and ask for his blessings on your task. Tell him of the things that you know you must do to complete these goals. Never ask him to give you power or strength, but ask him to help you find the strength within yourself. This is the key. Place the jewelry back between the candles and allow them to burn out, charging it with perseverance, growth, and success. Now wear your empowered Green Man symbol every day as a reminder of his guidance, and never, ever give up.

We should always remember that we have a friend in the spirit of the Green Man. After all, it's his energy that feeds all of life on earth. His growing and life giving force is what maintains us. When we try to make a conscious effort to keep that balance in our everyday lives, the rewards can be abundant and manifest in ways both spiritual and physical.

Adventures of a High Priestess:

What You Need to Know about Building and Running a Coven

by Ellen Dugan

So are you thinking about starting your own coven? I don't know whether to applaud you—or offer to go get you a good stiff drink. All kidding aside, you are taking on a lot of work so you better be prepared for it on an emotional, intuitive, and physical level. Do you believe you are up to this task? To begin, you will need a few things: a great sense of humor, the patience of a saint, and finally, the organizational skills and the nerves of steel of a middle school phys ed teacher.

Remember gym class in middle school? Take a moment and build a mental picture. Mass chaos . . . kids running around the gymnasium, screaming and laughing at top volume, trying to look cool and coordinated. See over there? Those couple of show-offs who can do every sport perfectly? Then there is the rest of the gang who just wants to play, and another few kids who just want to blend in and not stand out—or to get picked on? Remember those days?

Why did I use this analogy? Because basically as the head of a coven or High Priest or Priestess, (which I will refer to here as the HPS), there are times when you are going to feel like the only adult in the room. Chaos will ensue and everyone else just wants to play—not be organized—and, sadly, you do NOT get a shiny silver whistle to get everyone's attention.

You could try turning the lights off on them and see if that gets a reaction.

Seriously though, running a magickal group is not for the faint of heart. Nor is it for those who are prone to whining. Why do I have to do everything? Can't someone else step up and lead for a change?

If you want to build a group and run a circle or a coven, you have to put whining aside. Sure, you can indulge in a little private

pity from time to time, but for the most part, ditch it. It will not be of any use to what you are trying to accomplish.

So how come I know all of this? Well because I am an HPS of my coven. My group was originally an open, mixed-magick tradition circle, which served us pretty well for the first few years. However, after a while, the lack of rules or structure almost destroyed the group.

So after much debate and soul-searching, we cleaned house. There were different magickal traditions in my coven, which made it a challenge, but also kept us sensitive to the similarities and the differences of our members. Keeping that in mind, we gathered the remaining members and all sat down together. We discussed what our goals were, and then worked on building a degree system, decided how to handle adding new members, and designed a code of conduct.

Was it easy? Hell no! Was it quick and nonstressful? Umm, excuse me. Do you think getting seven Witches to agree on anything is simple or quick? It only took about four months longer than we imagined to put everything in place. Then a few months later, on the first Full Moon of the year, we did a big formal group initiation ritual, which ended with handing out the degrees, dedicating the coven, and officially re-forming that circle into a coven.

That my friends, was the easy part. The tough part came afterward. But don't panic. Here are a few tips that will help you so your coven will run smoothly and successfully.

Tips to Running a Successful Coven

Get organized! Make a contact list. On this contact list should be the names of the members, their addresses, emails, home phones, and cell numbers. Make copies and hand 'em out. Get three-ring binders and start filling them up with your coven's info and rituals. That way you have everything together—a portable Coven Book of Shadows that you can grab and take with you when the group gets together.

Write a mission statement. Got any wanna-be writers in your coven? Get them busy. Choose a coven totem or colors, design a coven logo, and slip it in the front of your three-ringed binders. See what you can make or create. You could even create custom coven T-shirts and wear them when you attend a festival together.

Plan your meetings well in advance. My coven, for example, does this at our Yule get-together every year. Everyone brings along their new calendars for the coming year and we plot out our gatherings—for the whole year. Trust me, it really works out better.

Set up a free, private Yahoo group. This lets you send messages to the whole group quickly. You can also post pictures, rituals, recipes, spells, and coven business in files that only group members can access. A very handy tool.

Take turns hosting the coven meetings. Nobody wants to be the one to get stuck hosting every time. Give all your initiated and established members a chance to host. (Don't dump this on a newbie or a dedicant of the group. Give them at least a year to get comfortable.) Oh, and if you are all new, then take turns anyway, and things will go much more smoothly.

Whoever hosts the sabbat or Full Moon is responsible for writing and running the ritual. This gives everyone a chance to spread their wings and to grow. It also will give your group a chance to experience different magickal styles and personalities.

Keep everyone involved by taking turns teaching a topic at each meeting. Nobody should be sitting on the sidelines all the time. Plan this out in advance just like the meetings. For example: If Sally is hosting Midsummer, then Jet will talk about herb magick. Have yet a different person give a half-hour long lecture on a topic they know well. It gives them a chance to share, and it allows everyone to learn something new.

Remember, covens are classically about teaching, training, and personal advancement. Work toward increasing your skills, gaining your degrees within your own coven, and teaching the new members.

Have everyone bring a dish to share at the coven gathering. This way the host/hostess doesn't get stuck buying all the food. This is more friendly, practical, and fun.

Magick and study first—food and chatting last. Otherwise you gab all night and nobody feels like working any magick later. Been there, done that. However, if you keep the focus on the magick and the spirituality—not just the social aspects—your group will thrive.

Watch the gossip. What happens in coven, STAYS in coven. Yes, you will know all about Gillian's goofball of a spouse and the problems with Janie's job. But keep your mouth shut to outsiders. Think of it like family. Yes, you and your sister can certainly discuss your Mom's horrific habit of wearing loud paisley prints, but if someone from outside the family makes a remark about it—on cue and together—both of you go to war at the insult.

Yes, you will bitch and complain about each other from time to time, but you should also be willing to go to the wall for each other as well. A coven is a magickal family. You are all sisters and or brothers in the Craft. When I call a covenmate "Sister," I mean it. You are a family. No one can make you as happy or as miserable as family, so think about it.

Do things socially together. Do something fun. Go to the movies, go shopping, go fishing, go hiking. You could take a class or exercise together, or attend Renaissance Fairs or Pagan festivals as a group. If you have a local Witches Ball, reserve a table, get everyone to bring their spouses or significant others, and go have a blast!

Managing the Growth of the Coven

Don't be too quick to bring in new unknown people. Basically, you should choose a possible candidate and then slowly get to know them on a social level first. They should not be trolling for a group. There is nothing wrong with someone making a polite inquiry; however, you have the right to politely say, no thanks.

Now if someone tries to strong-arm their way in . . . if they start the whole, "I am very powerful—you need me to bring balance to your group . . . ." or the dreaded, "I'm afraid to do magick alone" shtick, or my least favorite, "I am DESPERATE to join a coven" (any emails sent in all capital letters tick me off—it's like they are shouting at you). Avoid these folks. Honestly, group work isn't for sissies. It's about having the guts to believe in yourself to the point that you are willing to mix your energies and your magick with other people. That takes courage, daring, and wisdom. Not whimpering.

Oh, and while you are trying to get to know this possible candidate for your group, be careful. If you meet them for lunch and they stiff you with the expensive food and wine bill, are generally obnoxious and over the top, and then cap the afternoon off by

trying to talk you into looking over their book idea—that's a good clue that you need to refuse this person. (Don't laugh. That happened to me a few years ago.)

Also consider this . . . . If your coven is just beginning, starting to grow nicely, or is at a good spot—leave it as is for a while. It's not how quickly you get big—it's about how well you all work together.

On the other hand . . . if the addition of a new member or two will help the coven grow and boot it out of complacency, then yes, it is time to add someone new. But don't rush the process. Think about what we just discussed. (My coven has a six month get-to-know-you process we call it the "guest" phase.) After the guest phase, it takes a year to become dedicated into our coven—and another year after that to be initiated. Why is the wait so long? Because we have learned a few things the hard way, too. Also, it's important to keep in mind that once you have initiated a new member into your group, you will have a magickal and psychic bond with that person forever.

The circle of coven members expands and contracts. People may come and people may go. Sometimes people move away, have personal issues, or leave the coven for various reasons. You may have personality clashes that can't work themselves out. Members can become envious or unhappy. Or they may simply develop a different perspective on the Craft and want to make their own group. So when these situations occur, take a deep breath, embrace the lessons, and keep going forward. "Ever the circle continues . . ."

~

For more information, refer to my book, *Natural Witchery*. I devoted an entire chapter to starting a circle in the book, and those basic guidelines will assist you if you have a hankering to start your own coven. And yes, there is a ritual in chapter 5 for dedicating a group if you don't want to write your own.

Bottom line? If you want a crash course in running a successful coven—then start one. There is no better way to learn than to try it yourself. Use your common sense, get organized, and have fun. May the God and Goddess bless you and your group as you all grow, evolve, and thrive.

The Three R's of Chant Writing: Rhyme, Rhythm, and Repetition

by Ember Grant

Imagine a ritual in moonlight or a darkened room, the aroma of incense—a truly magical atmosphere—disrupted by fumbling with paper to read a chant and trying to see the words by candlelight. Most of us have had this experience. It's so much easier to recite chants from memory, without having to worry about a script. Since chants are such an important part of magic, learning to write simple, effective verses can add power to your rituals—freeing you from distraction and allowing you to focus more fully on your intent.

Rhythmic drumbeats and the harmony created by voices and musical instruments influence our consciousness and moods in many ways, inducing a trance-like state—the state of mind most often used for magical practice. Chanting does this as well. Words and sounds have power. The words themselves may not be magical, but the effect that sound has on us provides an avenue for magical intent. This is why the ability to write a good chant is so important—in order to effectively use a chant to reach an altered state of consciousness, the words should be easy to remember and effortless to use. To accomplish this, use the three Rs: rhyme, rhythm, and repetition. Let's examine these techniques and learn some ways to use them.

Rhyme: Not Just for the End of the Line

Rhyming helps people remember the words. It's a predictable pattern—when you have some idea of the expected sound, it's easier to recall the next word. In the oral tradition,

ballads were used to tell stories, and these songs used rhyme. In fact, rhyme is universal among languages. It also has roots in magic. Some traditions insist that ancient spells will not work in translation because the magic is in the words and sounds. I'll leave that up to you to decide.

There are many rhyme schemes you can work with. Start by looking for ways to rhyme the sound at the end of each line, or alternating lines. Rhyme schemes at the end of lines are usually depicted using letters like this: ABAB or ABBA. The first example means that the word used at the end of each alternating line would rhyme, such as cat, dog, bat, frog. The second example would be this pattern: cat, dog, frog, bat. Use whatever pattern you like, or create your own.

Don't worry if your rhymes don't seem original or clever. The point is to focus energy and avoid having to pay too much attention to the words. So what if everyone wants to rhyme flower with power, or spell with well? Chant writing is not a competition. However, you can practice with new ways of combining words to create your own style. Just don't feel too pressured to make every chant or spell a perfect work of art. Have fun! If you'd like, use the Internet or a thesaurus to locate words that don't immediately come to mind. Make lists of words that rhyme. Go through the alphabet and exhaust all the possibilities (by sound, not just by the letters) and you may come up with a new idea. Light rhymes with bright, right, and night, but it also sounds like rite, write, and ignite. And there are so many other choices: alight, sight, slight, plight, might, height, and delight. And don't forget about internal rhyme—see if you can find matching sounds within words and lines. Also remember you can get creative with your sounds, using internal vowel rhymes: Moon and smooth, for example. They both have the same "oo" sound in the middle. Focus on creating the best combination of words and sounds that you can.

In addition to rhyme, the sounds of language are like musical notes. Speaking from a poetic standpoint, there are some specific ways you can work with sound. For example, consonance is the repetition of similar consonant sounds, usually at the end of words or in the middle:

I can't think; my mind is blank. (nk)
The mammal is a camel named Sam. (am)
She likes soft sheets of silk. (s and sh)

Assonance is the use of similar vowel sounds to create internal rhyme:

I often muse in solitude. (u)

Alliteration is the repetition of the first consonant:

Welcome water, welcome wind.

Here's a line from one of my poems:

languid yellow light curled quietly in corners

(alliteration and consonance using c, q, and l)

The mechanics of human speech creates sounds that have particular characteristics. Think of the shape of your mouth when you say the words. Typically, words that resonate in the back of the throat are deeper and have a lower frequency, while words that use sounds created toward the front of the mouth are higher. You can easily evoke mood with the right choice of words. For example, vowels are like a rainbow of colors—be sensitive to their sounds. Some tend to be "darker" sounds. Lower notes, like aw, oo (the lowest sound), and oh, are used to convey large, ominous, gloomy moods. Some are "lighter" or higher sounding notes, like ee or a short "I" sound—think of small and bright—teeny weeny or itsy bitsy. Consonants have a variety of sound characteristics as well. There are "liquid" sounds—these flow around the tongue—L and R, sometimes W; there are whispers and hisses—ss or sh. Stops are more dramatic: p, b, t, d, k, g. These sounds cut off air flow abruptly in the mouth by using the tongue.

There are some words referred to as "gut" words because, often, the "uh" or "ugh" sound can be unpleasant—think of words like mud, ugly, slum, bum, grunt, repulsive, bug, and slug. But, sometimes this sound can be pleasant: yum, hug, summer, lullaby, love. Either way, "uh" is often a sound that is linked with human response to something we like or dislike—it's tied to our emotions.

Rhythm: Feel the Beat

There is rhythm in the universe itself—in nature, and in our bodies—a pattern of recurrence, cycles, seasons, and all life. Rhythm is very important in chants; it drives the words, like the beat of music.

We dance beneath the bright glow of the Moon.

Remember your Shakespeare from high school? These lines are iambic pentameter—five stresses (also called accented syllables) per line in a pattern of deeDUM—an unstressed beat followed by an accented one. This is the pattern of the human heartbeat—it's the most popular rhythm. But using five beats creates a long line; tetrameter, four beats, is shorter and often easier for chanting.

We greet the Moon, we greet the Sun,
A change of season has begun.

There's lots of rhyme here—Sun and begun, but also Moon and Sun both end in "n" and have one beat. In addition, the repetition of the word "greet" adds to the rhythm. Note the four beats, or stresses in each line.

We greet the Moon, we greet the Sun,
A season of magic has begun.

Can you hear why this second line is not as effective? Even though there is an end-rhyme, the rhythm is not consistent. There are too many syllables or stresses in the second line—it's not even with the first one. It's not wrong, but it could be better, especially if it's intended to be a spoken chant.

Practice your rhythm using a drum, or just slap your knee. Clap or snap. You don't need to know the formal names of poetic meter or even use any of them. Just find a beat that you like. Think of it like music. Whatever beat you choose, stick with it throughout the chant. Changing rhythm can be confusing.

Here's a very simple chant with four beats per line:

Simple circle, Sacred rite
Goddess bless us on this night.

The "s" sound in simple, circle, and sacred displays alliteration and consonance; in addition, there is a shared "r" sound in sacred rite. Also, the "s" sound in goddess, us,

and bless creates consonance as well—these elements create a very musical chant.

Remember, too, that beats are not the same as syllables. The lines above have four beats per line, but each line has seven syllables. If it's easier for you, work with even numbers of syllables rather than stressed and unstressed syllables. Either way, be sure you have an even rhythm.

Repetition: Say It Again, and Again for Meaning and Rhythm

Your goal or intent will help you focus and decide how to structure the repetition of your chant. If something is important, repeat it—this is also the basis for a refrain. A chant leader can say a few lines, and a group can repeat the same lines or different ones. Repetition is also a good way to reinforce the purpose of your chant. Here's an example used by an African tribe:

> *New Moon, come out, give water for us.*
> *New Moon, thunder down water for us.*
> *New Moon, shake down water for us.*

The goal here is apparent: water from the sky, and the time of action is the New Moon. This chant asks the New Moon to bring rain. In our language, it doesn't rhyme, but you get the idea. A similar chant might go like this:

Rain will wash us
Rain will cleanse us
Rain renew us
Rain will fall

In the next example, the approach is a tone of asking:

Rain come wash us
Rain come cleanse us
Rain renew us
Rain please fall

Both examples repeat the goal (hoping for rain), and the number of syllables in each line is the same. In addition, repetition of words like "come" or "will" help to recall the words of the chant. And, since "rain" and "renew" both begin with "r" that helps as well. Group members could easily memorize this chant for quick repetition, especially if the chant leader is familiar with it and can serve as a guide.

Always remember to practice your chant before teaching it to others. If you become tongue-tied while trying to speak the words, chances are that others will also have difficulty. Sometimes too much alliteration results in tongue-twisters. Practice chanting it several times to be sure it has even rhythm and the words are easy. Word play is fun, so enjoy it! Think of it as a game or puzzle, especially when trying your hand with complex rhyme schemes and meter. As with any magical art, crafting your words carefully can add extra personal energy to your work.

When in doubt, try it out. Practice your chant. Repeat it over and over while tapping out the rhythm. You'll be able to feel it. Chants that have good rhyme and rhythm are easy to repeat and remember, resulting in rituals that leave your hands free with no worries about a script to follow. This way, more attention can be given to focusing energy and reaching a magical state of mind—and that is the ultimate purpose of a chant.

For Further Study

Nims, John Frederick and David Mason. *Western Wind: An Introduction to Poetry*, McGraw-Hill, 1999.

The Fruits of Magic

by Peggy Wheeler

Ah, the sweet, juicy loveliness of fruit! Whether given in supplication as an offering to our deities, or used as elements in our sacred rituals and spellwork, fruit contributes to our spiritual sustenance. Across all cultures and on every continent, fruit appears as a leading character in our human-creation stories, myths, legends, and lore. There is an undeniable, traceable, recordable link between human culture, human spirituality, and fruit. But, what sets fruit apart from most growing things is that all fruits have within them magical properties, which are easy for anyone to access and connect to. The magic of fruit is so powerful that when used with a true heart and good intention, it will enhance the spiritual practice of anyone who simply chooses to respectfully place a single piece of fresh, fragrant fruit upon their altar.

Knowing which fruits to use in your spiritual practice is important, but since every type of fruit on the planet from the common western blueberry to the African Zulu marula has its own unique properties, to cover every fruit, its associated myths, cultural stories, and magical assets would require many fat volumes in a large series. This article focuses on a few fruits common in magical tradition. Figs, peaches, persimmons, strawberries, and of course apples and pomegranates are readily available. Rich in myth, legend, and lore, these fruits can be used in a number of spells and magical rituals.

Figs

In the Mediterranean, where figs were first cultivated, the fig tree is associated with wisdom, creation, and vigor. In Greek and Roman mythology, Dionysus (or Bacchus to the Romans) is closely linked to the fig, as is Priapus, a satyr who is a symbol of sexual desire. In Roman legend, the she-wolf who suckled Romulus and Remus rested beneath a sacred fig tree. Figs were given as gifts at the Roman New Year to ensure good fortune. The mother of

one of the Titans turned him into a fig tree when he fled from Zeus. Demeter, while searching for her daughter, Persephone, was given shelter by a man—and she rewarded by granting him the cultivation of fig trees. In classical Greece, figs were fed to lovers to enhance their lovemaking.

To the Buddhists, the fig tree is holy because it was under the Bodhi tree (a type of fig tree) where Siddhartha discovered enlightenment in 528 BCE and became the Buddha. In Eastern cultures, figs are eaten for vigor and are part of the Shaolin priests' diet because of their energy-giving properties.

In the Christian myth of the Garden of Eden, some say that after "The Fall," the leaf that Adam and Eve used to cover their nakedness was the fig leaf.

Figs in Modern Magic

Figs are used in spells and charms for love, health, and prosperity, but also figs are said to help produce vivid and meaningful dreams. For a charm to produce "Inspiring Dreams," you will need:

> Green fabric
> Yellow fabric
> Dried figs

Cut three 2-inch strips of green fabric, and four 2-inch strips of yellow.

Lay the strips on top of each other, alternating the colors so they form a star.

In the center of the fabric, place a few dried figs.

Gather the cache together and tie it.

Hang the amulet in a tree to absorb sunlight and wind for a full day.

Place the charm near your bed to provide you with good dreams to inspire, motivate, and encourage you during the day.

Peaches

Succulent, lovely peaches are associated in the West with warmth and the balmy days of summer. Juicy and sweet peaches are also associated with women's sexuality. In the East, peaches are closely linked to immortality, good health, hope, prosperity, and familial love.

There is a Chinese legend about "The Peach Tree of the Gods" that bloomed only once every thousand years. This tree yielded fruits that granted vibrant health, strength, and immortality to those who ate them. For many hundreds of years, the Taoist revered the peach as the most sacred of fruits. On ancient pottery, wall hangings, and other Chinese art, images often appear of Sau Sing Kung, one the three Star Gods, bearing a peach. According to the Chinese legend of the "Journey to the West," the Monkey God stole peaches from the garden of the Goddess of the West, Hsi Wang Mu, and attained immortality. Legends say peaches are served in the heavens to deities to honor their birthdays. Even today, the peach figures prominently in Taoist celebrations and rituals, and are often found in wedding feasts and during birthdays. Peaches are given as gifts to symbolize hope, good marriage, and longevity.

In a Japanese fable, a boy is born from a giant peach. Since he had no human mother, he was raised as a beloved child by foster parents who, sadly, were very poor. When the boy reached adulthood, he fought and defeated the demons on the Island of the Devils. He gave their riches to his foster parents who then prospered. In this way, the peach becomes a symbol of overcoming adversity, the love of family, and prosperity.

Peaches in Modern Magic

To attract good fortune, and to ensure a long healthy life for all who dwell in your home, place images of peaches on your altar, dining room, and living room. In the bedroom of a married couple or committed partners, peaches support a fruitful and long union and promote restful sleep.

In feng shui, to improve family relationships, place a peach (or the image of a peach) in the eastern sector of your home, the place designated on the *bagua* (feng shui tool) for family.

Persimmons

One of the most beautiful fruits of autumn is the brilliant, glossy red-orange persimmon. While its striking appearance is what gets your attention, its powerful properties make it a celebrated item. As the national fruit of Japan, persimmons are given at New Years because it brings "good fortune." Wild persimmons were first grown in China and are revered by the Koreans. For more than two thousand years, persimmons have been central to the practice of traditional Chinese medicine. They are thought to be imbued with "cold yin energy." The cold energy of persimmons helps promote fluid production, nourishes the lungs, reduces internal bleeding, dissolves blood clots, aids digestion, and cures hemorrhoids and hangovers. For hundreds of years, Asian women have rubbed persimmon skins on their faces to lighten and brighten their complexions.

Throughout Asia, myths are ripe with persimmons. Here is the popular folktale of "The Tiger and the Persimmon." In this story, a hungry tiger, under cover of darkness, stalks a domesticated ox. The tiger is about to pounce on the back of the ox, when he is stopped by the wailing of a baby inside the farmhouse. The child's mother attempts to shush the baby: "Don't cry, little one, lest you attract the attention of wild beasts or terrible monsters." The baby wails even louder. The tiger hears the mother say, "If you are quiet, I will give you a persimmon." Upon hearing this, the infant's cries immediately cease. The tiger thinks "A persimmon must be a ferocious beast indeed if the baby is so frightened at the mere mention of one it immediately stops crying!" The tiger is terrified as he imagines what a beast a persimmon might be. He wonders to himself, "What if a vicious persimmon is here right now!" At that exact moment, a thief who has also been stalking the ox leaps upon the back of the tiger, mistaking the tiger for the ox in the darkness.

The tiger, believing the thief is the ferocious persimmon, runs horrified into the forest trying to shake it from his back. The thief (once recognizing he's on the back of a tiger instead of the ox) desperately seeks ways to escape from the tiger. Finally, the thief grabs a low-hanging limb of a persimmon tree and frees himself. The thief vows to change his ways and never steals again. The tiger never again returns to the village.

Persimmons also are part of American folklore, literature, and poetry. Often, persimmons are used on American Thanksgiving tables in the Horn of Plenty because their golden color symbolizes prosperity. Below is a very old American poem about persimmons.

The Persimmon Tree

Raccoon up the 'simmon tree
Possum on the ground
Raccoon shake them 'simmons down
Possum pass 'em round
—African-American poem circa 1870, author unknown

Persimmons in Modern Magic

Persimmon weather forecasting folklore comes out of the Missouri and Arkansas Ozarks as long as two hundred years ago. However, using persimmons to predict winter weather is still in use, and many claim this means of weather prediction is not simply an old wives' tale, but is "good magic" because of its accuracy!

To predict winter weather with persimmons, you will need a ripe persimmon and a sharp knife.

First, cut the persimmon in half and then extract the seeds.

Examine the cavity within the seedless persimmon. (If you look closely, you will see the vague shape of a common eating utensil.)

If you perceive a spoon-like shape, there will be lots of deep snow. Expect to spend a lot of time shoveling walkways and driveways.

If the shape is knife-like in appearance, expect a long winter—so cold it cuts like a knife.

If the shape inside the persimmon resembles a fork, it will be a mild winter.

Strawberries

Members of the rose family, strawberries have long been associated with rebirth, love, and health. Strawberries were sacred to the goddess Friga. When the new religion consumed the old, Virgin Mary claimed this berry as her own. The Christian Virgin is said to accompany children on St. John's Day as they venture into the fields to pick strawberries. An old Christian myth is that infants ascended to heaven disguised as strawberries, and as a result, many early Christians avoided eating strawberries out of fear that they would be eating their own deceased babies.

Because strawberries are the first fruits to ripen in the spring, the Senecas of the northeastern United States associated these berries with spring and rebirth. The Senecas also believed strawberries line the path to heaven.

In Roman mythology, in grief over the death of Adonis, Venus wept so vigorously that her tears turned to heart-shaped strawberries when they dropped from her eyes to the earth. Some ancient cultures believed that strawberries have aphrodisiac properties and are eaten by lovers. Myth has it that a strawberry cut in half and shared with another will result in a love match. In Bavaria, during an annual spring ritual, farmers attach baskets of strawberries to the horns of their cattle. According to the Bavarians, the fruit attracts magical elves. The elves eat the strawberries and then repay the cattle ranchers by guaranteeing healthy calves and cows that produce an abundance of milk.

Strawberries in Modern Magic

Strawberries have long played a role in Beltane rituals. It is a fruit of love, abundance, and bright new beginnings. Below is a recipe for a Beltane Maywine said to contain powerful magical properties. It brings a bright touch of spring into the mouths and hearts of anyone who drinks it.

To make Maywine for a Beltane Circle, you need:

12 sprigs of woodruff
2 bottles of dry white wine
2 cups strawberry liquor or juice
1 cup sliced strawberries
Pink and red rose petals (to be added after all the other ingredients have been mixed together)

Soak the dried woodruff overnight in the wine. The next day, add the remaining ingredients, stir with a wooden spoon and allow the wine to steep overnight. Serve very cold in a punch bowl with the rose petals floating atop.

The Queens of Ritual Fruits

No story of the relationship between human culture, magic, and fruit would be complete without the apple and the pomegranate, the queens of ritual fruits. Apples and pomegranates, long associated with mythology and magic (particularly in Western Europe and the United States), have appeared in our spiritual teachings, our literature, and poetry for thousands of years.

Apples

Across cultures, apples signify fertility, temptation, peace, love, joy, youth, knowledge, and masculine energy. In European culture, the apple is best known as the "forbidden fruit" from the fabled Garden of Eden's Tree of Knowledge.

In exploring the spiritual meaning and ritual use of apples, you'll find the apple as a sacred image in many countries. In Celtic myths, the apple symbolizes immortality and is known as the "Fruit of the Gods." Ancient and modern Norse Pagans believe the apple is a symbol for eternal youth. The mystical Island of Avalon is closely linked to Apples. The root of the word "Avalon" is the Welsh word for apple, and in English mythology, an alternate name of Avalon is "The Isle of Apples." The goddess, Hera, received golden apples from Mother Earth as a wedding gift. Jason quested for the "golden apples." Apples figure prominently in the Trojan War, and are why the Goddesses Hera and Athena supported the Greeks. In China, apples are peace symbols, and their blossoms represent feminine beauty. Chinese women make apple offerings to Quan Yin, the Goddess of Mercy. Pomona, the Roman Goddess of Fruit Trees, is also known as "Apple Mother." An apple cut crossways reveals within it a perfect pentagram, the universal sacred symbol for Wiccans and Witches.

Apples in Modern Magic

For love rituals and spells, apples have been used from the Middle Ages until the present. A powerful and simple spell for attracting love is to first set your intention to attract a romantic partner. Never wish for a specific person. Instead, focus on specific qualities you find appealing in a potential mate. Be very clear about these qualities and have the goal of attracting the right person for

you. List your selected qualities on a slip of paper and place it on your altar beneath a red apple. Light a red altar candle.

A sip of apple juice or cider from a crystal goblet "internalizes and crystalizes" your intention and energizes your spell. When the candle burns down completely, eat the apple. It is said that love spells with apples are especially potent during Samhain, but apple spells are powerful in any season.

Pomegranate

According to Greek mythology, the first pomegranate tree sprung from the blood of Orion's wife, who had thrown herself off a cliff after being tricked by her rival, Hera, into believing she had killed her own children. Today, Greeks revere the pomegranate as the "fruit of abundance," and during holidays, pomegranates customarily appear on banquet tables.

The most well-known myth about pomegranates is the story of Demeter and Persephone. In this story, Persephone was picking flowers when Hades, God of the underworld, spied her. Hades was so taken by Persephone's beauty he kidnapped her and spirited her away to his underworld kingdom. Persephone's mother, the Goddess of Harvest, Demeter, was so grief-stricken she created winter and killed every living plant. The world's people began to starve. To save humanity, Zeus ordered Hades to release Persephone. But before she returned, Hades tricked her into partaking in the fruit of the underworld, the pomegranate. Before she realized her mistake, Persephone consumed seven pomegranate seeds. In exchange for the seeds she'd eaten, Persephone agreed to return to the underworld several months each year, during which time winter prevails and plants die. When Persephone returns to her mother in spring, the Sun shines; plants grow and thrive.

Bacchus is associated with the pomegranate because he turned a beautiful nymph who had rejected his advances into a pomegranate tree.

To Jews and Christians alike, the pomegranate has spiritual significance. To ancient Jews, its seeds represented the number of commandments in the Torah. Images of pomegranates were woven into their sacred vestments. To ancient Christians, pomegranate juice represented the blood of Christ. Pomegranates are associated with Mother Mary because she bore the "seed of Christ."

Ancient Romans associated pomegranates with marriage. Roman brides adorned themselves with wreaths made from pomegranate twigs.

The pomegranate is a fertility symbol because of its voluminous juicy red seeds. An ancient Chinese custom is to cut a pomegranate in half and count the seeds to know how many sons a woman will bear. A tradition among Turkish women is to drop a pomegranate on the ground. The number of seeds that burst from the pod upon impact forecasts how many children they'll have.

Pomegranates in Modern Magic

The myth of the pomegranate symbolizes the release of the earth from winter darkness and cold. Like the apple, they are often part of love spells. And, also like the apple, pomegranates are used in rituals and spells during fall and winter. But, at any time of the year, pomegranates are celebrated for their powers of fertility.

Here is a simple pomegranate abundance ritual. Sit quietly in the evening with a room lit only by green candles. Cut open a pomegranate, and remove the seeds one at a time. Speak a wish into each seed as you remove it from the pod. Consume each seed deliberately, slowly savoring its juice. Eat with a grateful heart. Thank the deities for the prosperity they bestow upon you. For thirty days thereafter, consciously note the abundance that comes your way.

Ecstasy Recipe

Keeping in mind each fruit's magical and mythical properties, combine three or more together into a smoothie or salad. Consciously feel each piece of fruit with your fingers. Is its skin supple, firm, soft? As you cut into each piece, hear the sound as the knife breaks the fruit apart. See how the fruit yields its juices and seeds. Inhale its rich fragrance. Then partake joyfully, because with each taste, and with every one of your senses, you are experiencing sweet, juicy magic.

Living Harmoniously with Non-Pagans

by Tabitha Bradley

Many practicing Pagans are living in situations where we come into contact with non-Pagan family members on a daily basis. This may be in-laws, parents, or spouses who do not practice the same religion as we do. If we're lucky, we are able to practice with little to no interference.

However, things come up occasionally that will challenge our personal spiritual comfort levels. What I'd like to do here is introduce some typical situations and offer some coping strategies and solutions to help you deal with the uncomfortable aspects of being Pagan in a family of non-Pagans.

As a Pagan who is a part of a larger Christian family that is aware of my religious choice and is choosing to either ignore it or "deal" with it, perhaps in a nonconstructive way, my experience is not unusual. In fact, most Pagans I know are faced with the issue of trying to live harmoniously in a larger Christian family structure. The keyword here is "harmoniously." Most young to middle-age families with children are at the point where they just want some kind of peace within the greater family and are sick of fighting with people whose minds are made up. Though this is the angle that this article is approaching the subject, I think these techniques can be used in similar situations, such as a teenage or adult child living at home, a student sharing quarters with other students, or a partner living with a non-Pagan partner or family.

Depending on how close you are with your parents or in-laws, you may be included in family gatherings that range from holidays at their home to dinners out. If the family you are a part of is overtly Christian, you may encounter uncomfortable situations that may be harder to deal with in a constructive way, particularly in public situations.

Prayer before meals in public restaurants is a common situation. This custom can bother nonreligious and agnostic people as well as non-Christians. There are families that insist on praying aloud in restraunts before meals and including everyone at the table—even if they are not of the same religious tradition. It can be embarassing as well as uncomfortable, because you are being induced to pray even if you do not pray (Buddhists, for instance, usually do not pray in the traditional Christian sense). What has worked for my little non-Christian family is to just sit quietly and either look into each other's eyes, lending each other silent emotional support, or say our own silent prayers to our gods, if that is our personal spiritual practice.

This has become more of an issue lately as my children are beginning to explore their own spirituality and have both told me public prayer makes them uncomfortable.

We do this at family gatherings at home as well. You may be in a situation where even gazing at your mutual Pagan family may not be permissible. In this case, simply saying your own prayers, mantras, or meditations in your head will ease the discomfort.

Many of you have children you are raising as Pagan or are sharing many sprititualies and allowing them to choose their own spiritual path. We are raising ours this way, answering questions about our own quite-different spiritualities (I am Wiccan and my husband is Buddhist), and directing them to appropriate people when we don't know the answer. While this is a great situation for kids seeking their own spiritual path in life, dictated by their own phi-

losophies and questions, it can be trying for parents if their families have specific ideas about how kids should be "raised up" in religion. We have been quite emphatic about our wishes with our families, emphasizing that the kids' choices are the most important ones—after all, this is their personal spirituality, not anyone else's. It's been a struggle, but we have put our foot down more in this area than we have in any other. I think this is because we both had Christianity forced on us when we were growing up, and we refuse to let that happen to our kids.

If you have kids, it's important early on to decide how you want to teach your kids about spirituality. If you're okay with letting the in-laws or parents teach the kids about their religion, make sure you set boundaries early, telling them what you want and don't want them taught. You always reserve the right to stop allowing family to teach your kids if they're being taught scary stuff or being pressured to practice when they don't want to.

On the kids' side, you want to reinforce good manners when they are being pressured to attend a religious event by family. Promises need to be kept, even if the child changes their mind later on. The best thing, of course, is to not let a child make a promise you know they won't want to keep. Some family members will try to wheedle and manipulate a kid into making a promise to attend church, which is a bad thing to do to a child, but it happens—even in the most "Christian" of families.

Balancing manners, promises, and family can be difficult—we also teach our kids not to cave to peer pressure, yet they are getting the exact same kind of pressure from people they love, like grandparents, aunts, and uncles. Children need to know it's okay to say "no" to grandparents who want them to attend church and that saying something like, "no thank you," is just fine. They aren't going to get in trouble as long as they are polite. Politeness goes a long way in dealing with problematic family members. Even if you're stuck in a conversation that has become extremely uncomfortable, as long as you're polite and refuse to argue about matters, you are a winner.

Saying no is difficult for many people, which is why it's so important to remember that you can and should say no if you are uncomfortable. Of course, the polite "no" is the best, and hopefully the only one you will need. However sometimes it becomes necessary to become more firm with your "no" if you are on the receiving end of pressure (also known as "the guilt trip"). A typical situation is the family Christmas or Easter event. Your little Pagan family may not even celebrate the holiday at all, but are part of an extended family that does. One pressure point with these holidays is church service attendance. Depending on the severity of pressure, it can cause distress on both sides, particularly if the family is using guilt to force you into attending their church. Many times, the family is being equally pressured by their church to bring family to the special services, so it is wise to keep in mind that your Christian family may also feel like they're in a vise. This makes holidays even more difficult for everyone.

It is best to make it clear as politely as possible that you are not interested in attending the event as you do not celebrate that holiday and are not a member of that religion. You don't need to add anything else, simply saying "No thank you, but thank you for inviting me" is plenty and polite. "I'd really rather not" isn't the best response here as it sounds too wishy-washy and it is important to be firm in this kind of situation. "No, thank you" is firm.

Sometimes the response will be an attempt to induce guilt by implying that someone will be hurt if you don't go. This usually seems to be more effective on blood relatives rather than in-laws. (For example: your partner's parents attempt to pressure him into attending even though you have made it clear you are not going.) You need to remain firm even if you're being pressured to attend, by continuing to say no even if you feel lousy doing it. The point here is that once you make your decision not to go, you should stick to it. If you back down, this will happen again because it means the pressure worked. Kids will have more trouble with this than adults, so be prepared to back your children's decisions as strongly as yours and your partner's.

When you are deeply involved in an extended family such as that of your in-laws—involved enough to goad you into participating in their customs—it's usually because the family wants to include you, despite the different religions. It's important to remember that while you're asking them to make allowances for your freedom of religion, that you must do the same for them. Some families are very involved in church activities and some of them can be a lot of fun, even for Pagan folks, as long as you are comfortable.

As an example, my in-laws' church has had a cute little "Trunk or Treat" event in the church parking lot every Halloween, which is a safe and fun event that is kind of unique and is popular with the community. It's absolutely mundane—no preaching or negative messages at all—and we love doing it every year even though the church community knows we're not Christian (we love stringing orange lights on the car!). We think it's the best Halloween event in town and the kids have a blast. We have our own Samhain at home, which is even more fun since we're already in the mood from the car trick or treating at the church. Amazingly enough, it's a very Pagan event at a very Christian church and nobody minds at all. I'll bet you can find things like this in your own extended family if you keep your ears and eyes open and ask if you hear something interesting.

Sharing in family activites that aren't religious also keeps harmony and balance active within the family, so finding things you have in common is a great way to connect with people. I am a science fiction writer and fan of all things SF and Fantasy. Discovering that my in-laws are big *Star Trek* fans was a great jumping off point for me. While I'm not as into *Star Trek* as they are (they have the little light-up tree ornaments, which are cute), I do have a solid working knowledge of the show and it was something we could talk about that we all liked. I share an interest in cute TV sitcoms with my sister-in-law and she got me hooked on *Friends* a few years ago. We both love the show and have fun chatting about it. I share a love of "trashy" romance novels with her as well, so we have shared books from time to time. Of course, the entire family are Disney-philes, so we have shared a group trip to Disneyland a couple of times throughout the years, which definitely brings the entire family together, Pagan and non-Pagan.

Being part of a large family can be a trial, even for people who share the same religion. Each family is unique and the fact that your family wants you to be a part of their lives is important, since there are many families who wouldn't even want to try. So if you show that you are trying to find harmony in your family by standing up for your rights, your efforts are going to be noticed and the people who love you will respect you for your strength of character, even if they don't agree with your religious choices.

It won't ever be perfect, but you can find the balance and harmony within your family by being firm and sticking up for your rights as well as those of your partner and children. You will get a return on your investment and will find an ease, at least a little bit, of your daily stress, making everyone's lives just a bit easier.

A Little Kitchen Magic: It's All in the Preparation!

by Boudica

The difference between "High Magic" and "Kitchen Witch" is that a Kitchen Witch does not need a stage, an audience, or props to make the magic. Rather, the focus is on intent, creating the maximum amount of energy, and doing the work.

But we find we do need a staging area; a place we can work in private and have all the tools we need to work our magic. For many women, it used to be the kitchen, where once upon a time, we spent most of our waking hours preparing meals and doing chores. In between stirring the cauldron and drying the herbs, we would find the time to set up a magical working on the kitchen table, read cards for a neighbor, or brew a love potion for a special friend.

Reality strikes—this is the twenty-first century. Most of us business types hardly see the inside of our kitchen except to brew coffee, and many of us ignore that small box they sold us as a kitchen when we bought the house. And if you live in an apartment, you know what I mean when I say "utility kitchen" and how very close it comes to "utility closet."

Nevertheless, we need to prepare a space for working. For most folks, this is a double-duty space where meals are prepared and magic is performed. Or maybe it will be storage space for pizza boxes and empty Chinese takeout containers that alternates with storing bottles of herbs and oils.

But no matter how large or small your kitchen, it will end up being the ideal place for working your magic. Why? Because it is the one place in the house with the storage space you will need and a countertop or tabletop to work your magic. It is also the one

place where we feel most at home, comfortable and secure. No matter how much time we spend in the kitchen, it is our hearth, the center of our life.

Magical real estate in the home should be set aside. Even if it is a shelf in a small closet, the storage of some oils and herbs should be away from the food stock and secure enough to keep prying eyes and fingers away from your "stash." I realize there may be children in the house, or husbands or wives who do not want to know what you are doing. A space should be agreed upon as your private space and as such, it should be respected and left alone. Having said that, we move on.

Not all your stock is going to be inedible. Most of your stock will hang out in the spice closet and the baking shelves. Most Witches I know have a spice closet (not a rack) that would rival most grocery stores, which is also a great place to get most supplies at a good price. Whole cloves, nutmeg, fresh cinnamon sticks, vanilla beans, cornmeal, and more can be purchased at a supermarket and are freshness dated. Freshness counts! Sorry, but I have been in "pagan" stores where the cinnamon sticks are twice the price, half the weight, and as old as the store itself. If you buy from a local Pagan store, demand freshness. And hold yourself to those same standards—clean out your magical cupboard

regularly so that fresh supplies are always on hand. The rule of thumb is if the product is a year old, it's time to get rid of leftovers and purchase or acquire fresh.

Oils are the same way. You can find many oils in health food stores, pharmacies, and department stores. While you will not find the specialty blends that are available at the Pagan store, you will find the basic ingredients. Please be advised, we are being frugal here. I will shop at the best Pagan stores for the special blends I want, but for my own blends, I shop fresh and affordable.

Candles are a whole different ball of wax. (Hmm... a pun.) Moving along, candles are a personal preference and depend entirely on the quality you need and your pocketbook. White utility candles are a staple. They can be used for everything and do not require a bank loan to purchase. But when we want specialty candles—specific colors, compositions, or scents—again, seek out your local Pagan store. The candles there are often handmade.

You can find beeswax and soy varieties, as well as candles that have solid color throughout. I hate it when you get a candle and it's only colored on the outside, the inside is plain white—cheating on the dye. I like solid color candles. But composition, that is your own choice. I find I only go for the beeswax when I want something special.

A walk in the park on a sunny weekend will yield a plethora of "extras" that may grace your closet essentials. Stones, leaves, acorns, and even the stray feather can be found in a park (and if it has a beach, sand and shells, too). Keep your eyes open because you never know what you might stumble across. Once, I hit a construction site that tore down a building that had brickwork. The old brick smashed up nicely into red brick powder. Not a bad deal—and ecological, too. Look to the natural world to supply you with the "extras" you may need for your working.

Then, of course, there are the hobby shops. A bag of the black river stones I like to use for protection spells come cheap in these stores—so does sprinkle sparkles for that touch of fairy dust; handmade paper for spellwork; and small wooden boxes, clay bowls, or colorful jars for spirit homes. Gemstones, paints, oils, candles, and even wooden binders for Books of Shadows can come from those lovely discount hobby stores if you look close enough.

So we come back to the kitchen space. A shelf in a closet for those things we cannot eat, and shelf space for those things we can eat. Those edibles will serve double duty and we can always be assured that they will be regularly replaced with fresh stock. However, I do recommend a separate set of mixing bowls. You really don't want to put your edibles in a bowl that had something that could leave behind oil or residue that is not good for your digestive system. I recommend a trip to the flea market or the Goodwill store for used bowls. Most secondhand shops have an interesting array of items. I found the perfect small cauldron, cast iron with three legs, at a Christian consignment store. It was labeled "fondue pot." Yeah, right. But it was mine for $5.00.

Setting up your working space is totally up to you. I keep a jar of kosher salt (I love the texture) on the counter. When working, I start by spreading some salt on the counter, get a clean, damp rag, and wipe the counter down. Cleaned and grounded. A little salt on the floor to remove any bad residue is a good idea as well. Mop and go!

Some folks like to "decorate" their working area. Small personal altar space with some stones or herbs or seasonal fruits or flowers always makes a nice display. A wooden cutting board with a lovely pentacle painted or carved into it makes a great portable workspace, and if you reserve it for spellworkings (and don't prepare food on it) you really don't need to worry about what you just cleaned on the surface.

A couple of candleholders discreetly placed will set the mood for the working. Colored light bulbs work well if you do not want to use candles. I've seen clear or colored lights running under kitchen cabinets that look like fairy lights and create a stunning effect for working in the kitchen. For those who are concerned about energy use, the new LED bulbs for under the kitchen counters are perfect for mood lighting.

If you have a center island or a kitchen table to work from, you are lucky you have such an ideal space. But for those who have a galley-style or utility kitchen, setting this up is going to be much more difficult. I suggest you get a stool, and set it next to the counter. It will get you closer to your work and make you more comfortable in close quarters.

Storage of your supplies and equipment should be considered. Kitchen canisters can hold candles, funnels, droppers, and more. I reuse candle jars for herbs and stones. I actually keep my candles in old plastic coffee containers—the big ones. I have a cookie sheet for burning candles on and working some spells. I have a bowl for water, a lovely deep cobalt blue. Great for scrying!

I also have a couple mortar and pestles. While a Cuisinart might be a choice for the modern Witch, I like to sit and contemplate what I am doing. I am slowly blending and bashing the herbs or stones I am adding to the mix, and in the process, I am adding energy and intent. And there is nothing like the smell of freshly bruised herbs to focus one's mind on the process at hand.

Which brings me to another topic—incense. We may clear our space with sage or burning herbs, but I am not all that great with smoke. In a confined space, smoke will build up quickly and can cause respiratory issues. I like oils in a diffuser. A candle under a small bowl of water and drops of essential oil is lovely to me. Or the smell of the herbs you are using and mixing with other oils. Why do I want to "flavor" the area with another smell if I am going to be using smell in my working? Try something different from incense. Let the aroma of the working fill your space.

Getting down to the real working, if you are going to mix oils for a special blend, you will need a few basic tools. Eyedroppers are essential. So are funnels. And small bottles.

For my "success" blend, I usually make about a dozen half-ounce glass bottles, sometimes more. (The cost per bottle is very reasonable if you buy from a wholesaler.) Use the Web to search for suppliers. A local store will provide cheaper postage. And, of course, there is always eBay. It's an afternoon's worth of work whether you make a large batch in a mixing bowl or mix it in the jars. I recommend making a larger batch of your special blend than you need. Although it will use up your supplies more quickly, you can sell the extras. (People are always asking for my success oil!) By adding a label to the bottle—Avery, or a cheaper brand printed from my computer printer—and a ribbon and a charm, they make very attractive gifts.

The last of the essentials is your "recipe book." A Book of Shadows is an essential in the kitchen when you are working. First, you keep the recipe. Second, you keep the incantation. Third, you keep the process. Finally, you keep the results. A spell-working is nothing unless you know whether it worked or not, and if you can repeat it exactly a second time and get the same

results. You should be working in that book before you even set foot in the kitchen. You should have your intent specifically laid out, your research done and verified, all your needed materials on hand and checked, and your plan written (down all the particulars) before you set up.

So, your workspace is clear, your BOS is worked up and open on the counter, and you have laid out all the ingredients and bowls on the counter. Here is a question I get a lot: Do I create a circle?

My question back to them is: What are you doing? If you want to create sacred space and call a deity to work with you on this project, then feel free. There are, of course, many Witches or magic practitioners who do not work with Deity. But I have some very different ideas.

I am drawing energy into this working, even with the help of my deity. And I will be sending this magic out to a project or person when it is completed. I am drawing energy into myself, coating it with intent, and then placing it into the project to add more energy, then releasing it. If I draw a circle around me to contain what I am doing, how am I going to collect the energy I need and how am I going to release it? If I am cooped up in my own bubble, how does all my working come in or go out?

Even if I am working something chaotic, I still need to draw in and then release. Forming a circle will impair that working.

Yes, I will call the elements or an element to my spellworking. Yes, I will draw all kinds of energy from that pool we all draw from to build my spellworking. And yes, depending on the work, I may call upon Deity to work with me to add an extra push to my working. When my intent is clear and I have built up to a point where the energy is at its peak, I will release it. I will then give thanks to the elements, to the energies, and to my Deity to for their assistance. But I will not create a circle to contain it. What I will do is clean up when I am done.

Cleanup is sometimes confusing. My working had a specific intent. If it is for me, that is one thing. I will draw that energy to me, allowing it to change me as it changes my world. But if that intent was for someone else, the energy is not mine to draw. I will salt down an area when I am done to remove any leftover energy. Candles will be removed and buried no matter who the working was for. Ashes will be buried. Any salt or stones or paper or inks or oils will be sent to the earth as well. These had intent, and the intent is released. Much of what I work with is "one-use only" when used for anyone else. My own materials, however, I will keep for reuse if I need to repeat the working.

At this point, you also should be writing in your BOS. What did you do? How did you feel? What did you feel? And what may have happened as you worked. Did you see something, or hear something? Was there an emotional response from your inner-self that should be noted? Was there an external response that you should note? And there should be follow-up. Was your intent answered? What was the final outcome of the working? Did you receive feedback from your client?

~

A final note: Working as a Kitchen Witch does not mean you have to work in the kitchen. If you have space elsewhere in the house you want to use, by all means use it. You are still a Kitchen Witch no matter where you work because you use what is at hand without all the glitz and glamour. Do not be restricted by name when you have the opportunity to set up a room for working that will serve as a personal private space. But again, do make sure you are prepared, make sure you have everything you need, and remember you don't always need the little trinkets or props. The key is intent, energy, and the desire to manifest change. A good kitchen Witch knows how to create the maximum amount of energy with the minimum amount of personal energy expended and without tools. Sometimes your finger is all you need.

The Strange Case of St. Expedite

by Denise Dumars

Pray to St. Expedite; he gets things done," the santera told me. St. Expedite? Who's that? Did such a saint really exist? If so, why had I never heard of him before, and why was I hearing about him for the first time from a practitioner of Santeria rather than from a mainstream Catholic?

As I would come to learn sometime later, practitioners of many Afrocentric magical traditions revere a figure with the unlikely name of St. Expedite, or San Expedito, as my prayer card calls him. On the card, he is clearly depicted as a Roman soldier, a cross in his right hand, some sort of plant in his left, one foot on a crow, the typical scrub-brush Roman helmet discarded on the ground behind him, and a halo now crowning him.

Ho-hum, I thought at first, yet another made-up saint supposedly converting to Christianity and preferring to die rather than to renounce his newfound beliefs. Surely "real" Catholics don't believe in such a figure. Or do they?

And yes, the friend who gave me this prayer card—purchased not at a botanica but at a Catholic church gift shop—was indeed Catholic and did believe in St. Expedite. And he was a bit hurt when I expressed doubt about his existence. So it seemed germane to try to right that wrong, or at the very least, track down the best versions of his story.

According to an Argentine website, Expeditus was a Roman legionnaire of Armenian ethnicity during the reign of Emperor Diocletian. One day, he was seized by an extraordinary desire to convert to Christianity. Immediately, an evil spirit in the body of a crow flew at him, squawking *"cras cras cras,"* the Latin word for tomorrow, and coincidentally, the Roman approximation of the sound a crow makes. The evil spirit tried to make him put off his decision until the next day, obviously hoping to talk him out of it. He refused, and said, "No, not tomorrow, NOW!"

Well, in AD 303, Diocletion had him beheaded for his refusal to renounce his conversion, and he is allegedly buried in Malatya, Turkey. His "official" feast day is April 19. His story is meant to act as a lesson to not put off until tomorrow what you ought to do today, especially when it comes to becoming a Christian—a banner on the cross St. Expedite carries often reads "today" in Latin. Or as hoodoo practitioner Dr. E says, "Don't proCRAStinate!"

According to SaintExpedite.org, an organization in Delaware, his story has been in and out of hagiographies for centuries, but he is not currently included in the Roman Catholic calendar of universally recognized saints. I looked at many, many Catholic sources, but never found him listed in any official calendar of saints' days, such as those that are recorded by the Franciscans on American-Catholic.org nor could I find his name in any form on any other official list of Catholic saints.

Then, miraculously it seemed, I found him on the Armeniapedia online! Clearly, at least the Armenians would like to acknowledge him for his ethnic heritage, if indeed he did exist, and the same Italian-made saint card that I was given showed up on an "Eastern Catholic" religious goods site. However, he was not listed on the official Armenian Catholic website. I had hit another dead end when it came to official sources.

Lore has it that his worship is "tolerated" by the Catholic Church, but not encouraged, as is true of many folk saints around the world. But that name? Come on. Must be a joke, right?

My original understanding of the myth (remember that one person's myth is another's religion) was that a large box marked "expedite," "spedito," or whatever version of the word in whatever language you want to use (I particularly like the tale that lists "special delivery" as the actual words on the crate) arrived by ship or washed ashore at A. New Orleans; B. Rio de Janeiro; or various other New World, primarily Catholic, port cities. Inside the box was a statue of our friend with the Roman uniform and the squashed crow. The cross in his hand clearly indicated that this was a statue of a saint. However, there was no packing list stating the saint's name or the name of the person who had ordered the statue. Since no one could remember ordering it, he was dubbed Saint Expedite. His arrival must have been a special delivery from God.

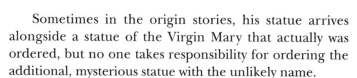

Sometimes in the origin stories, his statue arrives alongside a statue of the Virgin Mary that actually was ordered, but no one takes responsibility for ordering the additional, mysterious statue with the unlikely name.

St. Expedite is not just a New World myth; he is also immensely popular in parts of the Old World, specifically in Spain and France, where his origin has generated even more improbable stories, including one in which his famous crate appears in the Paris catacombs! Perhaps that is why a source quoted by Cat Yronwode refers to him in Creole French as "St. Espedee," and why the vodou practitioners see him as part of the Ghede, or death spirit family.

Legend has it that only two official Roman Catholic churches in the United States allow a statue of St. Expedite to be displayed. I could find only one—not too surprisingly—in New Orleans: Our lady of Guadalupe Chapel. So on a trip to New Orleans, I could not resist visiting Our Lady of Guadalupe Chapel on Rampart Street near the edge of the French Quarter, the closest church to St. Louis Cemetery No. 1. This church is important in the history of New Orleans for a variety of reasons.

Originally dedicated to St. Anthony, the church was rededicated to Our Lady of Guadalupe and is also home to the International Society of St. Jude, which is known locally as "St. Jude's" and as "The Voodoo Church." St. Expedite and his confederate, so to speak, St. Jude, a more mainstream Catholic saint, are both revered by the practitioners of vodou and hoodoo in Louisiana.

Known also as "the funeral church," Our Lady of Guadalupe Chapel was constructed in the early nineteenth century so that funerals for victims of yellow fever and other communicable diseases would be close to the cemetery and far from densely populated areas like the nearby French Quarter. For decades, the chapel has provided the official chaplain for the New Orleans Police and Fire Departments. The church was a sanctuary during Hurricane Katrina—the French Quarter and its environs did not flood nearly as badly as the rest of the city—and today it provides housing for homeless women as well as for students who come to help rebuild New Orleans.

The church's website is a font of information, including bragging rights to recording artist Aaron Neville, who sings there from time to time and is a follower of St. Jude, but nowhere on the site does it even mention that statue of St. Expedite, the one I saw with my own eyes when I was there!

Vodou queen Marie Laveau may have been a regular at the elegant St. Louis Cathedral in the French Quarter, but today, the "Voodoos" as they are called locally go to Our Lady of Guadalupe, and to the shrines of Sts. Jude and Expedite.

Hoodoo, Vodou, and Santería practicioners call on St. Expedite when something absolutely, positively, has to get done overnight. He is sought out specifically for particular financial needs—the more specific, the better. On Dr. E's site, for example, one college student stated that he needed a certain amount of money over and above what his initial financial aid award. He asked St. Expedite for the extra money, and the next time he went to financial aid office, he learned that the award had been amended to include the exact dollar amount he needed. He credits St. Expedite.

St. Expedite also, yes, expedites results that are moving too slowly. It gets very interesting here, for now our special delivery saint aids not just traditional adherents, but also those who work in contract jobs, freelancers, and anyone else who gets paid after they do the work, rather than getting a regular salary. One freelancer reports that a company was very slow in paying her for a project she completed, so she taped a St. Expedite card to her computer monitor and the money suddenly came through. There are self-described "computer geeks" who now count St. Expedite as their patron saint!

To ask St. Expedite for help, place his image, a glass of water, and a red candle on your altar, bureau, or computer workstation. Say the prayer on the back of the prayer card (or one of many found online), then ask him very specifically for what you need. The best time to do this is on Wednesday, the day of Mercury the messenger—in hoodoo and vodou, St. Expedite is associated with Papa Legba, Baron Samedi, Ellegua, and other "messenger" spirits. Light the candle every day until your wish is granted.

After he grants your wish, offer him flowers, a glass of water, and a slice of pound cake. According to Ray Malbrough, believers leave nine quarters by his statue at "the Voodoo church" with their offerings. New Orleans tradition has it that he prefers Sara Lee pound cake. How anyone figured this out is unclear. Here are two prayers to St. Expedite from St. Expedite.com; one is clearly in the Christian tradition, and the other is more ecumenical:

When in Urgent Need: Pray to Saint Expedite

Our dear martyr and protector, Saint Expedite,
You who know what is necessary and what
*   is urgently needed.*
I beg you to intercede before the Holy Trinity, that by
*   your grace my request will be granted.*
_____ (Clearly express what you want,
*   and ask him to find a way to get it to you.)*
May I receive your blessings and favors.
In the name of our Lord Jesus Christ, Amen.

For Quick Help: Pray to Saint Expedite

Saint Expedite, you lay in rest.
I come to you and ask that this wish be granted.
_____ (Clearly express what you want,
    and ask him to find a way to get it to you.)
Expedite now what I ask of you.
Expedite now what I want of you, this very second.
Don't waste another day.
Grant me what I ask for.
I know your power, I know you because of your work.
I know you can help me.
Do this for me and I will spread your name
    with love and honor
So that it will be invoked again and again.
Expedite this wish with speed, love, honor, and goodness.
Glory to you, Saint Expedite!

In addition, there are many videos on YouTube about St. Expedite, many of them made for the express purpose of thanking him for his help. His reach across religions is evident as the videos were created by followers of numerous belief systems from numerous countries: Wiccans from the United States and Candomblé followers from Brazil among them.

A statue of St. Expedite figures prominently in the film *Skeleton Key*, a fine supernatural thriller set in Louisiana that depicts some of the most authentic hoodoo I've seen on film, but he is never named in the film or even referred to…he's just there, for those in the know to recognize!

It's been more than twenty years since that santera told me about St. Expedite, and I'm happy that in 2009 I actually got to see his niche in "the Voodoo church." I'm taping his prayer card to my computer monitor right now.

For Further Study

Armenian Catholic Church. ArmenianCatholic. org. http://www.armeniancatholic.org/inside. php?lang=en&page_id=10.

Dr. E. *The Conjure Blog: Hoodoo at Its Best.* http:// conjuredoctor.blogspot.com/2009/02/saint-expedite.html.

Herczog, Mary. *Frommer's New Orleans 2009.* Hoboken: Wiley Publishing, 2009.

Malbrough, Ray. *Hoodoo Mysteries.* St. Paul: Llewellyn Worldwide, 2003.

San Expedito: Patron de las Causas Urgentes y Justas. http://www.san-expedito.com.ar.

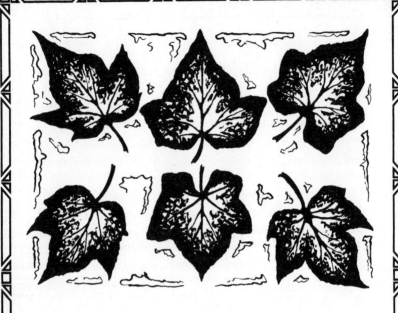

Nature Printing

by Autumn Damiana

One of the central themes to Paganism is the changing of the seasons. As the wheel of the year turns, we mark the passing of time by taking our cues from Mother Nature and her plant life. Sometimes the way we celebrate these changes is through seasonal crafts. We gather bouquets, dry flowers, carve pumpkins, dye eggs, make cornhusk dolls, etc., when those items are abundant. Wreath-making is one of the few nature crafts not restricted to one season—they can be made out of flowers, wheat, grape vines, pine boughs, and holly—which might explain its popularity. However, I would like to share another craft that can also be done any time of year, and that is the craft of nature printing.

The term "nature printing" means the art of using an object from nature as a "stamp," usually by loading it with paint or ink and then creating a copy of the object by pressing it onto a surface. Nature printing has been used for centuries the world over as scientists, explorers, and artists sought to document newly "discovered" species, or to simply preserve their beauty in memory. Herbs, leaves, and flowers are the most common subjects of a nature print, but branches, feathers, shells, nuts, fruits and vegetables, and even rocks can be printed. In some cases, insects, animals, and even things like spiderwebs and honeycombs have been used. There are different ways to prepare each subject. Solid, three-dimensional objects (such as a pine cone or a fish) usually just need to be washed clean and dried off before adding paint and making a print. More delicate pieces (like a daisy or a lettuce leaf) can also be printed as they are, but will make much more accurate and detailed prints if first pressed flat.

Here are the basic, all-purpose instructions for making a nature print. The first three items (nature object, printing surface, and craft paint) will change depending on what you are making. Then there are three sample projects that can be made using these same directions, with a few variations. For your first few tries, I recommend using fairly flat, broad, fresh green leaves of any type. These will be the easiest to manipulate until you get a feel for how the process works.

Items needed:
Nature object (leaves, flowers, herbs, etc.)
Printing surface (paper, cardstock, cloth, wood, etc.)
Appropriate craft paint (acrylic, glass paint, fabric paint, etc.)
Waxed paper
Paper towels
A paint tray (I prefer to use something recycled, such as a
    rinsed-out foam container that meat is packaged in, or
    a plastic margarine lid. Two or three clean paper plates
    stacked together work equally well.)

A variety of small paintbrushes (Pick an inexpensive acrylic or watercolor set—synthetic is best, because cheap natural brushes will "shed" hairs)

A pair of tweezers

A flat, dull knife

A heavy book (a large dictionary or encyclopedia)

Several bricks, or a stack of other heavy books

Paper to cover your work surface (newspaper, butcher paper, grocery bags, etc.)

Optional: markers or watercolors, glue, and embellishments (such as glitter, sequins, ribbons, beads, confetti, etc.)

Directions: Select your leaves for printing, and choose a book in which to press them. Tear two sheets of waxed paper (larger than the pages in the book). Open your book somewhere in the middle, and place one sheet of waxed paper on the right-hand side of the open book, taking care to line up the piece of waxed paper as close to the left-hand side (down in the "crack," near the book's binding) as possible. The remaining three sides of the waxed paper should extend beyond the book's page. This ensures that the pressed leaf does not contact the book, as the moisture from the leaf could potentially damage the pages.

Arrange your leaves on the waxed paper. Do not let the leaves extend beyond the perimeter of the book's page, or they will not be pressed when you close the book. Also make sure that the leaves do not touch or overlap, as this will prevent the leaves from being pressed evenly. Now take your other sheet of waxed paper, and line it up on the left-hand page in the same way as you did before on the right. If you followed these directions correctly, you should have two mirror-image pieces of waxed paper covering the opened book, with your leaves spread out on the right-hand side. If this is the case, carefully close the book. Do not slam the book shut, as this will disrupt your leaf layout.

If you have other heavy books, stack them on top of the book you just closed. Two or three bricks will work just as well. Wait at least three to four hours for the leaves to be pressed flat. When in doubt, opt for a longer press time. Generally, the thicker the veins and/or stem on a leaf, the longer it should press. If you are using particularly thick, gummy, or resinous foliage, you should also consider layering paper towels between the waxed paper sheets and the pages in your book.

When you think that your leaves are ready, carefully open the book and look at them. Are they flat? Do they have a mashed-down, "wilted" appearance? If so, grab one of your leaves by the stem (use the tweezers if necessary) and gently peel it off of the waxed paper. The leaf should be completely collapsed and pliable. (If not, replace the leaf, and press the whole batch for a few hours more.) The leaves should also peel off easily; however, if they have pressed out a residue or are particularly delicate, you may need to use a flat, dull knife to separate them from the waxed paper. Lay each leaf on a paper towel. Pat them dry if necessary.

Now, arrange whatever paper you are using as a makeshift blotter to keep the mess off your workspace. Squirt a tiny dab of each paint color you will use into your paint tray. Lay your first leaf onto a clean paper towel, with the side you wish to print facing up. Use a paintbrush to spread the color(s) in a thin layer onto the leaf. Now flip the leaf over (again, using the tweezers if necessary) onto a sheet of paper, and gently press down with your fingertips over the entire surface of the leaf. Peel the leaf off by the stem to reveal your print. Repeat these last steps several times on scratch paper (using different leaves if you like) to perfect your overall technique. Perhaps you want to use less paint, or print the other side of the leaf. Experiment until you are happy with the results. (Note: to print any nonpressable object, simply clean the object, dry it off, apply paint, and "roll" it across your printing surface. Again, make a few practice prints first to see how they come out.)

Book of Shadows Pages

If you have followed the directions above and produced a few prints that you like, then you know everything you need to know to print on paper. What better place to start than your BOS? Using liquid acrylic paint, press and print pictures of herbs you use frequently, along with any herbal spells, recipes, and correspondences. Basil, mint, and sage are easy to find in any grocery store, and simple to print. Try adding some decorations to your other pages as well. You can print shells on any ocean or water-themed pages, feathers on pages having to do with the air element, fruits and veggies on recipe pages, and flowers and leaves just about anywhere. Use markers or watercolors to enhance your prints, and add glitter or other embellishments if you like.

Autumn Leaf Altar Cloth

As the title suggests, cloth will be needed for this project, in addition to some fabric paint in several fall colors. If you happen to be handy with a needle and thread, you can make your own altar cloth from scratch in whatever size and shape you wish. Purchasing a ready-made tablecloth is the next best thing, and using a plain bandanna will work perfectly for a small altar, or as an accent on a larger table. Whatever covering you decide to work with, select a thick, preferably natural cloth, such as cotton, which is easy to print and will keep paint from bleeding through.

You will want to choose a color appropriate for the season that will also complement your paint colors. I suggest brown, black, golden yellow, or maroon. As for foliage to print, any large deciduous leaf, especially one that is easy to recognize, is a great choice. Use oak for protection or strength, maple for money or longevity, or birch for purification. Try scattering leaf prints every which way over a smaller cloth, while a larger piece of material might look better with a leaf border or with prints concentrated at the corners and in the center. You can also dress up your design with gold outlines, beadwork, or embroidery.

Apple Pentacle Dish

For this project, you will need an eight-inch clear glass plate for your printing surface, at least one apple, some apple tree leaves, and preferably apple blossoms as well. Other necessities for this project include glass paint and a white grease pencil (sometimes called a china marker.)

To start with, you need to prep your apple. Slice through the apple along its equator (through the center from side to side, not up and down, as you would normally cut an apple). Look inside the two halves. There should be five seed pockets inside the apple that form a pentacle. Choose the side that displays the pentacle more beautifully, cut it off in a one-quarter–inch slice, and discard the seeds. (Keep cutting slices off either half of the apple if your first cut fails to yield the pentacle

pattern.) Take two paper towels and fold each into quarters. Place one folded paper towel on a flat surface, such as a cutting board, followed by your apple slice and the remaining folded paper towel. Now place a piece of waxed paper on top of that. Finally, put the book or heavy brick on top of the pile. Check your apple every half-hour, replacing the paper towels as they become soggy. After two or three hours, the excess juice in the apple slice should be gone.

Press the leaves and blossoms using the directions above.

Next you will need to assemble your design. I recommend printing on the back of the plate, which requires a bit of fore-thought. First, trace the outline of the plate onto the paper you have spread onto your work surface. Now, place the apple slice in the center of the plate, arranging the leaves and blossoms to frame it, overlapping if you like. When you are satisfied with the results, place the glass plate on top of your arrangement. Use the grease pencil to outline each shape on the top of the plate. Now you can flip the plate over, and print each piece on to the space you have outlined on the front of the plate. If you have leaves and blossoms overlapping the apple slice, make sure to print these first. When the paint is dry, you may turn the plate over again and wipe away the grease marks. Don't forget to also follow the instructions on curing/baking time for the glass paint.

~

After you've tried your hand at nature printing with a variety of objects, paints, and surfaces, there really is no end to the projects you can apply it to. Try making your own Pagan-themed greeting cards, recipe cards, wrapping paper, or simply frame your prints and hang them on the wall. Decorate your ritual robes, clothing, book bags, or drapery. You can print on tiles to make trivets and coasters or embellish plain, inexpensive pottery, glass, and ceramic for beautiful, nature-inspired gifts and altar furniture. Let your creativity run wild and see what you can come up with. Happy nature printing!

Sacred Geometry in the Home
by Tess Whitehurst

In our homes, geometry is everywhere we look: the round kitchen table, the tiled floor, the striped curtains, and even the floor plan and structure of the home itself. When we become aware of the presence of the ancient magical principles behind all these shapes and patterns, we are lifted out of the illusion that our everyday reality is "mundane," and we arrive at the truth—that every single thing we see is sacred. Not only that, but we discover that the home is in fact an alchemical symphony, and we are empowered to magically conduct this symphony in order to create positive conditions in every area of our lives.

The Magic of Your Home's Floor Plan

You may be familiar with an ancient mathematical construct that is known as the "magic square." Present in the magical and alchemical systems of many countries, it's essentially a grid with a number in each square. Each row of numbers in a magic square adds up to the same number whether you add vertically or horizontally. There is a specific type of magic square known in the Hermetic tradition as the "square of Saturn," and in Taoist alchemy as the *lo shu*. This is a nine-square grid (like a tic-tac-toe board), with rows of numbers that each add up to the number 15. (See illustration.)

In feng shui (a branch of Taoist alchemy), the lo shu is strategically placed over the floor plan of one's home, and each of the nine areas in the home corresponds with a major life area. Interestingly, this corresponds to the Hermetic name for the lo shu—the "square of Saturn." Saturn is the planet of time, limitation, stability, and karmic lessons. Not only does the degree of stability we feel in our homes mirror the degree of stability we feel in our lives, but our homes are also our own little designated areas of the planet, where we literally contain and confine our belongings and personal space. Furthermore, each major life area encapsulates the karmic lessons and challenges that we are experiencing at this particular moment in time.

To discover the magical floor plan of your home, follow these simple steps:

Sketch or obtain a simple line drawing that shows the wall and door placement, as well as any attached covered patios or attached garages. If you live in an apartment, the drawing only needs to depict the walls and doors of your apartment (not the entire building).

Draw an arrow just outside the front door of your home, pointing inward. (Note: this should be the front door as intended by the architect, or the "technical" front door—not just the door you usually use.)

If necessary, rotate the page so that the arrow is pointing upward.

If the outline of your home (including attached garages or attached patios) is not a perfect square or rectangle, make it into one by extending the edges as necessary.

Draw a tic-tac-toe board over the square or rectangle that is your floor plan, so that you divide it into nine equal parts.

Write in the numbers as in the illustration (e.g., with the number four in the upper left corner).

4	9	2
3	5	7
8	1	6

Here's a key to the significance of each numbered area:

4 – Wealth, prosperity, abundance, gratitude, and blessings of all types

9 – Fame, reputation, radiance, shining your unique light, sharing your gifts, and how you are known and seen in the world

2 – Romance, love, marriage, receptivity, intimacy, and harmonious co-creation

3 – Physical and emotional health; family and family-like relationships; connection with ancestors, elders, and deceased loved ones; ancient wisdom, and harmonious coexistence within the household

5 – Grounding, centering, balance of all life areas, holistic wellness

7 – Creativity, playfulness, joy, lightheartedness, birthing (of babies, projects, or conditions), relationship with children, relationship with the inner-child

8 – Serenity, stillness, self-love, meditation, spirituality, study, exercise, self-improvement

1 – Career, life path, integrity, depth, intuition, authenticity, inner truth

6 – Synchronicity, miracles, divine guidance and assistance, help and support from other people, communication, travel

Take some time to think about these areas of your home. How does the current arrangement and use sync up with your life in the context of the lo shu.

The Magic of Shapes

Each simple shape has magical properties all its own. Contemplating these properties (especially when combined with an awareness of the nine life areas that make up our floor plans) allows us to see how they're already at work in our homes and to consciously wield sacred geometrical principles in order to create the feelings and conditions we desire in our lives.

Circles

Circles are a symbol of infinity, the wheel of the year, the heavenly/invisible/otherworldly realm, and protection. They also evoke still or gently swirling water, as it appears in lakes, ponds, fountains, cups, and pools, as well as the (Chinese) metal element, which represents precision and the conscious mind. Bringing circles into your home is a good way to soften and balance the natural excess of squares and rectangles found in most modern spaces. Here are some ideas:

A wreath on the front door employs the power of the circle to protect the home from negativity and/or bless the home with a celebratory and uplifting reminder of the wheel of the year.

A round (or oval) mirror is like a meditative reflecting pool and can be especially positive in the area that corresponds with the number "1" to help you to align with your natural flow in life and your truest and most authentic self. A round or oval mirror can also be wonderful above a fireplace to balance the fire energy and vitalize a room.

Polka dots activate the fun and creative aspects of the conscious mind and intellect, and, if you're drawn to them, they're especially positive in the area that corresponds with the number "7."

A round (or oval) rug can move the energy around a room in a harmonious way and aesthetically unite all aspects of a room. You might also choose a smaller-sized round rug for your meditation area and sit in the middle of it to feel protected and focused during meditations, visualizations, and rituals.

A round table promotes feelings of equality and harmony among those seated at it, and is therefore ideal for the kitchen and dining areas (or oval if appropriate to the space and number of diners).

Round or oval coffee tables are also ideal. Square and rectangular coffee tables can cause the energy to feel boxy, awkward, or stagnant while round or oval coffee tables move the energy in a softer, more elegant, and more dynamic way while simultaneously balancing the (usually) square or rectangular shape of the walls and room.

Round shapes in artwork, frames, throw pillows, and elsewhere activate the general energies mentioned above and are especially positive in the areas that correspond with the numbers "1," "7," and "6."

Squares

Ah, the square. Simplicity itself. Square one. In Taoist alchemy, square shapes represent solidity, grounding, centering, nourishment, and the earth element.

It should not be surprising, then, that in Native American, Wiccan, and other earth-based cosmologies, the number four plays a major part, as in the four elements, the four seasons, and the four cardinal points or directions. Similarly, modern science notes that protons, neutrons, electrons, and electron neutrinos are the four particles that make up all matter. Four is a solid number that grounds us in the magical cycles and earthy sensuality of our everyday existence here on this planet.

And, in our modern spaces, it often seems that four's most basic geometric incarnation—the square (or its close relative the rectangle)—appears everywhere, from cupboards to tiles to doors to entire buildings.

The best places to put extra squares (in addition to all the cupboards, picture frames, etc.) would be the areas that correspond to the numbers "5," "2," and "8"—all areas that have to do with stillness, grounding, and receptivity.

Triangle

Triangles are fiery and dynamic, like rays of the Sun or the edges of a flame. Because triangles bring in the fire element, triangles and triangle-heavy patterns and prints are generally positive in the area that corresponds with the number "9," where they can enhance its associated energies.

An equilateral triangle can represent the health and harmony associated with living so that one's mind, body, and spirit are all equally and abundantly nourished.

Three is a very mystical number that represents the birth of all things from the marriage of the divine masculine and feminine principles (yin and yang). And, as the most basic geometric representative of three, triangles (especially equilateral) hold this mystical energy as well. Chapter 42 of the *Tao te Ching*, as translated by Stephen Mitchell, begins:

> *The Tao gives birth to One.*
> *One gives birth to Two.*
> *Two gives birth to Three.*
> *Three gives birth to all things.*

Rectangle

Rectangles have very similar qualities to squares in that they bring in the earth element and are consequently very grounding. For this reason, they are excellent in the center of the home, also known as the area associated with the number "5."

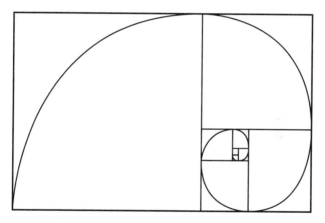

And then there is a special type of rectangle, known as the "golden section" or "golden mean" rectangle.

This type of rectangle mirrors the spiral shape found in nature (see illustration) and visually demonstrates the sacred geometric construct known as the "golden ratio." The golden section rectangle is used often in art and architecture because it's perceived as particularly beautiful and harmonious.

Hexagon

Bees love hexagons—you can tell by their hives. The prodigious, synchronized, and highly organized existence of bees is the perfect illustration of the energy of the hexagon, which represents the place where our hard work and preparations meet and are blessed with divine orchestration.

Six is a very divine number, and represents heavenly help and miraculous orchestration. Snowflakes are a case in point, gently falling from heaven to earth, each intricate six-sided shape a breathtakingly beautiful reminder of the universe's unflagging inventiveness and truly incomprehensible attention to detail.

Hexagons often appear in our homes in the form of tiling, but can also appear in other forms, including plaques, prints, mirrors, charms, or geometric art.

The energies associated with (you guessed it) the area that corresponds to the number "6" area are perfectly in alignment with the magical qualities of the hexagon. Placing a hexagon or hexagons in this area will help you to experience miracles and to consistently be in the right place at the right time.

Being in divine flow is a prerequisite to experiencing true abundance. For example, notice how it helps the bees to harvest their sweet, golden treasure trove of abundance (honey). And so, another positive placement for a hexagon or hexagons is the area associated with the number "4."

Spiral

Spirals have, since ancient times, universally symbolized life, planetary movement, and the cosmos. Interestingly, we now know that our galaxy appears in the form of a spiral (as do more than half of all other known galaxies).

Hurricanes also appear as spirals, and hurricanes—while often maligned—do get energy moving in a healthy way by stirring things up and bringing greater balance to temperature and climate.

Water moves down the drain in the form of a spiral, wind patterns are often invisible spirals, many seashells are spirals, feathers and some parts of plants fall through the air in spirals, and some birds move along a spiral path as they hunt their prey. These are just a few of the many examples of spirals in nature. It's a shape that Mother Nature loves.

Spiral shapes are excellent in the area associated with the number "6," as they bring in the energy of the cosmos and divine harmony. In the area associated with the number "8," they can help align us with our spirituality and connect us to the Divine.

A rug containing a spiral shape or shapes, when placed in the center area of the home (a.k.a., area number "5"), can help stir things up in your life if you've been feeling stagnant or stuck, especially if you prepare by clearing out all the extra clutter from your home. Then, when you feel ready, bring in the rug and perform a ritual to magically empower it with your intentions.

The Language of Sacred Geometry

Once you become aware of the interplay of sacred geometrical principles in your home, you'll begin to become aware of the interplay of sacred geometrical principles everywhere. Little by little, this ancient science will come alive to you and reveal its own secrets in ways that are meaningful to you personally. You will see what underlies and defines the fabric of existence, and unites all things. And, eventually, you will become fluent in the magical language of sacred geometry.

For Further Study

Gauding, Madonna. *The Signs and Symbols Bible.* New York: Sterling, 2009.

Lundy, Miranda. *Sacred Geometry.* New York: Walker and Company, 2001.

Lundy, Miranda. *Sacred Number.* New York: Walker and Company, 2005.

Spitzer, K. D. "Magic Squares." Llewellyn's 2009 Magical Almanac. Woodbury, MN: Llewellyn, 2008.

Tzu, Lao and Mitchell, Stephen. *The Tao Te Ching*. New York: Harper Perennial, 1991.

Whitehurst, Tess. *Magical Housekeeping: Simple Charms and Practical Tips for Creating a Harmonious Home*. Woodbury, MN: Llewellyn, 2010.

Air Magic

Academic Patrons for College Students

by Blake Octavian Blair

Venturing off to college is an exciting time. For many, it is their first time living away from home. A time for exploration and examination of the self, college can be an opportunity to further develop one's path in life. Although some may not readily admit it, I think most students would like and could benefit from a little spiritual help during the experience. A terrific start is to find an academic patron who can help you with your field of study and serve as a guide not only during your college years but also throughout your career.

There are a number of ways to go about finding your own academic patron. If you already have a specific cultural pantheon you like to work with, by all means start there. There is a good chance you will find a deity you connect with in that pantheon who presides over the domain you are studying. If not, or if you do not feel a connection with that specific deity, don't be afraid to expand your search. A natural place to start is by researching which deities are historically associated with your field of study. Throughout history and across cultures worldwide, there have been deities who have presided over certain professions. Remember, even if you have already devoted yourself to a patron deity, your academic patron may or may not be a different god, goddess, or spirit. Therefore, it is still advisable to go through a bit of exploration to see which deity might best fit your academic ventures. (Later in this article, we'll look at some examples of deities who can serve as academic patrons for some common and intriguing areas of study.)

Another more intuitive approach can be used to find your academic patron, especially if you're having trouble deciding which deity (out of several possibilities) with whom you should work. You can perform a simple ritual and meditation asking a patron to make itself known to you. I have always believed that patron deities choose their devotees, rather than the other way around! This method facilitates that philosophy.

Here is an example of a ritual in the spirit of this intuitive approach that you can use to help find your academic patron. After you have familiarized yourself

with the various deities presiding over your major or area of study, gather a yellow candle (yellow represents intellect, the mind, and the element of air) and a secure holder. Prepare a simple offering such as incense and bread or fruit, and a book related to your major. For example, if you were going to medical school, choose an anatomy book. Arrange the items on your altar and light the candle. Address the gods and goddesses of your profession and ask that the deity who would best serve as your patron to come forth and make itself known to you. Explain that you have left the offerings as a gift of your gratitude. Let the candle burn out (keeping an eye on it, of course). If your result does not immediately come to you in a vision, it will likely come to you in the next few days in the form of a vision, omen, or other sign associated with the deity. You will likely know without a doubt when they make contact.

It is important to remember that deities quite often have overlapping spheres of interest and may provide guidance in more than one area of study. For instance, the Celtic goddess Brigid is known to preside over not only education, but to have an affinity for writers of all kinds, as well as being a patroness to healers and midwives. Thus far, we can already see Brigid as a possible patron for those studying in such diverse fields as medicine and nursing, as well as English, literature, and poetry. Furthermore, another aspect to Brigid is as a goddess of the forge and blacksmiths, also making her a possible patron for the study of various technical trades. Due to this diversity, it would be impossible to mention each sphere or domain each deity could possibly serve. However, here is a brief overview of some popular and growing areas of study, as well as common and intriguing possibilities for academic patrons.

Medicine is an ever-expanding field with a growing need for an array of doctors, nurses, and various types of technicians. The array of possible patrons for these fields is equally expansive. As mentioned earlier, the goddess Brigid is a popular deity for healing professions; however, she is often particularly associated with midwives and childbirth, making her an excellent choice for those going into obstetrics and pediatrics. The African-diasporic spirit Ogun, from the religions of Vodou and Santeria, is also associated with healing. Although well known as a god of iron and of warriors, in the form of Ogun Balendjo, he takes the role of the healer. He is the spirit of the Ogun River and is seen to preside over healing waters. Perhaps due to his combined association with metal, war, and healing, he might be a good choice for someone who may end up working in an ER or perhaps treating those wounded by war, violence, or other trauma.

Deities who preside over and are associated with the crossroads can serve as excellent patrons for those studying to enter fields relating to counseling and social work. Patients and clients that seek the assistance of these professions are usually experiencing events that represent some type of metaphorical crossroads in their life. Of course, for many Witches, the very term "crossroads" evokes associations of the Greek goddess Hecate. Hecate is a quite a fine choice of patron for those entering counseling professions as she is not only the guardian of the crossroads, who has access to all realms, but also a healer. She is considered a torchbearer—a bringer of light. This is a wonderful blend of qualities for someone studying to counsel those in need. Another crossroads spirit that may be sympathetic to your studies in social services would be Legba. In the African-diasporic traditions, Legba is the spirit who presides over the crossroads, where he is found with his walking stick, perhaps awaiting to assist on your journey. He helps devotees navigate important decisions and improve communication. However, Legba is a trickster, and if not kept happy, he will play tricks upon you. So it is best to make sure you acknowledge him respectfully and leave offerings in return for his guidance. If a crossroads deity seems up your alley, you might choose to perform the ritual given earlier for finding a patron at a crossroads and leaving your offerings there.

For students studying scientific paths such as chemistry, engineering, and physics, the ancient Egyptian god Thoth might be eagerly waiting to guide you. Admittedly, Thoth's spheres of influence are quite vast. However, he is notably seen in Egyptian mythology as being the creator of, among other things, mathematics, engineering, geometry, as well as alchemy and spellcraft—an excellent combination of qualities for a scientifically academic Pagan, if I do say so myself! Perhaps he'll even be willing to help you navigate Calculus 3!

The Hindu goddess Laxmi has been known to provide assistance and guidance to those studying business and accounting. While Laxmi is more multifaceted than indicated by her reputation as a goddess of money and wealth, she does indeed have a powerful influence over these areas that cannot be denied. She is quite approachable and caring of her devotees, which is not uncharacteristic of deities of good fortune and happiness. In fact, she can be quite the helpful goddess to have on your side as you live the life of a college stu-

dent, no matter your major or area of study! However, be aware that Laxmi becomes easily displeased with those that come to her only to ask for money. I'm sure you'd become upset too! It is important to remember that the wealth Laxmi governs over extends beyond the monetary realm and into that of happiness, friendship, home, and family. So be sure to acknowledge her for her wisdom in addition to her other abundant qualities.

If your chosen field of study involves English, literature, poetry, and related areas, the array of deities waiting to guide you is voluminous. Another Hindu goddess, Sarasvati, is an excellent choice to consider, as she is considered matron of literature and wisdom. She is also believed to favor musicians and students of the musical arts, which comes as no surprise considering that images of Sarasvati are easily identified by her holding of a large sitar. Another wonderful choice would be Egyptian goddess Seshet, who, among other things, is patroness over books, writers, and librarians. Seshet also happens to be Thoth's wife. For those specifically studying poetry, an interesting selection is the Norse god Bragi, the son of Odin. Bragi is patron of poets. For the ancient Norse it was a poet's duty to open spiritual gateways within the consciousness so that a person could receive messages. Perhaps Bragi can help you find and instill purpose within your writing and carry on the great tradition of the poet.

Fields involving work with the natural world and the environment are increasingly popular as the need for said work continues to grow. Deities such as the Green Man, Pan, Dionysus, and Shiva all lend themselves as excellent choices for fields such as agriculture, horticulture, ecology, and environmental engineering. It has been my personal experience that in general the gods are quite adaptable beings who do not mind updating with the times. For example, it is often overlooked that Dionysus is not simply just the god of wine, but also a god of the natural world and the wild. Also, Hindu god Shiva is often known as Lord of Beasts, presiding over the world's animals. He may perhaps be a fitting patron for those going into veterinary medicine or zoology. While these are certainly nontraditional applications of these gods' areas of influence, one can clearly see that they are not off track and are in fact quite an appropriate fit in a modern context.

However, it is important to acknowledge that not every Pagan seeking higher education finds themselves on the track for a traditional four-year degree. Many will choose specialized trades that require attending special institutions. For example, those attending cosmetology school may feel an alignment with the spirit of New Orleans Vodou Queen Marie Laveau; now considered a Vodou Lwa, she is known to keep an eye out for hairdressers!

As Pagans, we are familiar with the cycle of life, death, and rebirth. Thus, we know that there will always be a need for those who do mortuary work. If you should choose to study funerary sciences, look into any spirit who is considered a psychopomp for your patron. Psychopomps are deities or spirits who escort and assist those newly departed from this realm to the afterlife. In Egyptian culture, Anubis is a god who presides over the rituals, preparation, and mummification of the bodies of the deceased. Other popular psychopomps are Archangel Michael, Santisima Muerte, and Hecate.

Once you have found your academic patron, remember to honor and communicate with them frequently. Personally, the Hindu god Ganesha is my general and academic patron. All during my college years, and to this day, I keep a small statue of him on my desk, in front of which I place offerings and say prayers. You can similarly set up a small shrine at your desk or study space. Honor the deity each day when you sit down to work or before you head out to class, and thank it for its continued guidance. Another way I've done this is by keeping a key ring in Ganesha's image attached to a zipper on my backpack for continued inspiration throughout the school day. A similar idea for keeping a reminder of your patron with you through your class schedule is to print out an image of your patron and affix it to the cover of a three-ring binder you use for classes, or by wearing spells, charms, and accessories aligned to your god or spirit. Regular, humble connection and communication with your patron will help strengthen your bond with them. Now, venture forth into your studies with the confidence that you have divine assistance on your path!

For Further Study

Krasskova, Galina. *Exploring the Northern Tradition: A guide to the Gods, Lore, Rites, and Celebrations from the Norse, German, and Anglo-Saxon Traditions*. Franklin Lakes NJ: New Page Books, 2005.

Illes, Judika. *Encyclopedia of Spirits: The Ultimate Guide to the Magic of Fairies, Genies, Demons, Ghosts, Gods & Goddesses*. New York: Harper One, 2009.

Grimassi, Raven. *Encyclopedia of Wicca & Witchcraft: 2nd Edition Revised & Expanded*. Woodbury, MN: Llewellyn Publications, 2000 & 2003.

Kinsley, David R. Hindu Goddesses: *Visions of the Divine Feminine in the Hindu religious Tradition*. Los Angeles, CA: University of California Press, 1986.

Glassman, Sallie Ann. *Vodou Visions: An Encounter With Divine Mystery,* 2nd Edition. New Orleans, LA: Island of Salvation Botanica, 2000.

Petitions and Incantation:
The Magic of Speaking Out

by Dallas Jennifer Cobb

Sounds have powerful effects on the human psyche, stimulating strong mental, emotional, and instinctual responses. Gentle running water can produce an experience of calm, a heart beat sound is commonly used to comfort babies and young animals, and the deep rumbling sound of thunder often evokes fear. Of all the sounds we know, perhaps the most powerful is the sound of the human voice. The human voice can affect all who hear it, produce feelings of love and security, provide direction and purpose, and instill order.

The voice is also a powerful tool. Even when we are alone, feeling powerless and weak, and think we are without defense, we can use our voice to break the bonds of silence, and speak our truth.

The vibration or resonance of voice can uplift the spirit, focus intention, change consciousness, and shape reality. Whether use it for speaking, whispering, shouting, or singing; or employ it in a purposeful and productive manner through incantation, enchantment, petition, charm or mantra, the voice can be used to work magic.

Following the Universal Laws of Nature[1] that describe how energy behaves and the patterns it moves in, we know that sound vibration has an energy signature, and that it affects the objects and subjects that it touches, influencing them and changing their vibration. Quite literally, sound has the power to change the energy of a person, interaction, thought, or feeling.

A powerful magical tool, be sure to learn how best to use your voice. Words have always been used to cast spells and state intentions. They have been chanted, recited, and written down, engaging the vibration of the voice and its transformative power in the working of magic.

Incantation

According to the online source, The Free Dictionary, an incantation is "the ritual recitation of verbal charms or spells to produce a magic effect." The origins of incantation are from the Middle English *incantacioun*, the old French *incantation*, the Late Latin *incantation*, and the Latin *incantatus*, the past participle of *incantare*, to enchant.[2]

Traditionally, an incantation was a ritual recitation of a (usually rhyming) phrase. It could be whispered, chanted, spoken, sung, or droned. The verbal uttering of a spell had only to be audible for it to have outward effect in the world, and the silent, internal recitation of an incantation had inward effect on the person reciting it.

Used during a magical ceremony, spell, or ritual, incantations were used to harness the energy of the individual or group for the purpose of creating magical results. Frequently used in spell

---

1 A lot is written about Universal Laws. For popular, modern sources see Milanovich, Dr. Norma J. and McCune, Dr. Shirley D., *The Light Shall Set You Free* Scottsdale, AZ: Athena Publishing, 1998 or Dyer, Dr. Wayne, *The Secrets to Manifesting Your Destiny*, Niles, IL: Nightingale-Conant Corporation, 2002

2 The Free Dictionary, http://www.thefreedictionary.com/Incantation (Accessed August 9, 2009).

work and healing ceremonies, sound vibration dissipates negative energy, replacing the vibration with positive energy via the waves.

The power of the voice in enacting magical change is renown, not only in Pagan circles, communities, and covens, but in the world of protest, social unrest, and social change. Think of the freedom fighters chanting *"we shall overcome"* and the cumulative effect of their voices upon the consciousness of America.

While we all sometimes feel powerless and unheard, we can learn to use the immense power of our voice to transform everyday situations. Whether you open your mouth to tell your family and friends how you feel, speak up at work to contribute your opinion; write letters to local government officials or letters to the editor of the paper; or create petitions to raise awareness, ignite dialogue, and unite people; the voice is a powerful tool to use in working magic.

History of Incantations

Traditionally, incantations were written in metrical form, consisting of an even numbered set of rhyming phrases that were uttered aloud and often repeated. Common to the languages of early Pagan peoples, early incantations are evident in Old English, Old Latin, Greek, Hebrew, Germanic, and early Norse languages.

Hidden from the conquering (and dominating) cultures, incantations often were hidden in hymns, prayers, poetry, and storytelling/mythology. The use of songs as incantations is age old, as the word incantation is derived from the Latin *incantare* (*in*, meaning "into" or "upon," and *cantare* meaning "to sing"). So incantation is to chant a magical spell upon someone, or into something.

Enchantments

Like an incantation, an enchantment is a term used to describe the use of works spoken during a ritual to produce a magical effect. Derived from the Old French *enchantement*, it meant, like the Latin, "to sing energy into or onto something." Enchantement led to the terms enchanter and enchantress titles for those (male and female, respectively) who used enchantments.

Enchantements were common throughout ancient France, so much that the term has survived into modern usage. In French custom, it is common to hear someone murmur enchante after being introduced to an attractive and or seductive person (usually a woman). The use of the terms harkens back to the notion that an enchantress was frequently depicted as a woman able to use magic to seduce, charm, or deceive people. To be enchanted was to be under the effects of an enchanting spell.

Charms

A charm is an object, either an amulet or talisman, which has been magically affected through the use of an incantation that instills a particular task or energy upon the object. Traditionally, charm bracelets were started when children were small. At each major event or turn of life, the child was given a small charm that had been magically imbued, usually with the task of protection for the child.

While the practice of magic and the instilling of magical energy into an object has moved from being an everyday practice to one practiced by a few (those of us who identify as Pagans), the use of magical charms continues even without specific Pagan intent. So often tiny angels are given to "watch over" someone, and religious symbols are also common gifts of protection and blessing.

Mantras

Mantras are words or phrases repeated by someone either silently or aloud for the purpose of affecting consciousness. From the Sanskrit *man* means mind, and *tra* means vibration. So literally *mantra* is to use vibration to shape or change the mind.

The recitation of a mantra, like an incantation, has an energetic effect on the person reciting the mantra and on those who hear it. Mantras are sacred utterances or chanting that are Vedic in origin, and were originally written in Sanskrit.

Not limited to the Hindu tradition, many spiritual practices throughout the world practice the use the voice to produce a desired effect. Whether they consider it as a tool to raise consciousness, produce peace, or find assistance, it is akin to working magic as they use the voice to produce a desired effect.

Buddhist monks chant and drone mantras to raise their level of consciousness to achieve inner peace and find enlightenment. Gregorian Monks were renowned for their chanting that produced calm in all who listened. Christians recite the Rosary for penance, a process of cleansing and uplifting, and some recite the "Our Father" prayer in times of need, a plea for their God to aid them. Not limited to religions, people on a spiritual path also use the voice the change consciousness. Recovering addicts recite the serenity prayer or the 12 Steps to produce a feeling of surety.

In India, scientists have been studying the effects of Mantropathy—the use of mantras to produce healing and cleansing of the environment. Their data supports the notion that daily chanting of a mantra can produce positive results.[3]

Mentally, mantras help to produce calm, focus concentration, and relieve stress. Biofeedback has been used to chart the positive effects (lowered blood pressure, slowed pulse) that mantras have on humans.

However mantras are used, they are effective because the sound of the human voice, its vibration and rhythm, are instruments that produce strong energy, affecting change. The results testify to the effect—inner calm, increased focus, and spiritual uplifting.

Petitions

Living in a democratic society, we have come to know petitions as long paper forms that state the will of a group and are signed by many people who support the cause being petitioned for.

Petitions are a powerful tool for raising community awareness—a way to engage people who otherwise might not have involved themselves in an issue or action to support or reject something. By capturing the energy of a large community through the transference of information to them and garnering of signatures and concern from them, a petition holds enormous power—the energy and vibration of all the people who touch it, and sign it.

Not just a method for communicating community concerns to government, petitioning can be used by an individual to ask for assistance from their higher powers. In Pagan ceremony and ritual, the gods or goddesses are called in, asked to aid the magic

---

3 Rajhans, Gyan, "The Power of Mantra Chanting," Hinduism http://hinduism. about.com/od/prayersmantras/a/mantrachanting.htm (Accessed August 13, 2009).

being worked, and lend their energy to the ritual. Calling upon a god or goddess in this manner is petitioning them for help.

An individual can also privately petition a God or Goddess through incantation, prayer, meditation, or even by writing out their intentions.

Speak Your Will

The voice has significant power not just magically, as in incantations and spell work, or spiritually, as in prayer and medication, but socially, too. Speaking your will is a technique that can produce huge social change. Speaking out can dramatically alter your perceptions, experience, and reality, and finitely affect change all around you. All you have to do is open your mouth and let the vibration out to work its magic on the surrounding objects and subjects.

Think of speaking your will as a technique for focusing intentions and making them manifest in the physical world. Through words, energy can be focused and directed with transformative powers. The power of a person stating what they think or feel is enormous, and when these thoughts or feelings are spoken genuinely, and from a first person singular position (using "I think," or "I feel"), they are virtually inarguable. It is easy to argue with a person who says *war is evil*, but someone who says *I fear war* makes a statement that is fully true for them, and cannot be refuted. The power of speaking your will is enormous, and worth the effort spent learning how to make "I" statements—those personal, powerful and irrefutable words that speak your will.

Speaking your will, speaking out, and speaking your mind also empower you. Too many times people hold their tongue, stay silent at times when maybe they thought or felt they should have said something, and felt impotent and powerless as a result. While speaking out doesn't guarantee that things will go your way, it does guarantee that you were not silent, and did not suppress the power of your own voice. Whether or not the people around you were able to hear you or heed the vibration of what you were saying, it is almost insignificant compared to the power found in speaking out.

Many communities who have been historically silenced (children, youth, women, people of color and elders) have been gradually finding their voices in our communities. As they learn and exert their right to speak out, our perceptions of these communities shift. No longer defined by what is said about them, communities who speak out define themselves and change how they are perceived in the world. There is enormous power in shifting the perceptions of people when a previously voiceless or silenced community starts to speak out, defining their likes, dislikes, and unique identity.

Like a silenced community, when an individual starts to exert their right to use their voice, they are able to define themselves rather than being saddled with outside definitions, they are also able to become a subject in the world, and no longer an object to be spoken about.

Learning specific techniques to speak your will can be useful in day-to-day living, making you better able to confront abuse, affirm affection and discuss ideas. In your magical practice, speaking your will can enable you to focus your intention, making manifest the energy of your thoughts, feelings and desires.

Working Your Will

1. You will need a quiet space, scented oil, and a plain candle. You can consult Llewellyn's website for articles about choosing a candle color conducive to the magic you want to work and for more information on the magical and healing properties of essential oils. For this protective spell, I chose a white candle for purity and protection, and lavender oil to promote feelings of safety, soothing, and calm. While rosemary has the power to protect psychically, I chose to use lavender oil for this spell because it also helps to integrate spiritual qualities into everyday life, and will aid you as you learn this technique of working your will magically.

2. Create a quiet, private space to work your magic in. Take time to breath deeply and center yourself.

3. In your mind, envision what you want to make manifest in the world—the embodiment of your will—in as much detail as you can. For this protection spell I envisioned my house filled with sunshine, my daughter playing on the floor in the play room, and feeling safe, calm, and happy as I watch her. I conjured up the quality of the hardwood floor in the sun, was able to hear my daughter's laughing voice, and feel the calm within my body, knowing we were safe in this happy house.

4. Craft a simple incantation or chant that best summarizes your will. The most effective chants or incantations are simple rhyming couplets with identical meter in each stanza. The rhythm and rhyme are conducive to repetition.

> *Bless this house with love and light,*
> *Keep it safe both day and night.*

5. Envision the reality of safety in your home, repeat the chant aloud, and slowly anoint the candle with the essential oil, charging the candle not just with the oil, but with your energy and intention. Visualization and chanting/incanting both help to transfer your energy signature and positive intentions to the candle.

6. Use this candle on your altar or in a position of significance in your home. Burn it frequently and regularly. Each time you light it affirm your intentions and what you charged the candle with through incantation.

I bless this house with love and light,
It is safe by day and night.

7. As the candle burns it will release the scent of lavender oil into the air. Know that this oil has a protective quality carried in its energy vibration, and know that, like the oil from the candle, your will wafts through the house creating protection and safety for all who dwell within it.

∼

This article is a starting place to get you thinking about the power of your voice. Add your own energy and vision to the process of incantation, petition, and spellcasting. As you find your voice, let it vibrate out into the world to make magical change.

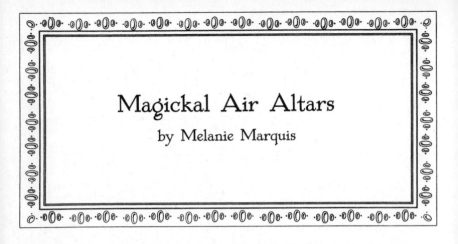

Magickal Air Altars
by Melanie Marquis

There's nothing like a windy day to freshen the spirit and stir up excitement in your magickal routine! When a breeze is blowing, the power of the air element is evident, the atmosphere is infused with its swift and determined force. As a magickal power source, the air is a friend the Witch can't do without. It is the agent of movement, the breath of life, providing energetic channels on which magick can travel quickly. Regardless of the type of spell you're performing, asking the air element to help it along will speed up the magickal process and more swiftly bring results. It is a fluid current, and on that current, your magick can rapidly flow.

The next time you open your door and find a nice wind kicking up, why not take advantage? Set up an altar designed especially to celebrate the air element, and experience new ways to utilize this amazing magick. Here's how.

Altar Design

Air altars can be well-planned, permanent fixtures or temporary, spur-of-the-moment constructions. While it's nice to have a long-standing home altar dedicated to the air element, the wind tends to be unpredictable, so the ability to set up an impromptu altar space wherever you happen to be is wonderfully useful. An air altar can be erected solely with intent, or with nothing more than the handkerchief in your pocket and the dandelion fluffs in the yard. But when you do have the opportunity to put more thought and detail into your air altar design, you'll be rewarded with a ritual space destined to facilitate an unforgettable experience.

The first step in designing your air altar is to find a place for it. You might choose to set up your air altar under a tree, or even in a treehouse nestled amongst the branches. A field of grass also makes a prime spot, as the wind blowing through the vegetation makes a pronounced visual display. If you prefer to work magick indoors, or if you simply don't have a nice outside area for your air altar, just open a window or door and place a small table or box in front of it. A wide windowsill could work nicely as well, or even a hanging basket. See what kind of space you have available, and make it work.

Once you've chosen an area, it's time to purify and enchant the place. Blow gently across the area you have chosen, clearing

out old energies and readying the altar space for the air element to enter.

Next, lay out a piece of cloth to cover the altar surface, or delineate an area by tracing a circle in the dirt. The air likes to feed the fire, so add candles to your altar as a visible display of the effects of this elemental interplay. Smoke is another way to see the air, so light incense or place a steaming cauldron or kettle near the altar.

To add a touch of whimsy and to showcase the air element in action, set up a row of pinwheels, poking the ends into the soil and firmly packing the dirt around them. Put even more magick and movement into your air altar with scarves and ribbons. Tack shorter scarves or fabric strips onto the edge of your altar table, and tie longer ribbons onto tree branches, letting them flutter in the breeze. You can also incorporate ribbons and scarves into your ritual attire; simply tuck them into your belt until you're ready to wave them in the sky and release the spell at hand.

What better way to communicate your joys and sorrows to the air than with the music of a wind instrument? Powered by your own breath, wind instruments put air into an audible and melodic form. Set a flute, recorder, clarinet, pipes, didgeridoo, pan flute, or other wind instrument on your altar so you'll have a way to get your magickal messages across to the sky powers loud and clear.

You might also try giving a voice to the air element by adding wind chimes and bells to your altar. Anoint them with a favorite oil or use string to tie on springs of herbs associated with the air. Hang the chimes and bells from a tree, dangle them out a window, or simply keep them handy until you're ready to pick them up mid-ritual and swing them into magickal action.

You might also add air symbols such as representations of clouds, miniature kites, or leaves to the altar. Look around your house and your yard, and see what inspires you. When possible, keep color symbolism in mind when choosing props. White, yellow, and gold are widely associated with air, and you can also include silvers and grays, reminiscent of clouds and mist.

Finally, sprinkle the altar with herbs associated with air, such as parsley, dill, almond, star anise, lavender, sage, or peppermint.

Try sipping a peppermint tea at your air altar, or sprinkle your magickal workspace with lavender to invite the power of the winds. Now whistle, sing, or blow gently, calling on the air element to infuse the place with its power.

Drawing Down the Air

Now that your altar is set up, it's time to make a real connection. There are many ways to connect with the air element. Focusing on the breath is one method. Simply breathe in deeply, letting the air element fill your lungs. Feel its power absorbed into every cell in your body as you hold your breath for a second or two. As you exhale, push the air element out through your mouth, letting it seep out slowly through your pursed lips. After a few slow, deep breaths, make your breathing faster and shallower. Notice how panting affects your emotions and internal energy. Play around with your breath, alternating between long, slow draws of air and quick puffs. Allow the air element to take effect, transforming you as you regulate how quickly or how slowly it is brought into and back out of your body. Let the air relax you, invigorate you, arouse you. Welcome it into your being and harness it; become one with the wind and your power will flow.

Movement is another method of calling on the air element. Dance, leap, wave your arms in the sky. Let your body move freely, as if you are being blown around by the breeze. Let the air element guide your movements, inviting it into your body. Be an open channel through which this natural power can fully express itself. Dance, jump, flail, twirl, whatever you feel led to do, leaving inhibitions by the wayside.

If you really want to train yourself to connect with the air element on deeper levels, try this exercise that involves singling out the senses. Sit or stand at your air altar, experiencing the air element through sight, sound, and touch. After a few moments, take away one of your means of observation. Insert earplugs and experience a heightened sense of the air through sight. Put on a blindfold and revel in the feel of the air on your body. For an intense sensory experience, deprive yourself of both sight and sound, and wrap your body in a sheet so that only your face is exposed. Focus on the air element brushing across your lips, flowing in and out of your open mouth as you breathe. Exercises like this make our senses sharper. As we learn to focus our perception and stretch our consciousness further, we gain a more complete understanding of the forces comprising reality, and this understanding can forge a friendly magickal collaboration between you and the elements.

Calming Winds Ritual

The wind can carry away your worries and woes, if you let it. Once you've connected with the air element and you feel it present at the altar, try working some magick. Stand at your air altar and rub finely ground sage on your arms and chest, letting it absorb your doubts and dissolve any unnecessary walls and blocks within you. Think of the energies and emotions that hinder you, and direct these feelings away from your spirit and into the sage. Loosen the energy field surrounding your body, willing it to be more fluid. Allow the wind to carry away your anxieties, envisioning these feelings as a sort of psychic dust drifting away from your aura. Let the wind flow over you as you blow the herbs off your skin, and let the negative energies you've released float away. Bend in the breeze, shaking off any remaining woes. Invite the air element to infuse you with its power; feel it bring a lightness and quickness to your body. Breathe in the new energy, and relax.

Bubble Charms

Bubble charms are a fun type of magick to work at the air altar, invoking a childlike happiness and awakening your natural magick instinct. Make your own bubbles with dishwashing liquid and water, or buy some ready-made bubble solution at the toy store. As you stand at your air altar with your bottle of bubbles placed before you, think of your magickal intention, putting the wish into the form of an energy-infused image. Dip the bubble wand into the solution and blow gently, sending the thought-form representing your magickal intention into a bubble. As the bubble drifts off and eventually pops, the magick is released and the charm is activated.

Pinwheel Spell

For another fun magickal experience at the air altar, try a pinwheel spell. To create a pinwheel that casts a spell as it spins, simply draw magickal symbols or images that express your intention on the twirly part. For instance, you might draw a heart symbol to attract romance, a dollar sign to increase wealth, or a lunar glyph to enhance intuition. For added punch, try anointing the pinwheel with a corresponding essential oil, letting the scent waft through the breeze as an offering and energy exchange to the air elementals. Envision your goal and let the pinwheel spin freely to bring the magick into manifestation.

Air Altar Divination

Try this quick method of elemental divination to assess your fortune at the air altar. Choose a broad leaf, and write on it a single yes or no question you would like answered. Place the leaf on the altar and see what happens. If the leaf blows away quickly, the answer to your quandary is yes, while if the leaf stays stationary, the answer is no. If the leaf simply flutters or falls straight down off the side of the altar, it indicates an affirmative response, after a period of delay.

Easy, Breezy, Magickal

An air altar provides a place to both honor and harness the power of this essential element. As a part of nature, we feel the enchantment of a fresh breeze, the miracle of each breath. The air element is a part of our lives, and making it a part of your spell life will bring great benefit. With an air altar and a few creative spells at hand, your magick will reach the skies.

Find Your Personal Goddess

by Deborah Blake

One of the things that most of us have in common—
whether we call ourselves Pagans, Witches, or Wiccans—is a belief in the female divine. Many of us also acknowledge the existence of a male divine, albeit one that bears little resemblance to the God we may have grown up with, but it is goddess worship which sets us apart from other religions and brings us together in this one.

But which goddess? There are so many names by which we call her, it can be hard to decide which of the lady's incarnations is best suited to our own practice and personality. Yet for many of us, the search for our personal goddess is part of the path we walk as Pagans. How can we know which goddess to call on in our prayers?

Does She Need a Name?

The first question to ask, really, is does she need a specific name at all? Some Pagans are happy to simply refer to their female deity as "goddess" in the abstract, without attaching any particular name or tradition to her. (I often do that myself, although I have one goddess who I worship primarily, and often call on others for specific tasks or holidays.)

There are a few benefits to this approach: it is simple and easy, you can be sure that your prayer will get to goddess in one form or another, and you don't have to worry that you are addressing the wrong deity for your magickal work.

There is certainly nothing wrong with calling on a general all-purpose goddess. After all, most people who talk to "God" don't call him by any particular name. If you are just starting out, or haven't figured out a specific goddess who seems right to you, then it is absolutely appropriate to address your prayers and spells to "Great Goddess," "Mother of Us All," "Lady of the Moon," or any other generic term for the feminine one.

Why Call Her by Name?

If it were fine to simply call her goddess, why would you want to identify with one or more goddesses in particular? There are a few different reasons, depending on the person involved.

For some Witches, it isn't a matter of choice: their deities chose them. It isn't unusual for Pagans to feel that one or another goddess has called them to worship. This can happen in subtle ways (you continually see an animal that belongs to a particular goddess, or see her symbols everywhere), or as something more obvious (you hear her call your name, or she comes to you in a vision).

If you are searching for your personal goddess, it is always a good idea to keep your eyes, mind, and spirit open, just in case. Goddesses do not like to be ignored!

For Witches who have chosen to follow a path that comes from a particular country or area of the world, there will be goddesses who are part of that tradition. Celtic Witches, for instance, will probably call on one or more of the Irish goddesses, such as Brigid, Morrigu, or Cerridwen. Those following a Norse path might call on Freya, Frigga, or Hel. Egyptian magick has seen a recent resurgence in popularity as well, and includes goddesses such as Isis, Anuket, and Bast.

I have always been drawn to deities from the Greek and Roman pantheons (probably because they are some of the first mythologies I was exposed to). The goddess I felt most in tune with for many years was Hecate, who has roots in both the Greek and Celtic worlds.

But even if you have figured out which pantheon or country your personal magickal path is based on, you still may have a hard time deciding which particular goddess is the one for you. Here are a few suggestions for discovering her.

For the Solitary Witch

If you walk your path alone, here is a ritual you can use to try and find the name of your personal goddess. Of course, it can also be used by Witches who usually practice in a group; just pick a night when you will be by yourself instead of with your coven or circle. Since you are in search of the goddess, the best night to do this ritual is on a Full Moon— outside, if you can manage it. But inside works too, if you can't be out under the moonlight.

You will need: a quiet, dimly lit space (if you are outside, a bonfire is nice, but completely optional); rhythmic music (preferably without words) or a drum; a large white or silver candle to represent the goddess (a candle in a woman's shape is nice, but any good-sized candle will do); a large bowl filled with pure water; a slip of blank paper or parchment; a pen; and a sage smudge stick or any purifying incense.

Prepare your space by setting the bowl on a level surface (the ground, an altar, or a low table). Place the candle behind the bowl and inscribe it with your name if you wish; if you have a magickal name, use that. If you are using pre-recorded music, start it now. Place the slip of paper in front of the bowl along with the pen.

Light the sage or incense and waft it around the space and around yourself to clear and cleanse your energy. Then sit or stand in front of the bowl and light the candle. Breathe slowly and deeply, feeling the light of the Moon coming down from the sky and into your body. If you will be drumming, start now. As you drum or listen to the beat of the music, think about the rhythm of your heart. Feel that rhythm expand to fill the area around you, just as it did when you were in your mother's womb. Then, you could feel her

heartbeat, too. As you listen to the drum beats, hear the beating of the Great Mother's heart surrounding you.

You may enter into a light trance state, or you may just be relaxed and tuned in to the energy around you; either one is fine. Go with the beat as long as you want, and send out your desire to learn the identity of your personal goddess. Close your eyes and send that yearning out with all your heart, opening yourself to an answer.

When you are ready, open your eyes and look into the bowl. Can you see her? Do you see the form of a maiden, a mother, or a crone? Do you see birds or animals or symbols? You may even see her face or hear her name echoing in the music. If you need quiet now, turn off the music. Pick up the pen and paper and write down her name without out thinking about it. You might be surprised what will come to you.

If you don't get a clear answer right away, try putting the blank piece of paper under your pillow that night, with the intention of dreaming of her. In the morning, pull out the paper and write down whichever name pops into your mind first, while you are still half asleep. (Be sure to leave the pen by your bed.)

Don't be discouraged if the ritual doesn't work. Perhaps the time isn't right for you to know, or you are torn between two paths and the goddess is waiting for you to make the choice that will lead to her.

Coven Work

At the start of 2010, my coven, Blue Moon Circle, decided to focus on goddess work for the course of the year. The group happens to be made up of all women, and we agreed that we wanted to explore our connection with the feminine deity more deeply. Many of us were feeling a desire to either identify a personal goddess or that it was time to change the main goddess that we worshipped—but none of us had more than a glimmering of an idea of who it was we were meant to be following. (Although we were pretty sure the answer was a different one for each of us, which is why we usually just said "goddess" during rituals!)

Over the course of that year, we used a number of approaches to look at the various goddesses. Because we all love to increase our knowledge, the first thing I did was buy a number of books specifically dealing with female deities. Luckily, there are some great ones out there to help Pagans and Witches learn about goddesses from all sorts of historical, mythological, and ethnological backgrounds. (I'll give a short list of some of our favorites at the end of the article.)

We spent months taking turns picking one goddess each to read about and report on to the rest of the group. That way we managed to get a lot of information without any one of us having to do a ton of research. (Not that we wouldn't love to do that, but who has the time?)

When we gathered for New Moons or Full Moons (Sabbats were still dedicated to both goddess and god, since we tend to worship both at the holidays and the goddess in particular at the lunar rituals), we would go around the circle and read out loud a selection about the goddess we had chosen to focus on that month.

Sometimes we picked a goddess we were intrigued by, but other times we let the goddesses pick us, by using one of three "Goddess Card" decks. These decks were really useful tools for our goddess exploration, and I highly recommend them (they'll work for solitaries, too). There are a few different ones out there, but the ones we used were *The Gifts of Goddess: 36 Affirmation Cards* by Amy Zerner and Monte Farber (Chronicle Books, 2000), *Goddess Tarot Deck and Book Set* by Kris Waldherr (US Games, 1999), and Waldherr's *Goddess Inspiration Oracle* (Llewellyn 2007).

During this time, we also used these decks to get messages from the goddesses about the paths we were on. For instance, while doing a Full Moon ritual during the month proceeding Mabon, we wanted to know what things we needed to work on before the harvest season was done. The goddess affirmation cards were perfect for this.

One of the great benefits of using the various card decks to tell us which goddesses to research was that we ended up looking outside of our normal comfort zones and areas of interest. For instance, I pulled a card for Freya from the *Goddess Tarot Deck*. I am not very familiar with the Norse gods, and wouldn't ever have chosen to look in that direction. And yet, when I started exploring the Freya mythology more deeply, I could see that this was a goddess I could connect with in many ways.

By working together as a group, we were able to deepen our connection with the feminine divine in other ways, as well. We did a number of guided meditations aimed at appreciating the divine inside ourselves (using the "Feminine Power" spell from my book, *Everyday Witch A to Z Spellbook*), or listening for goddess wisdom. At the end of the year, some of us had the name of a new goddess to worship and all of us felt a much deeper relationship with her in all of her forms.

Questions to Ask Yourself

I can't tell you the right path for you to take to your personal goddess; no one can. Each Witch is different, and we walk many different roads to get to where we are going. I can, however, suggest a few questions for you to ask yourself as you travel.

Do I feel drawn to the goddess in her manifestation as Maiden, Mother, or Crone?

Is my goddess more light than dark or more dark than light?

Am I looking for a goddess from a particular pantheon, mythology, or culture?

Do I feel as special connection to any animals, birds, or totems?

Is my goddess more nurturing or is she a warrior?

Does my goddess have a consort I will also worship?

What do I want from this relationship? Support? Strength? Wisdom? Righteous anger on my behalf? Love? A kick in the butt? (Different goddesses will definitely give you different things—including the last, if you need it!)

If you can come up with a list that has the answers to these questions, as well as anything else you can think of that applies to your path and your practice of magick, you should be able to find the goddess you seek in one of the books listed below, or any of the myriad of other wonderful reference materials on Pagan deities.

In the end, the search is just as much a part of your magickal education as anything else you will pursue during the course of your magickal studies. And whether or not you find your personal goddess right away or continue to call on her in a more general form, rest assured that even if you don't know her name, she knows yours. And She hears your prayers, no matter what you call her.

For Further Study

Auset, Priestess Brandi. *The Goddess Guide: Exploring the Attributes and Correspondences of the Divine Feminine*. St. Paul, MN. Llewellyn, 2009.

Illes, Judika. *The Element Encyclopedia of Witchcraft: The Complete A to Z for the Entire Magical World*. Hammersmith, London. HarperElement, 2005.

Monaghan, Patricia. *The Goddess Path: Myths, Invocations & Rituals*. St. Paul, MN. Llewellyn, 1999.

Skye, Michelle. *Goddesses Alive!: Inviting Celtic & Norse Goddesses Into Your Life*. St. Paul, MN. Llewellyn, 2007.

Charm Play

by Janina Renée

African approaches to charm-making and symbolism can inspire us not just because they offer insights into another society, but because they suggest ways we can exercise verbal and visual artistry as we play with our own use of language in making magic. Whether the metaphorical imagery we utilize draws from clichés and other common usage, from folk sayings, or from pop culture, it provides "hypnotic keys" to help us focus on the changes we want to manifest—especially when we are working on self-enchantment.

To briefly explain the particular variety of charms that are a celebrated art form in the Kongo and extended central African cultural area, they are referred to in the singular as *nkisi* and in the plural as *minkisi*, and the person who composes them is called a *nganga*, which means "maker." A charm assemblage requires a container, such as a bag, pot, pouch, gourd, horn, or large snail shell, and the materials put into it are referred to as medicines or *bilongo*. Sometimes a charm container has external attachments, or it may be affixed to a statuette that suggests the character of the charm, or several charm bags may be strung together. As the ingredients are added, the nganga recites special sayings or affirmations to activate each one individually. As charm-making is part of a much larger cultural complex, much more could be said about all of the additional ritual actions, gestures, and preparations that go into making these charms, but there is too much to be covered here.

The completed charm is an entity with a name and personality, and it also incarnates a spirit being. Sometimes ancestor and nature spirits actually inspire the construction of charms to house them, because that way they can be effective in the world, helping the human community. Minkisi variations have made it to the New World, appearing as the pot with magical ingredients called *prenda*, which plays a role in Afro-Cuban religion, and as the little bundle wrapped in colorful cloth and ornamented with beads, sequins, and feathers, which is the *pacquet congo* in Haiti. The mojo bag is a streamlined version.

The bilongo ingredients that go into the charm assemblages most often include items that invoke elemental powers of water, earth, and air, or that engage principles of sympathetic, contagious, or imitative magic. (Traditional magical items are okay, too.) However, some other classes of charms are regularly included because of their metaphorical nature. Verbal and visual puns engage a sense of fun in playing with words and images, but they also have magical potency. For example, a common Kongo ingredient is *tondo*, which is a type of mushroom, because it connotes the word *tondisa*, "to praise," so that "the spirits be praised," or "that the magic and the magician be respected." Ingredients are also used for their natural symbolism, so a crab claw may be included to enhance the efficacy of a charm in its ability to hang on, or the color red is used to stop bleeding. Playing with verbal and visual symbolism is also part of African-American hoodoo practice, as in the use of sugar or syrup added to a spell for "sweet work," which may even require brown sugar for a person of color or white for a white person.

We can find similar principles in European magic, such as the use of the herb lovage to attract love, the efficacy of borage is enhanced because it rhymes with courage, and five-fingered grass (cinquefoil) is a Pennsylvania Dutch charm for attracting favors because its leaves suggest the welcoming, extended hand. In other folkloric examples, red beads were worn to counteract the inflammatory skin disease, erysipelas, and blue beads are worn to cool the withering heat of the evil eye. Despite the fact that other quaint and obscure European examples could be listed, and that auspicious wordplay is also very big in Chinese culture, the minkisi take the cake for being more elaborate, articulated, and embedded in Africa's larger, shared cultural heritage in its love of creative virtuosity.

While so many African *charm* objects depend on culture-specific puns, we can use their example to rediscover the metaphorical associations of common objects, and how they might be used in spellwork. What follows are a few suggestions, though the list is potentially limitless. If it is hard to obtain certain ingredients, such as the feather of a duck or rooster, images of most of these animals or objects are likely available as bracelet-type charms. (Bracelet charms also have a few advantages: they don't involve harming animals, won't decay as organic materials might, and can be attached to the outside of charm bags for extra ornamentation.)

Acorn: Add to a charm assemblage for long-term growth potential.

Battery: Conveys the idea of providing power for your spell, especially if it's an Energizer, due to the popular slogan, "It keeps on going." (Indeed, an image of the Energizer Bunny would also do the job.)

Bell: Bells have a traditional function in giving voice to the spirits of air and also chasing off evil spirits. However, ring-ing a bell while adding it to a charm is a prompt to revive memory.

Body parts: Metaphorical expressions including the hand for when you "need a helping hand;" the heart for when you are "putting your heart into it," or want to "win someone's heart," or "give your own heart" to another (though it could also be used to get "a sweetheart deal"); and the head for "getting ahead" or "making headway" in some matter. Ideal for use are silver charms called *Milagros*, which people in Hispanic and Mediterranean countries offer as votives for bodily healing. Doll parts could also be utilized.

Cake: Include a small piece of cake in a charm for easy success, as when something is "a piece of cake" or "a cakewalk." As alluded to above, something that "takes the cake" is the big winner. We also use cake to celebrate milestones and achievements, such as weddings and promotions. Round cakes suggest fulfillment as well as the Full Moon (and in parts of Africa, when the Moon is full, "things are fully happening").

Candy: Sweets that evoke wealth include "Good 'N Plentys," "Payday" bars, "100 Grand" bars, "Fifth Avenue" bars, and "Sugar Daddies." Other magical uses are suggested by "Life Savers," "Charm Pops," "Red Hots," and chocolate "Kisses."

Daisy: While this is a symbol of innocence, exuberant youth, and brightness—as well as a Sun symbol—due to the cliché and sometime advertising slogan, "fresh as a daisy," you could add daisy petals to keep your spell fresh.

Dog: A well-known symbol of loyalty, but the hair or image of a dog could be added to a spell to "dog the footsteps" of someone who needs to be closely followed for some reason. Toward a similar goal, one could include an image of a footprint (which used to be popular among California surfers as key fobs and other items), or a pinch of dust from someone's footprint, as is common in both African and African-American spellworking.

Duck: The term "lucky duck" came about because it rhymes, not because we are a culture that views ducks as auspicious (though the Chinese do and the ancient Celts did, too).

However, because words that rhyme come to be co-identified, a duck feather or image can indeed invoke luck.

Easy money: A number of popular expressions allude to "the good life," so clover expresses the desire to be "rolling in clover," a wishbone figures in wishing charms, but also suggests a "lucky break," and a miniature ship affirms that "your ship has come in."

Elvis: For many older people, Elvis will always be "the king." Curiously though, his iconic image could also access advice from the fairy folk, because his name is old Anglo-Saxon for "the wisdom of the elves."

Hardware: A nail can be added to a charm "to nail the matter," and a bolt painted blue can help your spell work like "a bolt out of the blue." A screw, besides having obvious sexual suggestivity, can be used while reciting Shakespeare's Lady MacBeth's exhortation to "screw your courage to the sticking point." Something that "wears hard" also suggests endurance.

Key: For gaining access and unlocking secrets. With a gold-colored key, you can use the Mexican saying, "A golden key unlocks all doors" as an activation phrase. This also reinforces the idea that charms are hypnotic keys, because the process of composing a charm is an induction to focus both the conscious and unconscious mind. The small keys that come with diaries and jewelry boxes could be used, while an old-fashioned skeleton key suggests universal access, and also brings in male-female symbolism.

Leaves: A leaf of ivy represents clinging devotion, which is enhanced by its heart shape. A number of other plants and trees have heart-shaped leaves.

Mushroom: Popular as a design motif in the psychedelic era, mushrooms hint at entry into other realities. However, "to mushroom" suggests something that pops up overnight, and could be used when you want your spell to manifest and spread rapidly.

Rooster: The feather or image could be used to give somebody "a wake-up call." A rooster is also known as a cock, with obvious sexual symbolism.

Safety pin: Good for sealing the bag of a protective charm.

Tea bag: Could be used in a spell to promote communication and frankness, because tea has some amusing pop culture associations, as "pour me some tea" is an invitation to share gossip. (All the better if it's Earl Grey—it contains bergamot, which facilitates communication.)

⁓

No doubt, many other ideas for verbal and visual puns will present themselves. This is such a rich field for play because so much of our everyday language is built on metaphors.

If you have a surplus of traditional spell ingredients, as well as items like those above whose verbal and visual symbolism make a magical statement, you might want to try another Kongo custom by setting out a *nkisi a babonsono*, which means "everyone's nkisi" and amounts to a community charm basket. Because some magically oriented Africans regard charm making as a contribution to the public good, they may keep a supply of the most common bilongo items in a central location in the village so people can help themselves. (A basket acting as a "magical convenience store" includes such things as quartz, red and blue glass trade beads, and seashells, along with various metaphorical items, such as a crab claw.) If you regularly get together with a magical group, invite your friends to contribute, too, and see if they can apply their imaginations to coming up with meaningful new ingredients. Using this kind of charm imagery can also suggest arts and crafts projects, including collages and other assemblages.

Note: I use the spelling "Kongo," because that is the usage preferred by Africanists who separate the idea of Kongo as a culture area from Congo as the term for a political entity set up by Europeans. The examples of Kongo charms that I cite here were collected by Karl Edvard Laman, and his information has been further analyzed by Wyatt MacGaffey in his book *Art and Healing of the BaKongo Commented by Themselves: Minkisi from the Laman Collection*, among other publications.

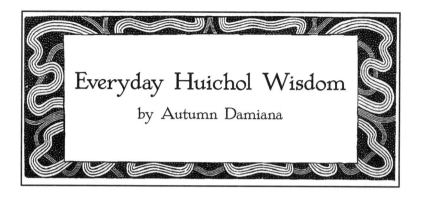

Everyday Huichol Wisdom
by Autumn Damiana

Years ago, I was vacationing in Puerto Vallarta, Mexico. Browsing the usual tourist attractions and shops along the city's seaside promenade and finding nothing of interest, I wandered down a meandering side street and discovered a gallery and store that held some of the most beautiful folk art I have ever seen. Fascinated by the bright colors and the intricacies of the craftsmanship, and charmed by the simple, yet obviously significant patterns and motifs worked into each piece, I wanted to know more about the people who had created such interesting and powerful works of art. This was how I first learned about the Huichol. However, it was years after discovering their artwork, through further study into Huichol culture and traditions, that I began to realize that the true beauty these indigenous people possessed was in their wisdom.

The Huichol (pronounced "wee-CHOL"), who call themselves *Wixáritari* ("the people"), are a native tribe that lives in remote areas of the Sierra Madre Mountains in central Mexico. These people are direct descendants of the Aztecs (which is reflected in Wixárika, their native language), and they are reportedly the only tribe in North America never conquered by European explorers. Because of this, thousands of Huichol still live by the same traditions as their ancestors did hundreds of years ago. Although many of them speak Spanish and may spend time working regular jobs away from home to help support their families, the deep connection they maintain with their land, people, religion, and heritage is what makes the Huichol so enlightened, blessed with an ageless wisdom that is just as pertinent today as it was in centuries past. However, in order to learn from the Huichol, it is necessary to understand their world.

For one, the Huichol live in isolation. This alone has proved to be extremely helpful in keeping to their traditional ways, as for centuries it was incredibly difficult for other native tribes, Spanish conquerors, Christian missionaries, and the more modern inhabitants of Mexico to access these people. Another factor involved is the Huichol tribe's deeply rooted spirituality. These people practice a pre-Christian shamanic religion that affects everything they do on a daily level. The Huichol celebrate life in all its cycles, and strive to understand the connectivity that all things have with each other. They do this in a number of ways: through tending their corn crops, sharing the history and mythology of their civilization through the use of storytelling (the Huichol have no written language, so knowledge of their history is passed down through the generations by word of mouth), through their artwork, and by ritual use of the peyote cactus.

Peyote, called *hicouri* by the Huichol, is central to Huichol culture and religion. Now known throughout the Americas as a psychedelic plant used in many Native American ceremonies to produce visions, the tradition of ingesting the peyote cactus for ritual use has been part of the Huichol way since ancient times. Within the tribe, everyone in the village, including youngsters, adults, and the elderly, make use of this "medicine" to interact with the world of the spirits. With the help of the tribe's shaman to guide and direct them, the Huichol see this practice as a completely natural way to converse with both their gods and the spirits of nature around them. The practice strengthens their reverence for the earth that sustains them, emphasizes their place within the world, and promotes feelings of connectivity to each other and to their environment. One major way that the tribe expresses these emotions and beliefs is through their artwork, the very same that I came across in Puerto Vallarta.

Huichol art manifests itself in a variety of different forms, from votive "gods eyes" and prayer arrows, to yarn paintings, to mosaic-like beaded gourds and sculptures. Each piece of Huichol artwork is created according to ancient customs. The patterns

that are chosen for each piece, as well as the colors themselves, all have religious significance in Huichol culture, and are taught and handed down as a tradition in the same way the stories are learned. The resulting symbols and images that emerge out of the patterns serve as a record of the people's beliefs, legends, visions, dreams, and prayers. However, these are more than mere pieces of art—they are also ceremonial offerings to the gods. In the Huichol way of life, every act—from harvesting corn or preparing an evening meal, tending the fire or working meticulous patterns with yarn or beadwork—is an act of worship and an act of prayer.

One of the most overtly spiritual activities in Huichol life is the holy pilgrimage to Wirikuta. Almost every member of the Huichol tribe will participate in this pilgrimage at least once in their lifetime. Wirikuta is a desert in central Mexico believed to be the home of the gods and ancestral spirits, and it is also where the Huichol go to gather the sacred peyote. This journey is one of the most important events every year, with preparations beginning weeks (sometimes even months) ahead of time. Throughout the pilgrimage itself, the participants dance, sing, fast, pray, and meditate. Strict codes of conduct are observed, and the many offerings that have been prepared beforehand are left at sacred sites along the way. Led by the shaman, the pilgrims travel hundreds of miles in this manner, stopping at times to pick up or join with other parties. When at last all have reached Wirikuta, the pilgrimage reaches its summit when the assembled group ritually harvests all the peyote that will be consumed by each village in the upcoming year's ceremonies. The next spring, when the peyote has been exhausted and another year has been completed, there will be another pilgrimage to Wirikuta, and the cycle will continue.

So what can we learn from the Huichol? Although it may seem on the surface that these people are far removed from the modern world and all its trappings, I believe that much can be gleaned from the Huichol mindset that is relevant to us all. Here are five examples of Huichol teachings that we can incorporate daily into our contemporary lifestyles:

1. Be Present in all You Do

Because every act is sacred to the Huichol, every moment is spent being present. This sounds simple, but is in fact very difficult to do consciously without practice. How often do we rush through a tedious task, such as laundry or doing the dishes, or "zone out" at work trying to make the day go by more quickly? If we learn to live as much as possible within the moment, each moment will take on meaning, and our lives will be much richer as a result.

2. Give as well as Receive

This message is also deceptively simple. What it calls for is a conscious spirit of giving, not an attitude of reciprocity. "Reciprocity" implies mutual exchange, and who among us can really give back as much as we receive every day? In any case, we can always give back spiritually. Yes, we need to remember to be thankful for our many blessings (however grand or humble as these may be) and to share generously with others. But the Huichol also know well the concept of "paying it forward." Long before they harvest or even plant their crops, they have made an offering to the spirit world thanking it for the bounty of corn. This is not sympathetic magic in which the desired outcome is visualized as having already happened; rather, the Huichol are thanking the spirit of the corn for even existing in their lives to be planted and harvested at all.

They know that in the natural ebb and flow of life there will be both times of plenty and of scarcity. This does not deter them from giving back what they can, when they can, and on all levels. To give IS to receive; they are two sides of the same coin.

3. Each of Us is never Alone

And yet, feelings of alienation, loneliness, disharmony, and opposition are widespread in individuals of today's world cultures. The Huichol are only human, and therefore suffer from these feelings, too. However, when these emotions arise, the Huichol know that they need only go out among nature to find another branch of their family waiting for them. As a tribe, they believe in a cosmology that includes *Yurianaka*, "Mother Earth"; *Taupa*, "father Sun"; *Metserli*, "grandmother Moon"; and *Tatewari*, "grandfather fire" who is embodied by a constantly burning communal village fire. Other influential figures are the blue deer Kayumari, and the aforementioned spirit of the peyote, Hicouri. In their belief system, everything in creation has a spirit (including plants and animals, lakes, rivers, mountains, etc.) that is kin to the Huichol. Furthermore, each one of these is just a part of the Great Spirit or God or Goddess, who is in all things and surrounds each of us constantly. Wherever we are, we are never truly alone.

4. Ritual and Ceremony are Necessities

The idea that the sacred is separate from the mundane and that religion must be practiced to experience spirituality is a thoroughly Western concept, one that the Huichol cannot grasp at all. To the Huichol, religion is lived every moment, life is one big ceremony, and everything is steeped in ritual. As such, they honor, recognize, or celebrate everything important in their lives, from major events such as births, deaths, marriages, and holidays to life changes or rites of passage, to simple day-to-day occurrences. By involving ourselves in ritual and ceremony as the Huichol do, we can each become more spiritually and psychologically balanced and healthy. Simple daily or weekly observances in between major events such as praying, meditating, grounding and centering, energy cleansing, or time spent introspectively will also enhance personal growth.

5. Strive always to Live in "Right Relationship"

"Right relationship" can easily be interpreted as "sustainable living." Outlined here is the notion that everyone and everything is interconnected and that every action committed ripples outward and affects all, sometimes for generations to come. This is the most important and timely message of the Huichol: one of ecology, conservation, and social consciousness. Although the Huichol exist mostly in seclusion, they *are* aware of the social and environmental disconnect in other cultures. The spiritual pilgrimage to Wirikuta has been a tradition since ancient times, but in recent decades, another focus of the trek has been to help heal the wrongs that are being committed to Mother Earth and her children. Because the Huichol embrace the concept of oneness and understand more fully the synergetic connections we have to nature and to each other, they see it as one of their spiritual responsibilities to help offset the evils of the world until the rest of us begin to live more consciously. Therefore, it is up to each of us to find our personal life paths of "right relationship," and to live them as the Huichol do in order to carry us all into a promising future.

~

Sadly, Huichol culture is disappearing. Many of the Huichol have left their native lands and gone to more metropolitan areas of Mexico to seek their fortunes. Fewer Huichol are learning Wixárika, and some of the younger generations are attending recently built Protestant churches. Still more Huichol have been invaded by "progress" in the form of other religious missionar-

ies, alcoholism, poverty, and the steady and persistent encroachment on their traditionally held lands by roads, airstrips, borders, and property divisions. Popularization of Huichol culture and art throughout the global community (mostly via the internet) has been both a blessing and a curse. The constant outside scrutiny of the tribe, which has strived for centuries to simply be left alone, is both eroding the Huichol way of life and helping to preserve it at the same time, mainly through sales of Huichol art. It is also currently possible to take a bus tour out of Puerto Vallarta to visit a supposedly "authentic" Huichol village, where Huichol dancers in native dress put on a "welcome ceremony" and handicrafts can be bought. It is difficult to say whether or not purchasing Huichol artwork and visiting their homeland is exploiting them or helping to support their civilization. I personally feel that the best way to keep the Huichol culture alive is to learn from the wisdom of the Huichol, and live day-to-day according to their teachings.

Crafty Ways
to Rummage and Recycle

by Emyme

A soft-edged triangle of arrows, tip to end, forms an endless rotation. More than forty years old, the symbol for recycling is used and known the world over. Practitioners of magic know recycling is by no means a 'new' idea. Throughout history many have lived by the mantra of "make it do, use it up, wear it out." Earth-based religions have incorporated natural "recycling" into their practices for thousands of years. The ability to see past a broken item to its use as a new item is a certain—special—type of positive, powerful magic, even to those who do not believe in or understand it. Discarded, broken, and unused items continue to contain original energy. In addition, extra energy is often transferred from the action of the recycler. It is in the transfer of that energy from the discarded into the serviceable where true, potent magic lies. Repair, re-fashion, recycle. Here are just two examples of how past generations of my family have incorporated eco-friendly hobbies and magical actions in ways that benefited our immediate family and the greater community.

~

Waste disposal, trash collection, the junk man—this was very different when I was a child. Our city landfill was not huge towering heaps of smelly refuse. Rather, a large pit was filled, truckload by truckload. Later this pit was covered with dirt and grass and became soccer and softball playing fields. The trash trucks were not owned by some mega-corporation, but by our city. The trash

men—they were always men—were respected laborers, and people we knew. Caught up in the prosperity that followed WWII, too often a barely broken bicycle ended up at that landfill. My grandfather saw whole, where others saw damaged. Living across the street from the "dump" was something of a joke, but to my grandfather it was a vast market of free parts. Every so often he would drive his pickup truck over to the landfill and look for bicycles. After a few hours he returned home and unloaded his finds. He spent hours in his garage dismantling the bent frames and degreasing the broken chains. Various pieces and parts were laid out on his workbenches and along the concrete floor. One complete bicycle was eventually found and formed from all of the miscellaneous and mismatched bits.

Although there was no ritual cleansing, the handling and re-handling of parts must have acted as a sort of filter through which energy was sorted. His care and patience would be enough to cancel the negative; no smudge stick or salt bath could have accomplished more. Occasionally, new accessories were required for his finished product—plastic handgrips, colorful streamers, bells, and baskets. Sometimes he needed to touch up the paint. But for the most part he only needed two or three of a child's formerly favorite plaything to create one sturdy, fully functional, two- or three-wheeler. When he had prepared three or four, the "new" bikes were placed at the end of his driveway, and he sat in a lawn chair off to the side and waited. Never sold for more than $10.00, his bikes were quickly purchased by families unable to afford those sold in the department and hardware stores in town. He was not the only person performing this service to the community. Over my lifetime I recall seeing repaired bikes at the edge of many properties, and the practice continues to this day. My grandfather was a quiet man. I never knew him to say a cross word, act rashly, or to even raise his voice. He was well-known and respected. Some of that slow, calm personality had to have been imparted to those bicycles via his repairs. Take the creative energy of the original laborer, plus the cheerful energy of the original owner riding, and add the honest energy of my grandfather rebuilding, and the happy energy of new owner/rider. Creative and cheerful, honest and happy = magic. The magic of positive power multiplied and poured into metal and rubber, gears and brakes.

The repairing magic my mother's father performed sent energy back out into the community to strangers.

~

On the other side of the family, my father's mother worked her re-fashioning magic and kept it within our relatives and friends.

Widowed before she was sixty years old, my grandmother sought out something to fill her time. Her mother had been an accomplished quilter, a talent sadly not passed down. But the feel for and the love of fabric was there, and she took up the hobby of braiding rugs. Whether from visiting yard sales, rooting through heaps of clothing at church rummage sales, or taking donations from family and friends—fairly soon a pile of cloth became a fixture on the floor next to her couch. Braided rugs are not something to be created in a day. The steps involved are complicated and time consuming. It is a solitary and contemplative enterprise, and countless hours went into every rug. In simplified terms—the clothing is cut into strips, which are then sewn together at the ends to make longer pieces. These long strips are folded into themselves, forming a sort of fabric tube. Three of these long tubes are braided. Starting at the center and working out, the braids are sewn together forming ovals or circles. Finished products range in size from a rather small eighteen by twelve inch oval to several large circles almost four feet across. The rugs can be heavy, and in the summer, with no air conditioning, it is hot work. Yes, there is magic in the actual creation of the rugs—making something useful out of discards, and pride in work well done. However, even more positive energy flows from the imagination of the creator.

Fabric was not just slapped together. Although there was the occasional rug made up from remnants, the majority of the rugs are glorious artwork—many of which have coordinated color and patterns. Among the nearly two dozen rugs still in the family are a matched set of three ovals in yellow and brown, another oval set of blues and tans, and a predominately red and green circle for holiday use. Polyester was the fabric of choice—it was plentiful in the 1970s and '80s—and it holds up remarkably well. Once in a while experiments were conducted with other fabrics. A personal favorite is a velvet rug, made just for my mother, which for years was the first thing she stepped on every morning and the last thing every night. Again I must point out no specific cleansing was performed. Complete transformation from a jacket, skirt, or trousers; the literal handling and re-handling of fabric; and the recipient's delight also contributed to the removal of any potential residual negativity. My grandmother was a smoker, with a loud laugh and a somewhat naughty sense of humor. She was a wonderful cook, and always had homemade baked goods in her kitchen. She and her circle of friends could be found a few afternoons a week at someone's dining table, playing serious cards under a cloud of cigarette smoke with little piles of change next to the ashtrays. Creating was deep in her being as a woman: creating family, food, and fun.

Re-creating came to her later in life. Where others saw unusable, unwanted clothing, she saw useful, unique floor coverings. Foresight and imagination combined to make healthy happy practical magic.

It is in the very nature of earth-based belief systems to be eco-friendly. However, earth-based belief systems are not the only religions to place eco-friendly acts in high regard. And of course there is magic small and large in the everyday lives of anyone who looks for it. Besides the examples cited, past generations of my family performed magic in a myriad of ways: an aloe plant on the kitchen windowsill for burns, healthy and ful-filling meals created with limited resources, and sand carved out of the earth for the manufacture of glass. The whir of the sewing machine and the whine of the saw were well-known sounds on visits to my relatives' homes. The lessons learned from my past generations have enabled me to seek out ways I can be a better citizen in my community, be it local or global. If it is broken—fix it. If it does not fit—refashion it.

Make do, use it up, wear it out. Repaired bicycles for sale at the end of the driveway and re-fashioned area rugs on display in front of the fireplace were two lessons I learned in how to love my Mother Earth.

Repair, re-fashion, recycle.

Magical Artistic Expression: An ARTicle for Creative Magicians

by Raven Digitalis

So many Pagans and magicians are natural artists. There's something alluring and comforting about the abstract, the mysterious, and that which cannot be fully grasped without some level of interpretation. The gods, the spirits, the profundity of nature . . . these forces can be felt on a level that transcends the mere physical realm. Though the seasons clearly shift, the Moon clearly changes, and the Sun clearly illuminates and descends, there are spiritual forces working deeply under the surface, penetrating the life-force of everything on earth. Mystics tap into these forces and visionaries interpret them spiritually. Artists, similarly, reach into their own unseen landscape and bring forth personal interpretations for others to respond to and reinterpret. Religion and art, naturally, have gone hand-in-hand since humankind's beginnings.

It took me years to come to terms with referring to myself as an "artist." I don't feel much of a calling to paint, I don't create music, I occasionally doodle rather than sketch, and the poetry I've written in the past can be considered mediocre by the best of critics! My only potentially artistic expressions beyond that were, and still are, writing (obviously!), black and white photography (with scenes staged in a creative manner), DJing (playing *other* peoples' music), and dark alternative fashion (clothing and makeup). Aside from the photographic artwork, many pieces of which I still consider good creative work, why did I struggle with calling myself an artist? Much of it is due to the intimidation of the word "artist" itself.

Thinking about the great artists of the past—Beethoven, DaVinci, Waterhouse, Shakespeare, etc., etc.—I felt a certain anxiety with such an identification. Now, however, I realize the true scope of the term. Artists are people who choose to reach beyond the veil and express themselves and their views in *any creative manner*. Some art schools or elitist creators might project a sort of ownership over the term, or thrive on giving other creative people degrading criticism. This can force a person to feel inadequate in their chosen forms of self-expression and has, on more than one occasion, inspired people to *give up* on their visions! *Très mal.* My advice—if you're getting any sort of creative inspiration, and you create art of any type, you *are* an artist and should pursue your callings because it's part of your soul's calling.

The Creative Frequency

For people who feel an affinity with mystical spirituality, whether it's Hermeticism, Paganism, shamanism, mysticism, or anything else, artistic creation is of particular significance. It somehow taps into the Divine both within the self and cosmically. All art is magic and all magic is art—something that numerous magicians have long believed, including the legendary Aleister Crowley! Creating art is a therapeutic and cathartic activity that allows us to, in an arcane light, express what we feel and present it to ourselves and

140

to the world. Beyond that, the goal any non-self-absorbed artist is to touch peoples' lives. There is no greater gift than knowing that your creations speak to people on the levels you've intended, and may cause life-changing realizations in the viewer, opening certain doorways of perception. If it's meaningful to the creator, chances are it will be to others—even if it's not the artist's direct intention.

Artists often draw inspiration from the subtle realms, most notably from the alleged Akashic Records. The Akashic Records are an astral storehouse of information documenting the whole of experience: past lives, the present life, and future lives. Whether this is an "actual" place between the worlds, or whether the Records are a metaphor in humanity's collective mind, the fact remains that all of human experience, emotion, and thought is accessible to us all, and in many regards still resides in collective thought. Experienced astral travelers can access these so-called Records that usually take the form of "video projected" documentations. I've also witnessed channelers and psychics access these mystical or metaphorical Records with their eyes half-opened and fully conscious; everyone, like any mystic or artist, has a different method of utilizing their inherent abilities. (And, as an aside, I feel it only proper to mention that we are all artists on some level, just like everyone is psychic to one degree or another, empathic to one degree or another, and so on.) The form the Records take is different for everyone because the astral realm is created as a projection of the traveler's mind. Because many spiritually inclined people travel to the Akashic Records, certain elements like the "video projection" of past lives and the accompaniment of a "librarian" guide with the Records are often reported due to the thoughtforms built upon that particular terrain of experience.

I mention the Akashic Records because the act of creating art subconsciously accesses this and other astral planes, as the artist taps into feelings buried deep within the unconscious. Many artists take from the Akashic Records without even being aware of it; their creations end up being reflections of past or universal experience and the artist may be left wondering "where the hell did that come from?" Some art is created without the artist even having the vaguest idea of what the finished product is all about! Artists may also discover that people who experience their art interpret it in a highly significant manner that has little or no connection to the artist's original intention—true multidimensionality! In this, consciousness is filtered through the artist as a conduit and the product ends up being nothing but a construction of spiritual vibration, sometimes actually totally disassociated from the artist! This is a form of channeled trance, wherein the artist surrenders to the cosmos to construct images or feelings they may have never been seen or thought of before. Art doesn't always come directly from the conscious mind. At the same time, it depends on the artist's personal callings—there tends to exist art created from the rational mental plane and art created from the abstract emotional plane, which I will discuss in a second.

The first "channeling" artist that comes to mind is Tori Amos. I remember hearing a quote from her stating that many fans become rabid about their interpreted meanings of certain songs. "This song has this meaning; not *that* meaning!" they would adamantly tell her, extremely convinced of the meanings because of the deeply personal nature of the lyrics. Tori would respond that she hadn't thought of that meaning when creating the track, which only inspired the fans to become more frustrated—in a good way! Tori's response makes sense, considering that she describes songs as hugely expansive etheric forces, or "girls" that "come to her" that must be conducted, to the best of her ability, into the form of lyrics, music, and sometimes visual art. Numerous artists are similar in their artistic channelings, feeling as though some of their creations have very little to do with themselves, and are instead channeled for the benefit of the viewer or listener.

Other art, such as many forms of graphic imagery, writing, political art, or cartooning, are created predominantly from the mental plane and have precise meanings (rather than abstract or highly interpretive meanings) that evoke specific responses within the viewer or listener. Perhaps an artist is wishing to express social, political, or religious commentary in a way that conveys a specific meaning. Or maybe they wish to capture a memory they have from their youth. Or a historical expression of a nation or a people. Even a simple landscape, cityscape, or country scene serve as common examples. In these instances, the art is generally a straightforward piece that has a direct meaning. With most art, the end product is a combination of the artist's own creative mind and the spiritually channeled universal mind, whether or not the artist is consciously aware of it. All art is magic and all magic is art.

Mythologically Speaking...

In Greek mythology, there are nine daughters of Zeus (the "King God") and Mnemosyne (the embodiment of memory) who are known as the Muses, each of who rules over a particular artistic talent. Hesiod's *Theogony* is an allegorical text mapping the cosmology of the universe and genealogy of the Greek gods as revealed to the author. Preceding each of the book's major segments is a poetic verse invoking a Muse, asking the daughters to inspire him with creative energy to finish the work accurately and accordingly.

Modern Pagans and magicians, especially those following a Græco-Roman pantheon, may summon a Muse as a spiritual assistant for a specific undertaking. If you are studying the stars, ask Urania for inspiration. If you're creating a book of sacred chants, ask Polyhymnia for help. I don't, however, recommend calling upon them without doing more research into their histories. The Muses' energies work with yours and alter your consciousness, often without your knowledge of the magic working directly. When you invoke them, they are likely to channel through you; their plane to yours. If you want inspiration, you will get it! But beware of boundaries—where does your energy end and theirs begin? Then again, if your intent is pure, I don't see why theirs would be any different. The Muses' skills are as follows:

Calliope – Epic poetry
Clio – History
Erato – Erotic and choral poetry
Euterpe – Music and song
Melpomone – Tragedy and performance art
Polyhymnia – Hymns, religious poetry, and miming
Terpsichore – Light verse and dance
Thalia – Comedy and epic poetry
Urania – Astronomy and astrology

Flat-Surface Art

There are many forms of flat-surface art. Working with a canvas is one of the most popular forms of visual art. Using a flat surface as a creative medium allows one to create imagery directly from a blank slate. The creative mind fills the empty surface with whatever they wish (or whatever they channel). Canvas art can be created with paints, inks, chalk, watercolor, or a multitude of other mediums. Experiment with different forms of flat surface art to discover your own personal niche. Or experiment within a ritual space to fully allow yourself to surrender to your creative current!

Canvas art allows the artist to express absolutely anything they desire—landscapes, nature, people, animals, fantastical creatures, sci-fi, and historical images are but a few of the possibilities. There is no right or wrong way to create canvas art. One of the most magical activities is to paint or sketch in a magic circle, dedicating the piece of art as an offering to the Divine. If you are a devotee of a certain deity or pantheon, or if you have a spiritual affinity with certain animals, plants, trees, or seasons, why not channel your love for them into the piece and dedicate it in sacred space?

Taking the spiritual associations a step further into the magical realm, each work of art that a person does can be a spell in and of itself. Feelings can tumble out when creating; channeling them into the piece at hand is an ideal way to express them. If you're working with paint, you can paint a representation of your sorrow and pain. Let it dry, consecrate it as an implement of releasing, and add additional coats over time with the intention of inviting healing (or what-have-you) into the piece and thus into the issue. This is a wonderful example of a successful ongoing spell. A new painting could be drawn over the old to heal and banish the pain, replacing the inner darkness with light. For an extra boost, try using acrylic paint (or watercolor, for example) and paint the "negative" or "releasing" piece while burning a black candle (to its end). Follow up for seven nights by burning a white seven-day knob candle while painting the "healing" or "invoking" pieces overtop the original artwork.

Similarly, sketching and drawing can become magical acts by, for example, sketching a representation of pain and suffering, burning it upon completion and asking the universe to heal and transform the ill feelings. This can also, of course, be done with written art—burning a "petition" spell has long been commonplace in spellcraft and the magical arts.

One can apply this method to collage or scrapbook art. Cutting and pasting significant imagery will help create (or banish) specific forces. Just as with other art forms, this can be additionally aligned to lunar or solar cycles, personal cycles, and other magical alignments.

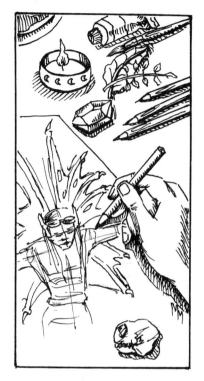

Creating collages (whether mixed media abstractions, assemblage art, or flat collages) is a form of artistic eclecticism. They allow the artist to borrow from a number of mediums and create an individual work from them. Flat collage pieces can include photographs, magazine and newspaper clippings, fabrics, cards, leaves, paint, and all sorts of flat items and graphics. Three-dimensional assemblages can include anything and everything, from wood to gears, gains to stones, mirrors to nails, found objects, and whatever else the creator desires.

Photography

I have found fine art photography to be a fantastic method of magical art-making, simply because it's one of my personal niches. The meaning of an artistic photo is often extremely open to interpretation. The artist fine-tunes his or her own perception to fit into a small visual space, frozen in time.

Many photographic artists use people as the central focus. Everyone can relate to a model in a picture, but the most important part is the energy conveyed through the model as a spiritual conduit. Metaphors are often strong in photographic artwork. If the artist wishes to express a feeling of hopelessness, the model may portray this emotional state with certain postures, expressions, makeup, and scenery. In more abstract pieces, the artist may capture representative images as metaphorical reflections of the emotion being conveyed. They may even take it a step further. About ten years ago, the photographic dark artist John Santerineross (who is one of my personal favs) brought the aforementioned idea to my attention, saying that he often includes imagery in his art that is a *representation of a representation* of a specific feeling. For example, a feeling of newly acquired personal freedom may be expressed by an image of broken chains or a lifted curtain. One may take this even further—a lifted curtain represents freedom, but what represents a lifted curtain? Perhaps it could be expressed as a stage play with masks, jesters, and costumery, reminiscent of an ancient fire festival! The mental process of association and representation is a cornerstone of artistic expression, which can easily be paralleled with sympathetic magic and the creative process of spellcraft.

If working with darkroom photography, take a photo constructed to represent the pain and another to represent healing. Develop the pictures yourself in a darkroom; develop a full print of the "releasing" photo and continue with a series of double-exposed pictures bringing the "healing" photo stronger and stronger into the series, ending with a fully exposed image of the "healing" picture. This represents the transformation from one paradigm to the next, and can also be applied to photographic artwork using digital manipulation.

Various effects are possible after capturing the original image. Some photographic artists are happy with the initial image taken, satisfied with it as a final piece. Others desire to expand upon the image at hand, developing or printing the actual piece in a more specific process. They may underdevelop, overdevelop, double-expose, play with lighting, scratch the negatives, or experiment with different chemical combinations to alter the piece. Learning these techniques require quite a bit of training and dedication by the artist.

Performance Art

Innumerable cultures and societies recognize theatre and performance as spiritual acts, not least of which is the post-apocalyptic, silent white-faced expressive art of Japanese Butoh, which is a relatively new form of Japanese dance—and is wonderfully terrifying to uneducated Western viewers! Likewise, one of my most beloved artists (both visually and musically) is a German project called Sopor Aeternus & the Ensemble of Shadows. Sopor incorporates extreme Butoh with Gothic and deathrock music and visuals—certainly a most rare and most beautiful combination! The eclectic and crosscultural nature of art is sacred and continuously evolving; a phenomenon that can easily be paralleled to magical and spiritual development across the world.

The ancient Greeks, who I mentioned earlier, also recognized the power of performance art. Their plays portrayed myths and histories of the culture, solidifying common cultural worldviews and carrying on their sacred tradition through living art. Most of their plays were tragedies or comedies that incorporated choir and song. The three most influential playwrights are often cited as Aeschylus, Sophocles, and Euripides.

Performers in Bali and Java (Indonesia) are known for their plays depicting stories from the Hindu epics *The Ramayana* and

The Mahabharata. This performance art derived from shadow puppet plays depicting the same epics, which made their way from India around the third to fourth century CE by way of the Silk Road trade route. These performers dress precisely like characters in the stories, including the deities. The actors will then perform the plays as if they were dolls themselves; their hand *mudras* and stiff movements—down to the very rolling of their eyes—will mimic puppetry, allowing the performers to become direct channels of the highly venerated tales. Children are schooled in proper acting methods from a very young age to carry on the unique tradition.

Artists across the globe are drawn to performance and theater. Acting allows a person to sidestep the ordinary cycles of reality and enter another reality altogether. Assuming different character types is a way to connect with different aspects of one's own personality and explore new types of expression. Many Witches ritually reenact mythologies attuned with seasonal shifts, melding the world of theatre and spirituality in the manner that many ancients themselves did.

The brilliant Stanislavsky acting style, also called method acting, calls for the actor to enter the mind of the individual portrayed. This is achieved by reminiscing on similarities in life experience between the character and the actor. Through regression, the actor recalls emotions felt when similar situations were experienced in their own life. For example, if the character being portrayed is to feel happiness, the actor recalls his or her own joyous experiences in life, resurfacing the feelings attached to it. Once this side of the personality is brought forth, the actor can act and react as if he or she were actually that person. The practice of realism-acting is incredibly similar to the process of Pagan invocation, where a Witch, mystic, or magician allows a god or spirit to enter their own body and channel through them. Invocation is also called "aspecting" or "godform assumption," depending on the tradition, and carries similar benefits and dangers to portraying another person through realistic acting.

Though the benefits are many, acting isn't always as harmless as sometimes believed. When the energy of another character is assumed, the actor's own personality gets pushed aside. Many actors are known to hold onto aspects of their character's personality and carry it into everyday life unknowingly. When one's original personality is not properly separated from the assumed character, the original personality gets muddled. A number of long-time actors and performers have such a difficulty separating themselves from their character portrayals in everyday life, that their every word and motion becomes an act—a constant performance for everyone to see. Performers who portray another individual *must* center themselves in their own body and own personality after performing, just as a magician who invokes a spirit or god must come back to center after channeling or assuming their guise. This is effective with meditation and grounding exercises of any sort.

Art is a broad term; there is no strict definition of "artist" or "non-artist." We all have that spark of creativity within us; it's just a matter of how much we wish to bring it out. If you are motivated in the realms of magic and wish to extend that to your chosen mediums of artistic expression, have at it; magic and art have always been intricately linked! If you are feeling the artistic call, but are unsure of how to express yourself, experiment with various mediums and come to find your ideal means of expression. Meditate, talk to the Muses and the spirits, and experiment with creative methods within a sacred space!

When art of any type becomes a spell or act of magic in and of itself, a particular potency is added that cannot be matched in any other way. Any spell or act of magic can occur through art; just use your imagination, intuition, and creativity! All art is magic and all magic is art. So mote it be.

Magic by Chance

by Magenta Griffith

Life is sometimes compared to a journey. But most journeys we take these days are tame and uninspiring. We commute to work, we visit family, we go on vacation. We travel the same paths, walk the same roads, over and over. Even when we go someplace we haven't been before, we focus on the destination, not the path. How can we turn our travel into something more inspiring and spiritual?

First, look for the unexpected. So much of our day we go through half asleep, ignoring our surroundings, barely noticing anything. Pay attention, and you might notice a new restaurant on your way home from work, a new shop near your sister's house, or a garage sale down the street from the gym. This is a good way to start paying attention. Once you start paying attention, it can be amazing what you'll find. It's the magic in the unexpected.

Magic can be defined as causing change in accordance with one's will; one decides a change is needed, and acts to cause what is necessary, be it healing or a new job. But magic also happens without decision, without need, without will. Magic can crop up when you aren't seeking it. This is a subtler magic, and it can be missed if you aren't paying attention. Sometimes it seems things are going wrong, and, suddenly or slowly, everything comes together to produce a wonderful result.

I remember a time when we were running late on our way to a retreat at a campground. It was raining. I had never been to the site before, and I wasn't entirely sure how to find it. Then an accident on the freeway and the ensuing traffic jam delayed us further. Would we miss dinner? Would we even find the place at all? Would the rain ever stop? Finally, it did. The traffic started to move, and as we came around a bend, there in front of us was the most stunning rainbow I had ever seen. A double rainbow, filling the sky in front of us, with all the colors distinct in both rainbows. We were on flat land with nothing in the way. It was so beautiful that I had trouble paying attention to the other cars. We didn't have a camera along, but the sight of that rainbow stayed imprinted on my mind to this day. Yet, I had been fuming that we were late, irritated that it was raining, and worried about the whole situation. But if it hadn't been raining, there would not have been a rainbow, and if we hadn't been running late and delayed, we might not have been at the spot where we could see the rainbow.

~

It's all too easy to ignore an offering out of the blue. I love fireworks, but I hate crowds, so I often avoid fireworks displays. Not too long ago, we were driving home from a small party when we heard booming in the distance. We came over a hill and saw fireworks exploding in the air ahead of us. For a few blocks we had an excellent view of the finale of a professional display. This was unexpected gift from the universe.

~

The Sun come up and goes down every day. It's free and available to everyone. If there are clouds, they often add to the display. Seldom is it so overcast that we cannot see the Sun at all. Yet how often do we actually watch the sunrise or set?

Many years ago, I drove with a friend from Minnesota to California. After dinner, as we were entering the foothills of the Rockies, we were driving almost due west. Before us was a scene that looked like a pre-Raphaelite painting of heaven, a sunset of blue, pink, and yellow, and masses of clouds with rays of bright light coming through. All that was missing was the angels. We hadn't been looking for a magnificent sunset; we were lucky enough for the universe to give it to us.

The journey doesn't have to be by car, either. We discovered one magical possibility of the train a few

winters ago whilie going through the Rocky Mountains in Glacier National Park. We were looking at the sunset until the Sun sank below a mountain, and we thought that was it for the day. A few minutes later, we came around a sharp curve, and there, to the west, was the Sun, not quite touching the horizon. We watched the Sun once again, and once again, it set. The day of two sunsets; I never thought it could happen.

~

Walking is a good way to travel as well. One of the first experiences that turned me to the path of being Pagan was on Spring Equinox when I was a teenager. I was walking north, out in the country where it was very flat, with no buildings. On my left the Sun was setting, and on my right the Full Moon was rising. Looking at the Sun, and the Moon, I knew that today—when day and night were the same length—was in balance, and I saw the Sun and the Moon exactly opposite each other, also in balance. The world felt very serene and solid, yet I knew this was just the balance point of an ever-changing cycle.

~

If we expect all magic to be exactly what we intend, what we think we want or need, we close off possibilities. We can never know what could be around the next bend in the road, one stop farther on the bus line, even a few blocks from home. There are opportunities in missed connections, delays, and detours. Just be receptive to chance and luck.

Let us seek to make every journey a pilgrimage that brings knowledge, even enlightenment. Whether you are taking the kids to school, or driving across the country, remind yourself that you are on your own course. When you travel, look for possibilities the universe will reveal to you. Open your eyes to new perspectives. See the spark of the divine in other people and sacred places everywhere. Magic is all around you.

Balloon Magick

by Melanie Marquis

They star in parades. They stand out at parties. They can bring both smiles and tears in seconds, and they float through the sky inspiring wonder and curiosity. Balloons are indeed magickal, both as delightful objects to amuse us and as powerful mediums for effective spellcasting.

As a kid, getting a balloon brought mixed emotions. On one side, there's the happiness and excitement of having the balloon in hand to hold and toss about, but on the other side, anxiety and anticipated sadness regarding the balloon's certain eventual fate. A world of fun while intact and inflated, but bursting suddenly at the slightest prick from a pin, balloons show us that reality is temporary and can be changed in a heartbeat. Balloons teach us to enjoy what we can't hold forever, while we can hold it. It's no wonder why balloons incite our fascination, and using them magickally has benefits.

Working with the same old spell mediums time and again can get repetitive, and balloons offer an unusual means for casting many types of magick. When we switch up our routines, our rituals become more enjoyable and we are more likely to be full-fledged participants in the magickal process. Manipulating candles for the thousandth time, for example, it makes it easy to simply go through the motions without really working the magick. But with the uncommon novelty of balloons at the altar, the Witch's attention is focused and interest is piqued, making for powerful spellcasting energy. If you're looking for something a little different to add to your magickal repertoire, grab a bag of balloons and get popping.

Expand It

Inflatable to many times their original size, balloons are perfect symbols of expansion and growth. Try this balloon expansion spell next time you want to create a magickal increase. Place a balloon on your altar and think about whatever it is you want to expand. Draw a picture or a symbol, or write a few words on the balloon's surface to represent your wish. For example, if you would like to increase your wealth, draw a money sign on the balloon. If you want to expand your romantic opportunities, draw a heart on the balloon or write on it the words, "more love." Now choose an essential oil you feel would be beneficial in achieving your spell goal. For a spell to magnify confidence, you might anoint the balloon with frankincense oil, while lavender oil might be appropriate for a spell to increase relaxation.

Symbols drawn and oils applied, think of your magickal goal and blow hard and steady into the balloon. See the balloon, now a representation of your spell's intent, expand and stretch as you fill it with air. Picture your goal perfectly manifested as you tie off the end of the balloon. Leave it on your altar for a day or so, then release the air, affirming that the magickal expansion is in full effect.

Abracadabra, Zoom!

If something in your life is moving more slowly than you'd like, balloon magick can bust through the sluggishness fast. Powered by air, the element of swiftness and motion, balloons can impart

a burst of speed to any situation. Here's how. Hold a balloon in your hands and envision the situation you would like to hurry along. State clearly your desire to speed things up. Slowly blow into the balloon, inflating it as you see in your mind the circumstances you want to occur playing out in fast forward, visualizing the steps toward your goal being reached in rapid succession. When the balloon is fully inflated, envision a very clear image of the end result you are hoping to quickly achieve. Release your hold on the balloon's end, letting your magick zoom off with it as the air rushes out, imparting an energy of fast-moving action to your spell.

Magick with a Bang

Balloons are also great magickal tools for use in banishing and repelling spells. When you have a need to expel a dangerous person from your life, try this simple balloon charm to banish your foe with a bang. Inflate a balloon while you think of the individual you need to repel. Focus on their personality and appearance as you blow up the balloon to full size. Write the name of the person on the balloon, and say it out loud, speaking clearly. Hold the balloon in one hand and a sharp knife in the other. Pierce the balloon, busting it with a loud bang as you adamantly say, "Now, go!"

Reduction Spells

Reduction spells are a useful form of magick, able to help shrink everything from debts to fears to waistlines. One way to work a reduction spell is with balloon magick. Inflate a balloon while thinking of the thing you want to reduce. Once it's nearly full of air, hold the end firmly closed, but don't tie it off. Keeping the balloon held tightly, draw an image on it that represents the focus of the reduction spell. For example, if you're hoping to give your exercise program a kick-start and reduce your weight, you might draw an image of your current body on the balloon. If you want to reduce a fear of heights, you could draw an image of yourself a top a tall building. Now gently release your grip on the balloon's end, letting the air seep out a little at a time as you watch the symbolic image shrink before your eyes. Know that the energies therein represented will be minimized just as the balloon's volume diminishes. The reduction spell is now cast.

Sneaky Magick

Sometimes all we need is a little opportunity, an open door, or a secret passage to get us where we want to go. When you're in steady pursuit of a goal and the only thing lacking is a lucky chance, balloon magick can help create opportunities to sneak your biggest ideas into manifestation. Blow up a balloon, leaving it not quite fully inflated, and tie it off. Through visualization, empower it to represent the Earth as a whole. If you like, draw the continents on its surface so that it resembles a globe. As an alternative, especially if you're seeking an opportunity with a particular individual or company, decorate the balloon to represent the specific person, place, or entity you're hoping will give you a boost up the ladder to success. Now take a small piece of transparent tape and write on it the word, "Chance." Stick the tape on the balloon's surface. Choose a thin needle and hold it in your hand, thinking of your ambition and feeling the emotion of achieving your biggest dreams. Send this energy into the needle, stroking it from eye to point. Now, very carefully and slowly slide the empowered needle into the balloon through the tape. Push it all the way through and leave it inside the balloon. Place the balloon in a hidden area of your home and let it deflate naturally. Once the balloon has fully deflated, untie it and remove the needle. Take the needle outside and toss it over your shoulder without looking, whispering to yourself and to the powers that be, "Get me in there!"

Bombs Away!

Air-filled balloons are versatile in their own right, but add water- and potion-filled balloons to your arsenal, and you'll have a whole new way to cast spells that really make a splash. To work a spell to cause a transformation, use chalk to draw an image of the thing to be transformed (as it looks in its current state) on concrete or on a large rock. Now take a balloon and place in it a small amount of an herb, or a few pieces of a stone, that is magickally associated with the change you wish to effect. For example, turquoise could be used to transform isolation into friendship, or cinnamon to transform timidness into courage. Fill the balloon up with water and tie it securely. Give it a good shake to mix the energies of the herbs or stones with the energies of the water. Your potion now made, throw the balloon hard at the chalk image so that it bursts, washing away the drawing and the energies it represents to jump-start a transformation.

Binding with Balloons

The symbolic twisting of words, images, and objects has been a technique common to binding magick since ancient times. Able to be bent, shaped, and twisted, "balloon animal" balloons provide a contemporary and unusual medium for casting familiar, old-fashioned spells. Whether you wish to do a balloon-binding spell to cut off potato chip cravings or to seal out termites, the basic format is the same. To start, pump up a balloon, the kind especially made for twisting into various shapes. Don't fill it up too much; leave a little room so that it can be manipulated without popping. The balloon placed before you, focus on the target of the binding spell. Envision the energy to be bound encased in the balloon; state out loud or write words on the balloon to identify it as a stand-in for whatever you intend to bind. Concentrating on your magickal need, twist the balloon at its center, giving it four sharp turns. Now bring together the opposite ends of the balloon and make another twist, forming the balloon into a roughly circular shape. Gather the circle in its middle and twist again, making a figure eight. Continue folding and twisting the balloon until it pops, audibly and visibly sealing the binding spell.

Charge It Up

Balloons can also be used in attraction magick. Try this science experiment turned spellwork the next time there's something you want to draw closer. Take an empty soda can and write on it words to express what you wish to attract. Depending on your goal, you might write something like, "More money," "True love," "Motivation," or "Opportunity." Now blow up a regular balloon and draw on it an image of yourself, your whole body or just your face. To strengthen the charm, attach a piece of your own hair to the balloon. Next, take a square of bathroom tissue and draw on this a symbol you feel has general magickal power. You might choose a Witch's knot, a pentacle, a crescent Moon, or other symbol you find meaningful and appealing. Now rapidly rub the square of tissue back and forth across the rounder end of the balloon, building up both static electricity and magickal power. Place the empty soda can on its side several inches away from the balloon. Watch as the static charge of the balloon pulls the can closer, envisioning the resources you want to attract likewise being drawn straight to you.

Latex Universe

For the Witch who is just beginning to discover the wide variety of magickal applications for balloons, taking some time to connect with balloons on a spiritual and mental level is enriching and inspiring. Used in meditations on the universe and its creation, balloons offer us a way to fathom the unfathomable, a handy model to aid our finite perceptions in envisioning the infinite. By expanding our understanding of reality and the abstract concepts that comprise it, our instinctual insights into the inner workings of magick reawaken.

Ever heard of Inflation Theory? It's the idea that the universe may have "began" as a single point of enormous density that "inflated" outward within fractions of a second after the Big Bang—expanding exponentially in every direction. Try using a balloon to illustrate this concept and better understand the magickal principles implied therein. Before blowing it up, use a marker or pen to draw a lot of tiny dots all over the surface of the balloon. These dots can represent stars, planets, or energy particles. Now gently inflate the balloon, noticing how dots that were once side by side are now separated by greater distance. Think about how the surface of the balloon is still the same substance, the same energy particles, as it was when it was flat and floppy. Contemplate the contagion principle of magick, the theory that substances or objects that come into contact "pick up" and retain the magickal charge or energetic pattern of that meeting, even when afterward separated by great distances. Look at those little dots on the balloon, thinking of them as the original magickal power of the universe, now spread throughout but still a connected network within our ever-expanding reality. Does this give you any ideas you can apply magickally? What spiritual concepts does this exercise bring to mind?

～

With their versatility and widespread availability, balloons are one of the easiest ways to blow new life into your magick. Play around with balloons. Let them inspire you, amuse you, and incite your imagination. The better you feel, the more power you can utilize in your spellcastings, so let loose and have a good time with your balloon workings. Balloons are serious magick, but they are also serious fun.

Almanac Section

Calendar

Time Changes

Lunar Phases

Moon Signs

Full Moons

Sabbats

World Holidays

Incense of the Day

Color of the Day

Almanac Listings

In these listings you will find the date, day, lunar phase, Moon sign, color, and incense for the day, as well as festivals from around the world.

The Date

The date is used in numerological calculations that govern magical rites.

The Day

Each day is ruled by a planet that possesses specific magical influences:

MONDAY (MOON): Peace, sleep, healing, compassion, friends, psychic awareness, purification, and fertility.

TUESDAY (MARS): Passion, sex, courage, aggression, and protection.

WEDNESDAY (MERCURY): The conscious mind, study, travel, divination, and wisdom.

THURSDAY (JUPITER): Expansion, money, prosperity, and generosity.

FRIDAY (VENUS): Love, friendship, reconciliation, and beauty.

SATURDAY (SATURN): Longevity, exorcism, endings, homes, and houses.

SUNDAY (SUN): Healing, spirituality, success, strength, and protection.

The Lunar Phase

The lunar phase is important in determining the best times for magic.

THE WAXING MOON (from the New Moon to the Full) is the ideal time for magic to draw things toward you.

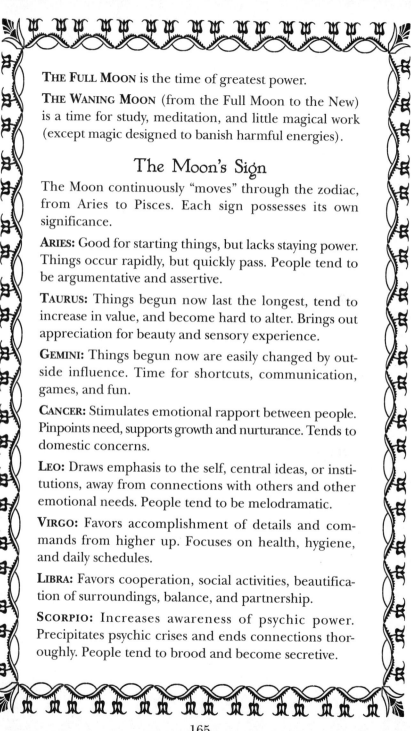

THE FULL MOON is the time of greatest power.

THE WANING MOON (from the Full Moon to the New) is a time for study, meditation, and little magical work (except magic designed to banish harmful energies).

The Moon's Sign

The Moon continuously "moves" through the zodiac, from Aries to Pisces. Each sign possesses its own significance.

ARIES: Good for starting things, but lacks staying power. Things occur rapidly, but quickly pass. People tend to be argumentative and assertive.

TAURUS: Things begun now last the longest, tend to increase in value, and become hard to alter. Brings out appreciation for beauty and sensory experience.

GEMINI: Things begun now are easily changed by outside influence. Time for shortcuts, communication, games, and fun.

CANCER: Stimulates emotional rapport between people. Pinpoints need, supports growth and nurturance. Tends to domestic concerns.

LEO: Draws emphasis to the self, central ideas, or institutions, away from connections with others and other emotional needs. People tend to be melodramatic.

VIRGO: Favors accomplishment of details and commands from higher up. Focuses on health, hygiene, and daily schedules.

LIBRA: Favors cooperation, social activities, beautification of surroundings, balance, and partnership.

SCORPIO: Increases awareness of psychic power. Precipitates psychic crises and ends connections thoroughly. People tend to brood and become secretive.

Sagittarius: Encourages flights of imagination and confidence. This is an adventurous, philosophical, and athletic Moon sign. Favors expansion and growth.

Capricorn: Develops strong structure. Focus on traditions, responsibilities, and obligations. A good time to set boundaries and rules.

Aquarius: Rebellious energy. Time to break habits and make abrupt changes. Personal freedom and individuality is the focus.

Pisces: The focus is on dreaming, nostalgia, intuition, and psychic impressions. A good time for spiritual or philanthropic activities.

Color and Incense

The color and incense for the day are based on information from *Personal Alchemy* by Amber Wolfe, and relate to the planet that rules each day. This information can be taken into consideration along with other factors when planning works of magic or when blending magic into mundane life. Please note that the incense selections listed are not hard and fast. If you cannot find or do not like the incense listed for the day, choose a similar scent that appeals to you.

Festivals and Holidays

Festivals are listed throughout the year. The exact dates of many of these ancient festivals are difficult to determine; prevailing data has been used.

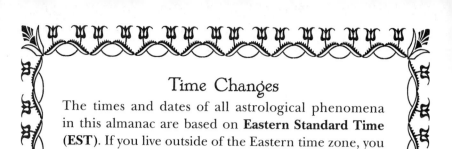

Time Changes

The times and dates of all astrological phenomena in this almanac are based on **Eastern Standard Time (EST)**. If you live outside of the Eastern time zone, you will need to make the following changes:

PACIFIC STANDARD TIME: Subtract three hours.

MOUNTAIN STANDARD TIME: Subtract two hours.

CENTRAL STANDARD TIME: Subtract one hour.

ALASKA: Subtract four hours.

HAWAII: Subtract five hours.

DAYLIGHT SAVING TIME (ALL ZONES): Add one hour.

Daylight Saving Time begins at 2 am on March 13, 2011, and ends at 2 am on November 6, 2011.

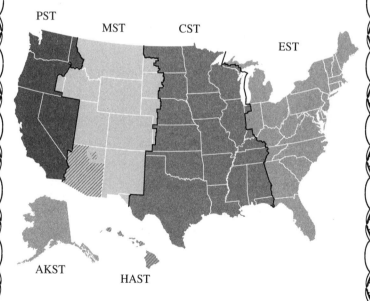

Please refer to a world time zone resource for time adjustments for locations outside the United States.

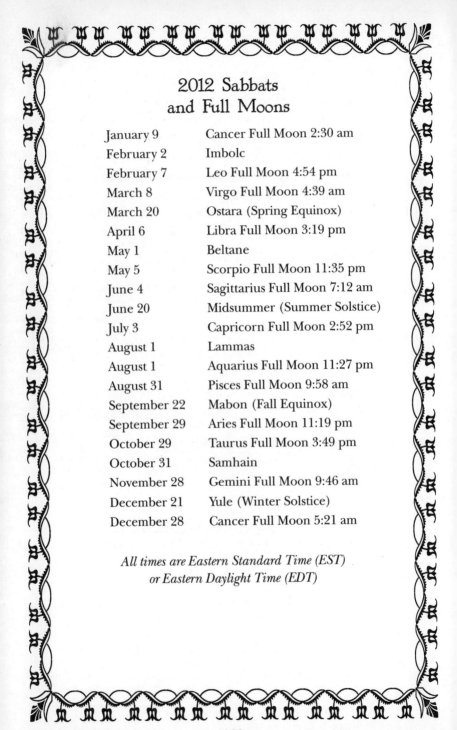

2012 Sabbats
and Full Moons

January 9	Cancer Full Moon 2:30 am
February 2	Imbolc
February 7	Leo Full Moon 4:54 pm
March 8	Virgo Full Moon 4:39 am
March 20	Ostara (Spring Equinox)
April 6	Libra Full Moon 3:19 pm
May 1	Beltane
May 5	Scorpio Full Moon 11:35 pm
June 4	Sagittarius Full Moon 7:12 am
June 20	Midsummer (Summer Solstice)
July 3	Capricorn Full Moon 2:52 pm
August 1	Lammas
August 1	Aquarius Full Moon 11:27 pm
August 31	Pisces Full Moon 9:58 am
September 22	Mabon (Fall Equinox)
September 29	Aries Full Moon 11:19 pm
October 29	Taurus Full Moon 3:49 pm
October 31	Samhain
November 28	Gemini Full Moon 9:46 am
December 21	Yule (Winter Solstice)
December 28	Cancer Full Moon 5:21 am

All times are Eastern Standard Time (EST)
or Eastern Daylight Time (EDT)

2012 Sabbats in the Southern Hemisphere

Because Earth's Northern and Southern Hemispheres experience opposite seasons at any given time, the season-based Sabbats listed on the previous page and in this almanac section are not correct for those residing south of the equator. Listed here are the Southern Hemisphere sabbat dates for 2012:

February 2	Lammas
March 20	Mabon (Fall Equinox)
May 1	Samhain
June 20	Yule (Winter Solstice)
August 2	Imbolc
September 22	Ostara (Spring Equinox)
November 1	Beltane
December 21	Midsummer (Summer Solstice)

❖

Birthstone poetry reprinted from
The Occult and Curative Powers of Precious Stones
by William T. Fernie, M.D.
Harper & Row (1981)

Originally printed in 1907 as
Precious Stones:
For Curative Wear; and Other Remedial Uses;
Likewise the Nobler Metals

January ♑

○ **Sunday**
New Year's Day • Kwanzaa ends
Waxing Moon
Moon phase: Second Quarter 1:15 am
Color: Gold

Moon Sign: Aries
Incense: Juniper

2 **Monday**
First Writing Day (Japanese)
Waxing Moon
Moon phase: Second Quarter
Color: Ivory

Moon Sign: Aries
Moon enters Taurus 5:16 pm
Incense: Narcissus

3 **Tuesday**
St. Genevieve's Day
Waxing Moon
Moon phase: Second Quarter
Color: Scarlet

Moon Sign: Taurus
Incense: Ginger

4 **Wednesday**
Frost Fairs on the Thames
Waxing Moon
Moon phase: Second Quarter
Color: Topaz

Moon Sign: Taurus
Incense: Bay laurel

5 **Thursday**
Epiphany Eve
Waxing Moon
Moon phase: Second Quarter
Color: Crimson

Moon Sign: Taurus
Moon enters Gemini 5:44 am
Incense: Nutmeg

6 **Friday**
Epiphany
Waxing Moon
Moon phase: Second Quarter
Color: Purple

Moon Sign: Gemini
Incense: Yarrow

7 **Saturday**
Rizdvo (Ukrainian)
Waxing Moon
Moon phase: Second Quarter
Color: Blue

Moon Sign: Gemini
Moon enters Cancer 4:05 pm
Incense: Sandalwood

8 Sunday
Midwives' Day
Waxing Moon
Moon phase: Second Quarter
Color: Amber

Moon Sign: Cancer
Incense: Almond

Monday
Feast of the Black Nazarene (Filipino)
Waxing Moon
Moon phase: Full Moon 2:30 am
Color: Lavender

Moon Sign: Cancer
Moon enters Leo 11:35 pm
Incense: Clary sage

---

10 Tuesday
Business God's Day (Japanese)
Waning Moon
Moon phase: Third Quarter
Color: Red

Moon Sign: Leo
Incense: Geranium

---

11 Wednesday
Carmentalia (Roman)
Waning Moon
Moon phase: Third Quarter
Color: Yellow

Moon Sign: Leo
Incense: Lavender

---

12 Thursday
Revolution Day (Tanzanian)
Waning Moon
Moon phase: Third Quarter
Color: Green

Moon Sign: Leo
Moon enters Virgo 4:44 am
Incense: Jasmine

---

13 Friday
Twentieth Day (Norwegian)
Waning Moon
Moon phase: Third Quarter
Color: Rose

Moon Sign: Virgo
Incense: Alder

---

14 Saturday
Feast of the Ass (French)
Waning Moon
Moon phase: Third Quarter
Color: Black

Moon Sign: Virgo
Moon enters Libra 8:28 am
Incense: Patchouli

January

15 Sunday
Birthday of Martin Luther King, Jr. (actual)
Waning Moon
Moon phase: Third Quarter
Color: Yellow

Moon Sign: Libra
Incense: Eucalyptus

○ Monday
Birthday of Martin Luther King, Jr. (observed)
Waning Moon
Moon phase: Fourth Quarter 4:08 am
Color: Silver

Moon Sign: Libra
Moon enters Scorpio 11:33 am
Incense: Lily

17 Tuesday
St. Anthony's Day (Mexican)
Waning Moon
Moon phase: Fourth Quarter
Color: Black

Moon Sign: Scorpio
Incense: Bayberry

18 Wednesday
Assumption Day
Waning Moon
Moon phase: Fourth Quarter
Color: Brown

Moon Sign: Scorpio
Moon enters Sagittarius 2:29 pm
Incense: Lilac

19 Thursday
Kitchen God Feast (Chinese)
Waning Moon
Moon phase: Fourth Quarter
Color: White

Moon Sign: Sagittarius
Incense: Myrrh

20 Friday
Breadbasket Festival (Portuguese)
Waning Moon
Moon phase: Fourth Quarter
Color: Pink

Moon Sign: Sagittarius
Sun enters Aquarius 11:10 am
Incense: Cypress
Moon enters Capricorn 5:40 pm

21 Saturday
St. Agnes' Day
Waning Moon
Moon phase: Fourth Quarter
Color: Blue

Moon Sign: Capricorn
Incense: Magnolia

January

22 Sunday

Saint Vincent's Day (French)
Waning Moon
Moon phase: Fourth Quarter
Color: Orange

Moon Sign: Capricorn
Moon enters Aquarius 9:53 pm
Incense: Frankincense

☽ Monday

Chinese New Year (dragon)
Waning Moon
Moon phase: New Moon 2:39 am
Color: Gray

Moon Sign: Aquarius
Incense: Hyssop

24 Tuesday

Alasitas Fair (Bolivian)
Waxing Moon
Moon phase: First Quarter
Color: Red

Moon Sign: Aquarius
Incense: Cedar

25 Wednesday

Burns' Night (Scottish)
Waxing Moon
Moon phase: First Quarter
Color: Topaz

Moon Sign: Aquarius
Moon enters Pisces 4:11 am
Incense: Honeysuckle

26 Thursday

Republic Day (Indian)
Waxing Moon
Moon phase: First Quarter
Color: Green

Moon Sign: Pisces
Incense: Clove

27 Friday

Vogelgruff (Swiss)
Waxing Moon
Moon phase: First Quarter
Color: Coral

Moon Sign: Pisces
Moon enters Aries 1:28 pm
Incense: Violet

28 Saturday

St. Charlemange's Day
Waxing Moon
Moon phase: First Quarter
Color: Brown

Moon Sign: Aries
Incense: Pine

January

29 Sunday
Australia Day
Waxing Moon
Moon phase: First Quarter
Color: Yellow

Moon Sign: Aries
Incense: Marigold

 Monday
Three Hierarch's Day (Eastern Orthodox)
Waxing Moon
Moon phase: Second Quarter 11:10 pm
Color: White

Moon Sign: Aries
Moon enters Taurus 1:28 am
Incense: Neroli

31 Tuesday
Independence Day (Nauru)
Waxing Moon
Moon phase: Second Quarter
Color: White

Moon Sign: Taurus
Incense: Ylang-ylang

January Birthstones

By her in January born
No gem save Garnets should be worn;
They will ensure her constancy,
True friendship, and fidelity.

Modern: Garnet   Zodiac (Capricorn): Ruby

February Birthstones

The February-born shall find
Sincerity, and peace of mind,
Freedom from passion and from care,
If they the Amethyst will wear.

Modern: Amethyst   Zodiac (Aquarius): Garnet

February

1 **Wednesday**
St. Brigid's Day (Irish)
Waxing Moon
Moon phase: Second Quarter
Color: White

Moon Sign: Taurus
Moon enters Gemini 2:14 pm
Incense: Marjoram

2 **Thursday**
Imbolc • Groundhog Day
Waxing Moon
Moon phase: Second Quarter
Color: Turquoise

Moon Sign: Gemini
Incense: Mulberry

3 **Friday**
St. Blaise's Day
Waxing Moon
Moon phase: Second Quarter
Color: Pink

Moon Sign: Gemini
Incense: Rose

4 **Saturday**
Independence Day (Sri Lankan)
Waxing Moon
Moon phase: Second Quarter
Color: Black

Moon Sign: Gemini
Moon enters Cancer 1:04 am
Incense: Patchouli

5 **Sunday**
Festival de la Alcaldesa (Italian)
Waxing Moon
Moon phase: Second Quarter
Color: Orange

Moon Sign: Cancer
Incense: Hyacinth

6 **Monday**
Bob Marley's Birthday (Jamaican)
Waxing Moon
Moon phase: Second Quarter
Color: Ivory

Moon Sign: Cancer
Moon enters Leo 8:24 am
Incense: Rosemary

☺ **Tuesday**
Full Moon Poya (Sri Lankan)
Waxing Moon
Moon phase: Full Moon 4:54 pm
Color: Maroon

Moon Sign: Leo
Incense: Ginger

February

8   **Wednesday**
Mass for Broken Needles (Japanese)
Waning Moon
Moon phase: Third Quarter
Color: Brown

Moon Sign: Leo
Moon enters Virgo 12:32 pm
Incense: Lavender

9   **Thursday**
St. Marion's Day (Lebanese)
Waning Moon
Moon phase: Third Quarter
Color: Purple

Moon Sign: Virgo
Incense: Myrrh

10   **Friday**
Gasparilla Day (Floridian)
Waning Moon
Moon phase: Third Quarter
Color: Rose

Moon Sign: Virgo
Moon enters Libra 2:54 pm
Incense: Vanilla

11   **Saturday**
Foundation Day (Japanese)
Waning Moon
Moon phase: Third Quarter
Color: Blue

Moon Sign: Libra
Incense: Sage

12   **Sunday**
Lincoln's Birthday (actual)
Waning Moon
Moon phase: Third Quarter
Color: Gold

Moon Sign: Libra
Moon enters Scorpio 5:01 pm
Incense: Frankincense

13   **Monday**
Parentalia (Roman)
Waning Moon
Moon phase: Third Quarter
Color: Silver

Moon Sign: Scorpio
Incense: Clary sage

◗   **Tuesday**
Valentine's Day
Waning Moon
Moon phase: Fourth Quarter 12:04 pm
Color: Gray

Moon Sign: Scorpio
Moon enters Sagittarius 7:56 pm
Incense: Cedar

February

15 **Wednesday**
Lupercalia (Roman)
Waning Moon
Moon phase: Fourth Quarter
Color: Brown

Moon Sign: Sagittarius
Incense: Bay laurel

16 **Thursday**
Fumi-e (Japanese)
Waning Moon
Moon phase: Fourth Quarter
Color: Green

Moon Sign: Sagittarius
Incense: Carnation

17 **Friday**
Quirinalia (Roman)
Waning Moon
Moon phase: Fourth Quarter
Color: White

Moon Sign: Sagittarius
Moon enters Capricorn 12:03 am
Incense: Orchid

18 **Saturday**
Saint Bernadette's Second Vision
Waning Moon
Moon phase: Fourth Quarter
Color: Gray

Moon Sign: Capricorn
Incense: Ivy

19 **Sunday**
Pero Palo's Trial (Spanish)
Waning Moon
Moon phase: Fourth Quarter
Color: Orange

Moon Sign: Capricorn
Sun enters Pisces 1:18 am
Incense: Heliotrope
Moon enters Aquarius 5:28 am

20 **Monday**
Presidents' Day (observed)
Waning Moon
Moon phase: Fourth Quarter
Color: Lavender

Moon Sign: Aquarius
Incense: Lily

☽ **Tuesday**
Mardi Gras (Fat Tuesday)
Waning Moon
Moon phase: New Moon 5:35 pm
Color: Red

Moon Sign: Aquarius
Moon enters Pisces 12:31 pm
Incense: Ylang-ylang

22 Wednesday
Ash Wednesday
Waxing Moon
Moon phase: First Quarter
Color: Yellow

Moon Sign: Pisces
Incense: Lilac

23 Thursday
Terminalia (Roman)
Waxing Moon
Moon phase: First Quarter
Color: Purple

Moon Sign: Pisces
Moon enters Aries 9:48 pm
Incense: Balsam

24 Friday
Regifugium (Roman)
Waxing Moon
Moon phase: First Quarter
Color: White

Moon Sign: Aries
Incense: Cypress

25 Saturday
Saint Walburga's Day (German)
Waxing Moon
Moon phase: First Quarter
Color: Indigo

Moon Sign: Aries
Incense: Rue

26 Sunday
Zamboanga Festival (Filipino)
Waxing Moon
Moon phase: First Quarter
Color: Amber

Moon Sign: Aries
Moon enters Taurus 9:29 am
Incense: Juniper

27 Monday
Threepenny Day
Waxing Moon
Moon phase: First Quarter
Color: Gray

Moon Sign: Taurus
Incense: Hyssop

28 Tuesday
Kalevala Day (Finnish)
Waxing Moon
Moon phase: First Quarter
Color: Black

Moon Sign: Taurus
Moon enters Gemini 10:27 pm
Incense: Basil

March

○ Wednesday
Leap Day
Waxing Moon
Moon phase: Second Quarter 8:21 pm
Color: Topaz

Moon Sign: Gemini
Incense: Honeysuckle

---

1 Thursday
Matronalia (Roman)
Waxing Moon
Moon phase: Second Quarter
Color: Turquoise

Moon Sign: Gemini
Incense: Balsam

---

2 Friday
St. Chad's Day (English)
Waxing Moon
Moon phase: Second Quarter
Color: Rose

Moon Sign: Gemini
Moon enters Cancer 10:08 am
Incense: Thyme

---

3 Saturday
Doll Festival (Japanese)
Waxing Moon
Moon phase: Second Quarter
Color: Blue

Moon Sign: Cancer
Incense: Sage

---

4 Sunday
St. Casimir's Day (Polish)
Waxing Moon
Moon phase: Second Quarter
Color: Yellow

Moon Sign: Cancer
Moon enters Leo 6:17 pm
Incense: Almond

---

5 Monday
Isis Festival (Roman)
Waxing Moon
Moon phase: Second Quarter
Color: Lavender

Moon Sign: Leo
Incense: Neroli

---

6 Tuesday
Alamo Day
Waxing Moon
Moon phase: Second Quarter
Color: Scarlet

Moon Sign: Leo
Moon enters Virgo 10:27 pm
Incense: Ylang-ylang

March

---

7   **Wednesday**
Bird and Arbor Day
Waxing Moon
Moon phase: Second Quarter
Color: Yellow

Moon Sign: Virgo
Incense: Bay laurel

Thursday
Purim
Waxing Moon
Moon phase: Full Moon 4:39 am
Color: Green

Moon Sign: Virgo
Moon enters Libra 11:50 pm
Incense: Nutmeg

---

9   **Friday**
Tibet Day
Waning Moon
Moon phase: Third Quarter
Color: Pink

Moon Sign: Libra
Incense: Alder

---

10   **Saturday**
Feast of the Gauri (Hindu)
Waning Moon
Moon phase: Third Quarter
Color: Black

Moon Sign: Libra
Incense: Magnolia

---

11   **Sunday**
Daylight Saving Time begins
Waning Moon
Moon phase: Third Quarter
Color: Amber

Moon Sign: Libra
Moon enters Scorpio 12:24 am
Incense: Hyacinth

---

12   **Monday**
Receiving the Water (Buddhist)
Waning Moon
Moon phase: Third Quarter
Color: White

Moon Sign: Scorpio
Incense: Rosemary

---

13   **Tuesday**
Purification Feast (Balinese)
Waning Moon
Moon phase: Third Quarter
Color: Gray

Moon Sign: Scorpio
Moon enters Sagittarius 2:54 am
Incense: Bayberry

March

○ **Wednesday**
Mamuralia (Roman)
Waning Moon
Moon phase: Fourth Quarter 9:25 pm
Color: Topaz

Moon Sign: Sagittarius
Incense: Marjoram

15 Thursday
Phallus Festival (Japanese)
Waning Moon
Moon phase: Fourth Quarter
Color: Crimson

Moon Sign: Sagittarius
Moon enters Capricorn 6:24 am
Incense: Apricot

16 Friday
St. Urho's Day (Finnish)
Waning Moon
Moon phase: Fourth Quarter
Color: Coral

Moon Sign: Capricorn
Incense: Thyme

17 Saturday
St. Patrick's Day
Waning Moon
Moon phase: Fourth Quarter
Color: Blue

Moon Sign: Capricorn
Moon enters Aquarius 12:11 pm
Incense: Patchouli

18 Sunday
Sheelah's Day (Irish)
Waning Moon
Moon phase: Fourth Quarter
Color: Gold

Moon Sign: Aquarius
Incense: Eucalyptus

19 Monday
St. Joseph's Day (Sicilian)
Waning Moon
Moon phase: Fourth Quarter
Color: Ivory

Moon Sign: Aquarius
Moon enters Pisces 8:05 pm
Incense: Narcissus

20 Tuesday
Ostara • Spring Equinox • Int'l Astrology Day
Waning Moon
Moon phase: Fourth Quarter
Color: White

Moon Sign: Pisces
Sun enters Aries 1:14 am
Incense: Geranium

March

21 Wednesday
Juarez Day (Mexican)
Waning Moon
Moon phase: Fourth Quarter
Color: Brown

Moon Sign: Pisces
Incense: Honeysuckle

☽ Thursday
Hilaria (Roman)
Waning Moon
Moon phase: New Moon 10:37 am
Color: White

Moon Sign: Pisces
Moon enters Aries 5:57 am
Incense: Mulberry

23 Friday
Pakistan Day
Waxing Moon
Moon phase: First Quarter
Color: Purple

Moon Sign: Aries
Incense: Rose

24 Saturday
Day of Blood (Roman)
Waxing Moon
Moon phase: First Quarter
Color: Brown

Moon Sign: Aries
Moon enters Taurus 5:43 pm
Incense: Sandalwood

25 Sunday
Tichborne Dole (English)
Waxing Moon
Moon phase: First Quarter
Color: Orange

Moon Sign: Taurus
Incense: Marigold

26 Monday
Prince Kuhio Day (Hawaiian)
Waxing Moon
Moon phase: First Quarter
Color: Gray

Moon Sign: Taurus
Incense: Rosemary

27 Tuesday
Smell the Breezes Day (Egyptian)
Waxing Moon
Moon phase: First Quarter
Color: Red

Moon Sign: Taurus
Moon enters Gemini 6:43 am
Incense: Cinnamon

March

28 Wednesday
Oranges and Lemons Service (English)
Waxing Moon
Moon phase: First Quarter
Color: Yellow

Moon Sign: Gemini
Incense: Bay laurel

29 Thursday
Feast of St. Eustace's of Luxeuil
Waxing Moon
Moon phase: First Quarter
Color: Green

Moon Sign: Gemini
Moon enters Cancer 7:07 pm
Incense: Jasmine

◐ Friday
Seward's Day (Alaskan)
Waxing Moon
Moon phase: Second Quarter 3:41 pm
Color: White

Moon Sign: Cancer
Incense: Mint

31 Saturday
The Borrowed Days (Ethiopian)
Waxing Moon
Moon phase: Second Quarter
Color: Gray

Moon Sign: Cancer
Incense: Rue

March Birthstones

Who in this world of ours, her eyes
In March first opens, shall be wise.
In days of peril, firm and brave,
And wear a Bloodstone to her grave.

Modern: Aquamarine
Zodiac (Pisces): Amethyst

1 Sunday
April Fools' Day • Palm Sunday
Waxing Moon
Moon phase: Second Quarter
Color: Gold

Moon Sign: Cancer
Moon enters Leo 4:35 am
Incense: Eucalyptus

2 Monday
The Battle of Flowers (French)
Waxing Moon
Moon phase: Second Quarter
Color: Silver

Moon Sign: Leo
Incense: Lily

3 Tuesday
Thirteenth Day (Iranian)
Waxing Moon
Moon phase: Second Quarter
Color: White

Moon Sign: Leo
Moon enters Virgo 9:53 am
Incense: Bayberry

4 Wednesday
Megalesia (Roman)
Waxing Moon
Moon phase: Second Quarter
Color: White

Moon Sign: Virgo
Incense: Lilac

5 Thursday
Tomb-Sweeping Day (Chinese)
Waxing Moon
Moon phase: Second Quarter
Color: Crimson

Moon Sign: Virgo
Moon enters Libra 11:32 am
Incense: Clove

☺ Friday
Good Friday
Waxing Moon
Moon phase: Full Moon 3:19 pm
Color: Coral

Moon Sign: Libra
Incense: Vanilla

7 Saturday
Passover begins
Waning Moon
Moon phase: Third Quarter
Color: Black

Moon Sign: Libra
Moon enters Scorpio 11:18 am
Incense: Ivy

April

8 Sunday
Easter
Waning Moon
Moon phase: Third Quarter
Color: Amber

Moon Sign: Scorpio
Incense: Heliotrope

9 Monday
Valour Day (Filipino)
Waning Moon
Moon phase: Third Quarter
Color: Ivory

Moon Sign: Scorpio
Moon enters Sagittarius 11:12 am
Incense: Hyssop

10 Tuesday
The Tenth of April (English)
Waning Moon
Moon phase: Third Quarter
Color: Maroon

Moon Sign: Sagittarius
Incense: Cedar

11 Wednesday
Heroes Day (Costa Rican)
Waning Moon
Moon phase: Third Quarter
Color: Brown

Moon Sign: Sagittarius
Moon enters Capricorn 1:02 pm
Incense: Marjoram

12 Thursday
Cerealia (Roman)
Waning Moon
Moon phase: Third Quarter
Color: Purple

Moon Sign: Capricorn
Incense: Myrrh

◖ Friday
Orthodox Good Friday
Waning Moon
Moon phase: Fourth Quarter 6:50 am
Color: Pink

Moon Sign: Capricorn
Moon enters Aquarius 5:48 pm
Incense: Orchid

14 Saturday
Passover ends
Waning Moon
Moon phase: Fourth Quarter
Color: Indigo

Moon Sign: Aquarius
Incense: Pine

April

15 **Sunday**
Orthodox Easter
Waning Moon
Moon phase: Fourth Quarter
Color: Gold

Moon Sign: Aquarius
Incense: Eucalyptus

16 **Monday**
Zurich Spring Festival (Swiss)
Waning Moon
Moon phase: Fourth Quarter
Color: Silver

Moon Sign: Aquarius
Moon enters Pisces 1:38 am
Incense: Clary sage

17 **Tuesday**
Yayoi Matsuri (Japanese)
Waning Moon
Moon phase: Fourth Quarter
Color: Red

Moon Sign: Pisces
Incense: Geranium

18 **Wednesday**
Flower Festival (Japanese)
Waning Moon
Moon phase: Fourth Quarter
Color: Yellow

Moon Sign: Pisces
Moon enters Aries 11:59 am
Incense: Lilac

19 **Thursday**
Cerealia last day (Roman)
Waning Moon
Moon phase: Fourth Quarter
Color: Green

Moon Sign: Aries
Sun enters Taurus 12:12 pm
Incense: Carnation

20 **Friday**
Drum Festival (Japanese)
Waning Moon
Moon phase: Fourth Quarter
Color: Pink

Moon Sign: Aries
Incense: Violet

🌑 **Saturday**
Tiradentes Day (Brazilian)
Waning Moon
Moon phase: New Moon 3:18 am
Color: Gray

Moon Sign: Aries
Moon enters Taurus 12:05 am
Incense: Sage

April

22 Sunday
Earth Day
Waxing Moon
Moon phase: First Quarter
Color: Orange

Moon Sign: Taurus
Incense: Almond

23 Monday
St. George's Day (English)
Waxing Moon
Moon phase: First Quarter
Color: Lavender

Moon Sign: Taurus
Moon enters Gemini 1:05 pm
Incense: Neroli

24 Tuesday
St. Mark's Eve
Waxing Moon
Moon phase: First Quarter
Color: Black

Moon Sign: Gemini
Incense: Ginger

25 Wednesday
Robigalia (Roman)
Waxing Moon
Moon phase: First Quarter
Color: Topaz

Moon Sign: Gemini
Incense: Lavender

26 Thursday
Arbor Day
Waxing Moon
Moon phase: First Quarter
Color: White

Moon Sign: Gemini
Moon enters Cancer 1:42 am
Incense: Jasmine

27 Friday
Humabon's Conversion (Filipino)
Waxing Moon
Moon phase: First Quarter
Color: Purple

Moon Sign: Cancer
Incense: Yarrow

28 Saturday
Floralia (Roman)
Waxing Moon
Moon phase: First Quarter
Color: Blue

Moon Sign: Cancer
Moon enters Leo 12:10 pm
Incense: Magnolia

April

○ **Sunday**
Green Day (Japanese)
Waxing Moon
Moon phase: Second Quarter 5:57 am
Color: Yellow

Moon Sign: Leo
Incense: Juniper

---

30 Monday
Walpurgis Night • May Eve
Waxing Moon
Moon phase: Second Quarter
Color: Gray

Moon Sign: Leo
Moon enters Virgo 7:02 pm
Incense: Lily

April Birthstones

She who from April dates her years,
Diamonds shall wear, lest bitter tears
For vain repentance flow; this stone
Emblem for innocence is known.

Modern: Diamond
Zodiac (Aries): Bloodstone

May

1 Tuesday
Beltane • May Day
Waxing Moon
Moon phase: Second Quarter
Color: Maroon

Moon Sign: Virgo
Incense: Cinnamon

---

2 Wednesday
Big Kite Flying (Japanese)
Waxing Moon
Moon phase: Second Quarter
Color: Yellow

Moon Sign: Virgo
Moon enters Libra 10:04 pm
Incense: Honeysuckle

---

3 Thursday
Holy Cross Day
Waxing Moon
Moon phase: Second Quarter
Color: Green

Moon Sign: Libra
Incense: Nutmeg

---

4 Friday
Bona Dea (Roman)
Waxing Moon
Moon phase: Second Quarter
Color: Purple

Moon Sign: Libra
Moon enters Scorpio 10:20 pm
Incense: Vanilla

☺ Saturday
Cinco de Mayo (Mexican)
Waxing Moon
Moon phase: Full Moon 11:35 pm
Color: Black

Moon Sign: Scorpio
Incense: Rue

---

6 Sunday
Martyrs' Day (Lebanese)
Waning Moon
Moon phase: Third Quarter
Color: Gold

Moon Sign: Scorpio
Moon enters Sagittarius 9:39 pm
Incense: Marigold

---

7 Monday
Pilgrimage of St. Nicholas (Italian)
Waning Moon
Moon phase: Third Quarter
Color: White

Moon Sign: Sagittarius
Incense: Narcissus

May

8 **Tuesday**
Liberation Day (French)
Waning Moon
Moon phase: Third Quarter
Color: Gray

Moon Sign: Sagittarius
Moon enters Capricorn 10:00 pm
Incense: Ginger

9 **Wednesday**
Lemuria (Roman)
Waning Moon
Moon phase: Third Quarter
Color: Yellow

Moon Sign: Capricorn
Incense: Bay laurel

10 **Thursday**
Census Day (Canadian)
Waning Moon
Moon phase: Third Quarter
Color: Turquoise

Moon Sign: Capricorn
Incense: Apricot

11 **Friday**
Ukai Season opens (Japanese)
Waning Moon
Moon phase: Third Quarter
Color: Rose

Moon Sign: Capricorn
Moon enters Aquarius 1:03 am
Incense: Thyme

☾ **Saturday**
Florence Nightingale's Birthday
Waning Moon
Moon phase: Fourth Quarter 5:47 pm
Color: Blue

Moon Sign: Aquarius
Incense: Ivy

13 **Sunday**
Mother's Day
Waning Moon
Moon phase: Fourth Quarter
Color: Orange

Moon Sign: Aquarius
Moon enters Pisces 7:42 am
Incense: Frankincense

14 **Monday**
Carabao Festival (Spanish)
Waning Moon
Moon phase: Fourth Quarter
Color: Lavender

Moon Sign: Pisces
Incense: Lily

May

15 Tuesday
Festival of St. Dympna (Belgian)
Waning Moon
Moon phase: Fourth Quarter
Color: Red

Moon Sign: Pisces
Moon enters Aries 5:45 pm
Incense: Ylang-ylang

16 Wednesday
St. Honoratus' Day
Waning Moon
Moon phase: Fourth Quarter
Color: Brown

Moon Sign: Aries
Incense: Lilac

17 Thursday
Norwegian Independence Day
Waning Moon
Moon phase: Fourth Quarter
Color: Crimson

Moon Sign: Aries
Incense: Myrrh

18 Friday
Las Piedras Day (Uraguayan)
Waning Moon
Moon phase: Fourth Quarter
Color: Coral

Moon Sign: Aries
Moon enters Taurus 6:03 am
Incense: Orchid

19 Saturday
Pilgrimage to Treguier (French)
Waning Moon
Moon phase: Fourth Quarter
Color: Black

Moon Sign: Taurus
Incense: Pine

Sunday
Pardon of the Singers (British)
Waning Moon
Moon phase: New Moon 7:47 pm
Color: Yellow

Moon Sign: Taurus
Sun enters Gemini 11:16 am
Incense: Hyacinth
Moon enters Gemini 7:05 pm

21 Monday
Victoria Day (Canadian)
Waxing Moon
Moon phase: First Quarter
Color: Gray

Moon Sign: Gemini
Incense: Rosemary

22 Tuesday
Heroes' Day (Sri Lankan)
Waxing Moon
Moon phase: First Quarter
Color: Red

Moon Sign: Gemini
Incense: Basil

23 Wednesday
Tubilustrium (Roman)
Waxing Moon
Moon phase: First Quarter
Color: Brown

Moon Sign: Gemini
Moon enters Cancer 7:31 am
Incense: Marjoram

24 Thursday
Culture Day (Bulgarian)
Waxing Moon
Moon phase: First Quarter
Color: Green

Moon Sign: Cancer
Incense: Clove

25 Friday
Urbanas Diena (Latvian)
Waxing Moon
Moon phase: First Quarter
Color: White

Moon Sign: Cancer
Moon enters Leo 6:11 pm
Incense: Alder

26 Saturday
Pepys' Commemoration (English)
Waxing Moon
Moon phase: First Quarter
Color: Brown

Moon Sign: Leo
Incense: Patchouli

27 Sunday
Shavuot
Waxing Moon
Moon phase: First Quarter
Color: Orange

Moon Sign: Leo
Incense: Heliotrope

◑ Monday
Memorial Day (observed)
Waxing Moon
Moon phase: Second Quarter 4:16 pm
Color: Ivory

Moon Sign: Leo
Moon enters Virgo 2:06 am
Incense: Clary sage

May

29 **Tuesday**
Royal Oak Day (English)
Waxing Moon
Moon phase: Second Quarter
Color: White

Moon Sign: Virgo
Incense: Cedar

---

30 **Wednesday**
Memorial Day (actual)
Waxing Moon
Moon phase: Second Quarter
Color: White

Moon Sign: Virgo
Moon enters Libra 6:46 am
Incense: Lavender

---

31 **Thursday**
Flowers of May
Waxing Moon
Moon phase: Second Quarter
Color: Purple

Moon Sign: Libra
Incense: Balsam

May Birthstones

Who first beholds the light of day,
In spring's sweet flowery month of May,
And wears an Emerald all her life,
Shall be a loved, and happy wife.

Modern: Emerald
Zodiac (Taurus): Sapphire

June

1 **Friday**
National Day (Tunisian)
Waxing Moon
Moon phase: Second Quarter
Color: Rose

Moon Sign: Libra
Moon enters Scorpio 8:31 am
Incense: Mint

---

2 **Saturday**
Rice Harvest Festival (Malaysian)
Waxing Moon
Moon phase: Second Quarter
Color: Indigo

Moon Sign: Scorpio
Incense: Magnolia

---

3 **Sunday**
Memorial to Broken Dolls (Japanese)
Waxing Moon
Moon phase: Second Quarter
Color: Amber

Moon Sign: Scorpio
Moon enters Sagittarius 8:32 am
Incense: Juniper

☺ **Monday**
Full Moon Day (Burmese)
Waxing Moon
Moon phase: Full Moon 7:12 am
Color: Lavender

Moon Sign: Sagittarius
Incense: Lily

---

5 **Tuesday**
Constitution Day (Danish)
Waning Moon
Moon phase: Third Quarter
Color: Red

Moon Sign: Sagittarius
Moon enters Capricorn 8:31 am
Incense: Cinnamon

---

6 **Wednesday**
Swedish Flag Day
Waning Moon
Moon phase: Third Quarter
Color: Topaz

Moon Sign: Capricorn
Incense: Lavender

---

7 **Thursday**
St. Robert of Newminster's Day
Waning Moon
Moon phase: Third Quarter
Color: Green

Moon Sign: Capricorn
Moon enters Aquarius 10:17 am
Incense: Jasmine

June

8 **Friday**
St. Medard's Day (Belgian)
Waning Moon
Moon phase: Third Quarter
Color: White

Moon Sign: Aquarius
Incense: Rose

9 **Saturday**
Vestalia (Roman)
Waning Moon
Moon phase: Third Quarter
Color: Black

Moon Sign: Aquarius
Moon enters Pisces 3:22 pm
Incense: Sage

10 **Sunday**
Time-Observance Day (Chinese)
Waning Moon
Moon phase: Third Quarter
Color: Amber

Moon Sign: Pisces
Incense: Eucalyptus

☾ **Monday**
Kamehameha Day (Hawaiian)
Waning Moon
Moon phase: Fourth Quarter 6:41 am
Color: Ivory

Moon Sign: Pisces
Incense: Hyssop

12 **Tuesday**
Independence Day (Filipino)
Waning Moon
Moon phase: Fourth Quarter
Color: Red

Moon Sign: Pisces
Moon enters Aries 12:21 am
Incense: Geranium

13 **Wednesday**
St. Anthony of Padua's Day
Waning Moon
Moon phase: Fourth Quarter
Color: White

Moon Sign: Aries
Incense: Honeysuckle

14 **Thursday**
Flag Day
Waning Moon
Moon phase: Fourth Quarter
Color: Turquoise

Moon Sign: Aries
Moon enters Taurus 12:22 pm
Incense: Nutmeg

June

15 Friday
St. Vitus' Day Fires
Waning Moon
Moon phase: Fourth Quarter
Color: Purple

Moon Sign: Taurus
Incense: Cypress

16 Saturday
Bloomsday (Irish)
Waning Moon
Moon phase: Fourth Quarter
Color: Brown

Moon Sign: Taurus
Incense: Sandalwood

17 Sunday
Father's Day
Waning Moon
Moon phase: Fourth Quarter
Color: Yellow

Moon Sign: Taurus
Moon enters Gemini 1:24 am
Incense: Marigold

18 Monday
Independence Day (Egyptian)
Waning Moon
Moon phase: Fourth Quarter
Color: Silver

Moon Sign: Gemini
Incense: Clary sage

☽ Tuesday
Juneteenth
Waning Moon
Moon phase: New Moon 11:02 am
Color: Maroon

Moon Sign: Gemini
Moon enters Cancer 1:34 pm
Incense: Bayberry

20 Wednesday
Midsummer • Summer Solstice
Waxing Moon
Moon phase: First Quarter
Color: Brown

Moon Sign: Cancer
Incense: Bay laurel
Sun enters Cancer 7:09 pm

21 Thursday
U.S. Constitution ratified
Waxing Moon
Moon phase: First Quarter
Color: White

Moon Sign: Cancer
Moon enters Leo 11:47 pm
Incense: Clove

June

22 Friday
Rose Festival (English)
Waxing Moon
Moon phase: First Quarter
Color: Rose

Moon Sign: Leo
Incense: Vanilla

23 Saturday
St. John's Eve
Waxing Moon
Moon phase: First Quarter
Color: Gray

Moon Sign: Leo
Incense: Rue

24 Sunday
St. John's Day
Waxing Moon
Moon phase: First Quarter
Color: Orange

Moon Sign: Leo
Moon enters Virgo 7:42 am
Incense: Almond

25 Monday
Fiesta of Santa Orosia (Spanish)
Waxing Moon
Moon phase: First Quarter
Color: Gray

Moon Sign: Virgo
Incense: Neroli

◗ Tuesday
Pied Piper Day (German)
Waxing Moon
Moon phase: Second Quarter 11:30 pm
Color: Black

Moon Sign: Virgo
Moon enters Libra 1:15 pm
Incense: Ylang-ylang

27 Wednesday
Day of the Seven Sleepers (Islamic)
Waxing Moon
Moon phase: Second Quarter
Color: Yellow

Moon Sign: Libra
Incense: Lilac

28 Thursday
Paul Bunyan Day
Waxing Moon
Moon phase: Second Quarter
Color: Crimson

Moon Sign: Libra
Moon enters Scorpio 4:32 pm
Incense: Carnation

June

29 Friday
Feast of Saints Peter and Paul
Waxing Moon
Moon phase: Second Quarter
Color: Coral

Moon Sign: Scorpio
Incense: Mint

---

30 Saturday
The Burning of the Three Firs (French)
Waxing Moon
Moon phase: Second Quarter
Color: Blue

Moon Sign: Scorpio
Moon enters Sagittarius 6:04 pm
Incense: Sage

June Birthstones

Who comes with summer to this earth,
And owes to June her hour of birth,
With ring of Agate on her hand,
Can health, wealth, and long life command.

Modern: Moonstone or Pearl
Zodiac (Gemini): Agate

1 Sunday
Climbing Mount Fuji (Japanese)
Waxing Moon
Moon phase: Second Quarter
Color: Amber

Moon Sign: Sagittarius
Incense: Almond

2 Monday
Heroes' Day (Zambian)
Waxing Moon
Moon phase: Second Quarter
Color: White

Moon Sign: Sagittarius
Moon enters Capricorn 6:51 pm
Incense: Narcissus

☻ Tuesday
Indian Sun Dance (Native American)
Waxing Moon
Moon phase: Full Moon 2:52 pm
Color: Maroon

Moon Sign: Capricorn
Incense: Ginger

4 Wednesday
Independence Day
Waning Moon
Moon phase: Third Quarter
Color: Yellow

Moon Sign: Capricorn
Moon enters Aquarius 8:26 pm
Incense: Honeysuckle

5 Thursday
Tynwald (Nordic)
Waning Moon
Moon phase: Third Quarter
Color: Turquoise

Moon Sign: Aquarius
Incense: Mulberry

6 Friday
Khao Phansa Day (Thai)
Waning Moon
Moon phase: Third Quarter
Color: Rose

Moon Sign: Aquarius
Incense: Violet

7 Saturday
Weaver's Festival (Japanese)
Waning Moon
Moon phase: Third Quarter
Color: Gray

Moon Sign: Aquarius
Moon enters Pisces 12:29 am
Incense: Ivy

July

8 Sunday
St. Elizabeth's Day (Portuguese)
Waning Moon
Moon phase: Third Quarter
Color: Orange

Moon Sign: Pisces
Incense: Eucalyptus

9 Monday
Battle of Sempach Day (Swiss)
Waning Moon
Moon phase: Third Quarter
Color: Gray

Moon Sign: Pisces
Moon enters Aries 8:14 am
Incense: Clary sage

10 Tuesday
Lady Godiva Day (English)
Waning Moon
Moon phase: Fourth Quarter 9:48 pm
Color: Red

Moon Sign: Aries
Incense: Cinnamon

11 Wednesday
Revolution Day (Mongolian)
Waning Moon
Moon phase: Fourth Quarter
Color: Topaz

Moon Sign: Aries
Moon enters Taurus 7:30 pm
Incense: Lilac

12 Thursday
Lobster Carnival (Nova Scotian)
Waning Moon
Moon phase: Fourth Quarter
Color: Green

Moon Sign: Taurus
Incense: Apricot

13 Friday
Festival of the Three Cows (Spanish)
Waning Moon
Moon phase: Fourth Quarter
Color: Pink

Moon Sign: Taurus
Incense: Alder

14 Saturday
Bastille Day (French)
Waning Moon
Moon phase: Fourth Quarter
Color: Indigo

Moon Sign: Taurus
Moon enters Gemini 8:26 am
Incense: Pine

15 Sunday
St. Swithin's Day
Waning Moon
Moon phase: Fourth Quarter
Color: Gold

Moon Sign: Gemini
Incense: Almond

---

16 Monday
Our Lady of Carmel
Waning Moon
Moon phase: Fourth Quarter
Color: Ivory

Moon Sign: Gemini
Moon enters Cancer 8:31 pm
Incense: Neroli

---

17 Tuesday
Rivera Day (Puerto Rican)
Waning Moon
Moon phase: Fourth Quarter
Color: Red

Moon Sign: Cancer
Incense: Basil

---

18 Wednesday
Gion Matsuri Festival (Japanese)
Waning Moon
Moon phase: Fourth Quarter
Color: Brown

Moon Sign: Cancer
Incense: Marjoram

☽ Thursday
Flitch Day (English)
Waning Moon
Moon phase: New Moon 12:24 am
Color: Crimson

Moon Sign: Cancer
Moon enters Leo 6:13 am
Incense: Carnation

---

20 Friday
Ramadan begins
Waxing Moon
Moon phase: First Quarter
Color: Coral

Moon Sign: Leo
Incense: Yarrow

---

21 Saturday
National Day (Belgian)
Waxing Moon
Moon phase: First Quarter
Color: Blue

Moon Sign: Leo
Moon enters Virgo 1:24 pm
Incense: Ivy

22 Sunday
St. Mary Magdalene's Day
Waxing Moon
Moon phase: First Quarter
Color: Yellow

Moon Sign: Virgo
Incense: Hyacinth
Sun enters Leo 6:01 am

23 Monday
Mysteries of Santa Cristina (Italian)
Waxing Moon
Moon phase: First Quarter
Color: White

Moon Sign: Virgo
Moon enters Libra 6:38 pm
Incense: Neroli

24 Tuesday
Pioneer Day (Mormon)
Waxing Moon
Moon phase: First Quarter
Color: Black

Moon Sign: Libra
Incense: Cinnamon

25 Wednesday
St. James' Day
Waxing Moon
Moon phase: First Quarter
Color: Yellow

Moon Sign: Libra
Moon enters Scorpio 10:29 pm
Incense: Bay laurel

◖ Thursday
St. Anne's Day
Waxing Moon
Moon phase: Second Quarter 4:56 am
Color: Purple

Moon Sign: Scorpio
Incense: Clove

27 Friday
Sleepyhead Day (Finnish)
Waxing Moon
Moon phase: Second Quarter
Color: Purple

Moon Sign: Scorpio
Incense: Orchid

28 Saturday
Independence Day (Peruvian)
Waxing Moon
Moon phase: Second Quarter
Color: Black

Moon Sign: Scorpio
Moon enters Sagittarius 1:18 am
Incense: Magnolia

29 Sunday
Pardon of the Birds (French)
Waxing Moon
Moon phase: Second Quarter
Color: Orange

Moon Sign: Sagittarius
Incense: Heliotrope

30 Monday
Micman Festival of St. Ann
Waxing Moon
Moon phase: Second Quarter
Color: Silver

Moon Sign: Sagittarius
Moon enters Capricorn 3:29 am
Incense: Narcissus

31 Tuesday
Weighing of the Aga Kahn
Waxing Moon
Moon phase: Second Quarter
Color: Gray

Moon Sign: Capricorn
Incense: Cedar

July Birthstones

The glowing Ruby shall adorn
Those who in warm July are born;
Then will they be exempt and free
From love's doubt, and anxiety.

Modern: Ruby
Zodiac (Cancer): Emerald

August

☺ **Wednesday**
Lammas
Waxing Moon
Moon phase: Full Moon 11:27 pm
Color: White

Moon Sign: Capricorn
Moon enters Aquarius 5:56 am
Incense: Lilac

2 **Thursday**
Porcingula (Native American)
Waning Moon
Moon phase: Third Quarter
Color: Green

Moon Sign: Aquarius
Incense: Balsam

3 **Friday**
Drimes (Greek)
Waning Moon
Moon phase: Third Quarter
Color: White

Moon Sign: Aquarius
Moon enters Pisces 9:58 am
Incense: Thyme

4 **Saturday**
Cook Islands Constitution Celebration
Waning Moon
Moon phase: Third Quarter
Color: Blue

Moon Sign: Pisces
Incense: Pine

5 **Sunday**
Benediction of the Sea (French)
Waning Moon
Moon phase: Third Quarter
Color: Gold

Moon Sign: Pisces
Moon enters Aries 4:59 pm
Incense: Juniper

6 **Monday**
Hiroshima Peace Ceremony
Waning Moon
Moon phase: Third Quarter
Color: Ivory

Moon Sign: Aries
Incense: Lily

7 **Tuesday**
Republic Day (Ivory Coast)
Waning Moon
Moon phase: Third Quarter
Color: Red

Moon Sign: Aries
Incense: Geranium

August

8 Wednesday
Dog Days (Japanese)
Waning Moon
Moon phase: Third Quarter
Color: Brown

Moon Sign: Aries
Moon enters Taurus 3:28 am
Incense: Lavender

◑ Thursday
Nagasaki Peace Ceremony
Waning Moon
Moon phase: Fourth Quarter 2:55 pm
Color: White

Moon Sign: Taurus
Incense: Jasmine

10 Friday
St. Lawrence's Day
Waning Moon
Moon phase: Fourth Quarter
Color: Rose

Moon Sign: Taurus
Moon enters Gemini 4:11 pm
Incense: Vanilla

11 Saturday
Puck Fair (Irish)
Waning Moon
Moon phase: Fourth Quarter
Color: Blue

Moon Sign: Gemini
Incense: Patchouli

12 Sunday
Fiesta of Santa Clara
Waning Moon
Moon phase: Fourth Quarter
Color: Orange

Moon Sign: Gemini
Incense: Frankincense

13 Monday
Women's Day (Tunisian)
Waning Moon
Moon phase: Fourth Quarter
Color: Lavender

Moon Sign: Gemini
Moon enters Cancer 4:27 am
Incense: Clary sage

14 Tuesday
Festival at Sassari
Waning Moon
Moon phase: Fourth Quarter
Color: Scarlet

Moon Sign: Cancer
Incense: Cinnamon

August

15 Wednesday
Assumption Day
Waning Moon
Moon phase: Fourth Quarter
Color: Topaz

Moon Sign: Cancer
Moon enters Leo 2:05 pm
Incense: Marjoram

16 Thursday
Festival of Minstrels (European)
Waning Moon
Moon phase: Fourth Quarter
Color: Green

Moon Sign: Leo
Incense: Myrrh

☽ Friday
Feast of the Hungry Ghosts (Chinese)
Waning Moon
Moon phase: New Moon 11:54 am
Color: Pink

Moon Sign: Leo
Moon enters Virgo 8:33 pm
Incense: Rose

18 Saturday
St. Helen's Day
Waxing Moon
Moon phase: First Quarter
Color: Black

Moon Sign: Virgo
Incense: Sage

19 Sunday
Ramadan ends
Waxing Moon
Moon phase: First Quarter
Color: Yellow

Moon Sign: Virgo
Incense: Marigold

20 Monday
Constitution Day (Hungarian)
Waxing Moon
Moon phase: First Quarter
Color: Silver

Moon Sign: Virgo
Moon enters Libra 12:45 am
Incense: Narcissus

21 Tuesday
Consualia (Roman)
Waxing Moon
Moon phase: First Quarter
Color: Gray

Moon Sign: Libra
Incense: Cedar

August

22 Wednesday
Feast of the Queenship of Mary (English)
Waxing Moon
Moon phase: First Quarter
Color: Brown

Moon Sign: Libra
Moon enters Scorpio 3:54 am
Incense: Lilac
Sun enters Virgo 1:07 pm

23 Thursday
National Day (Romanian)
Waxing Moon
Moon phase: First Quarter
Color: Turquoise

Moon Sign: Scorpio
Incense: Apricot

◖ **Friday**
St. Bartholomew's Day
Waxing Moon
Moon phase: Second Quarter 9:54 am
Color: Coral

Moon Sign: Scorpio
Moon enters Sagittarius 6:50 am
Incense: Mint

25 Saturday
Feast of the Green Corn (Native American)
Waxing Moon
Moon phase: Second Quarter
Color: Brown

Moon Sign: Sagittarius
Incense: Magnolia

26 Sunday
Pardon of the Sea (French)
Waxing Moon
Moon phase: Second Quarter
Color: Gold

Moon Sign: Sagittarius
Moon enters Capricorn 9:58 am
Incense: Marigold

27 Monday
Summer Break (English)
Waxing Moon
Moon phase: Second Quarter
Color: Ivory

Moon Sign: Capricorn
Incense: Rosemary

28 Tuesday
St. Augustine's Day
Waxing Moon
Moon phase: Second Quarter
Color: Red

Moon Sign: Capricorn
Moon enters Aquarius 1:38 pm
Incense: Ylang-ylang

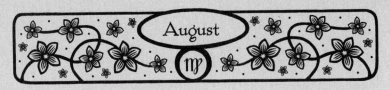

29 Wednesday
St. John's Beheading
Waxing Moon
Moon phase: Second Quarter
Color: Topaz

Moon Sign: Aquarius
Incense: Bay laurel

---

30 Thursday
St. Rose of Lima Day (Peruvian)
Waxing Moon
Moon phase: Second Quarter
Color: Purple

Moon Sign: Aquarius
Moon enters Pisces 6:31 pm
Incense: Jasmine

 Friday
Unto These Hills Pageant (Cherokee)
Waxing Moon
Moon phase: Full Moon 9:58 am
Color: Purple

Moon Sign: Pisces
Incense: Rose

❖

August Birthstones

Wear Sardonyx, or for thee
No conjugal felicity;
The August-born without this stone,
'Tis said, must live unloved, and lone.

Modern: Peridot
Zodiac (Leo): Onyx

September

1 **Saturday**
Greek New Year
Waning Moon
Moon phase: Third Quarter
Color: Gray

Moon Sign: Pisces
Incense: Sandalwood

2 **Sunday**
St. Mama's Day
Waning Moon
Moon phase: Third Quarter
Color: Orange

Moon Sign: Pisces
Moon enters Aries 1:37 am
Incense: Eucalyptus

3 **Monday**
Labor Day
Waning Moon
Moon phase: Third Quarter
Color: Lavender

Moon Sign: Aries
Incense: Neroli

4 **Tuesday**
Los Angeles' Birthday
Waning Moon
Moon phase: Third Quarter
Color: Black

Moon Sign: Aries
Moon enters Taurus 11:41 am
Incense: Cinnamon

5 **Wednesday**
Roman Circus • First Labor Day (1882)
Waning Moon
Moon phase: Third Quarter
Color: Yellow

Moon Sign: Taurus
Incense: Marjoram

6 **Thursday**
The Virgin of Remedies (Spanish)
Waning Moon
Moon phase: Third Quarter
Color: Green

Moon Sign: Taurus
Incense: Nutmeg

7 **Friday**
Festival of the Durga (Hindu)
Waning Moon
Moon phase: Third Quarter
Color: Pink

Moon Sign: Taurus
Moon enters Gemini 12:10 am
Incense: Orchid

September ♍

○ **Saturday**
Birthday of the Virgin Mary
Waning Moon
Moon phase: Fourth Quarter 9:15 am
Color: Blue

Moon Sign: Gemini
Incense: Pine

9 **Sunday**
Chrysanthemum Festival (Japanese)
Waning Moon
Moon phase: Fourth Quarter
Color: Yellow

Moon Sign: Gemini
Moon enters Cancer 12:49 pm
Incense: Hyacinth

10 **Monday**
Festival of the Poets (Japanese)
Waning Moon
Moon phase: Fourth Quarter
Color: Silver

Moon Sign: Cancer
Incense: Clary sage

11 **Tuesday**
Coptic New Year
Waning Moon
Moon phase: Fourth Quarter
Color: Maroon

Moon Sign: Cancer
Moon enters Leo 11:00 pm
Incense: Bayberry

12 **Wednesday**
National Day (Ethiopian)
Waning Moon
Moon phase: Fourth Quarter
Color: Yellow

Moon Sign: Leo
Incense: Lilac

13 **Thursday**
The Gods' Banquet (Roman)
Waning Moon
Moon phase: Fourth Quarter
Color: Crimson

Moon Sign: Leo
Incense: Mulberry

14 **Friday**
Holy Cross Day
Waning Moon
Moon phase: Fourth Quarter
Color: Purple

Moon Sign: Leo
Moon enters Virgo 5:30 am
Incense: Cypress

☽ **Saturday**
Birthday of the Moon (Chinese)
Waning Moon
Moon phase: New Moon 10:11 pm
Color: Brown

Moon Sign: Virgo
Incense: Ivy

---

16 Sunday
Mexican Independence Day
Waxing Moon
Moon phase: First Quarter
Color: Gold

Moon Sign: Virgo
Moon enters Libra 8:55 am
Incense: Almond

---

17 Monday
Rosh Hashanah
Waxing Moon
Moon phase: First Quarter
Color: White

Moon Sign: Libra
Incense: Lily

---

18 Tuesday
Dr. Johnson's Birthday
Waxing Moon
Moon phase: First Quarter
Color: Red

Moon Sign: Libra
Moon enters Scorpio 10:46 am
Incense: Basil

---

19 Wednesday
St. Januarius' Day (Italian)
Waxing Moon
Moon phase: First Quarter
Color: White

Moon Sign: Scorpio
Incense: Honeysuckle

---

20 Thursday
St. Eustace's Day
Waxing Moon
Moon phase: First Quarter
Color: Purple

Moon Sign: Scorpio
Moon enters Sagittarius 12:34 pm
Incense: Apricot

---

21 Friday
UN International Day of Peace
Waxing Moon
Moon phase: First Quarter
Color: Pink

Moon Sign: Sagittarius
Incense: Vanilla

September

♑ Saturday
Mabon • Fall Equinox
Waxing Moon
Moon phase: Second Quarter 3:41 pm
Color: Indigo

Moon Sign: Sagittarius
Moon enters Capricorn 3:20 pm
Incense: Patchouli
Sun enters Libra 10:49 am

---

23 Sunday
Shubun no Hi (Chinese)
Waxing Moon
Moon phase: Second Quarter
Color: Amber

Moon Sign: Capricorn
Incense: Juniper

---

24 Monday
Schwenkenfelder Thanksgiving (German-American)
Waxing Moon
Moon phase: Second Quarter
Color: Gray

Moon Sign: Capricorn
Moon enters Aquarius 7:32 pm
Incense: Hyssop

---

25 Tuesday
Dolls' Memorial Service (Japanese)
Waxing Moon
Moon phase: Second Quarter
Color: White

Moon Sign: Aquarius
Incense: Ginger

---

26 Wednesday
Feast of Santa Justina (Mexican)
Waxing Moon
Moon phase: Second Quarter
Color: Brown

Moon Sign: Aquarius
Incense: Lavender

---

27 Thursday
Saints Cosmas and Damian's Day
Waxing Moon
Moon phase: Second Quarter
Color: White

Moon Sign: Aquarius
Moon enters Pisces 1:23 am
Incense: Clove

---

28 Friday
Yom Kippur
Waxing Moon
Moon phase: Second Quarter
Color: Coral

Moon Sign: Pisces
Incense: Mint

September

☽ **Saturday**
Michaelmas
Waxing Moon
Moon phase: Full Moon 11:19 pm
Color: Black

Moon Sign: Pisces
Moon enters Aries 9:14 am
Incense: Patchouli

30 Sunday
St. Jerome's Day
Waning Moon
Moon phase: Third Quarter
Color: Yellow

Moon Sign: Aries
Incense: Hyacinth

September Birthstones

A maiden born when autumn leaves
Are rustling in September's breeze,
A Sapphire on her brow should bind;
'Twill cure diseases of the mind.

Modern: Sapphire
Zodiac (Virgo): Carnelian

October

1 Monday
Sukkot begins
Waning Moon
Moon phase: Third Quarter
Color: White

Moon Sign: Aries
Moon enters Taurus 7:26 pm
Incense: Clary sage

2 Tuesday
Old Man's Day (Virgin Islands)
Waning Moon
Moon phase: Third Quarter
Color: Scarlet

Moon Sign: Taurus
Incense: Cedar

3 Wednesday
Moroccan New Year's Day
Waning Moon
Moon phase: Third Quarter
Color: White

Moon Sign: Taurus
Incense: Lilac

4 Thursday
St. Francis' Day
Waning Moon
Moon phase: Third Quarter
Color: Purple

Moon Sign: Taurus
Moon enters Gemini 7:47 am
Incense: Clove

5 Friday
Republic Day (Portuguese)
Waning Moon
Moon phase: Third Quarter
Color: Pink

Moon Sign: Gemini
Incense: Violet

6 Saturday
Dedication of the Virgin's Crowns (English)
Waning Moon
Moon phase: Third Quarter
Color: Black

Moon Sign: Gemini
Moon enters Cancer 8:45 pm
Incense: Sage

7 Sunday
Kermesse (German)
Waning Moon
Moon phase: Third Quarter
Color: Orange

Moon Sign: Cancer
Incense: Hyacinth

October

Monday ☽
Sukkot ends • Columbus Day (observed)
Waning Moon
Moon phase: Fourth Quarter 3:33 am
Color: Ivory

Moon Sign: Cancer
Incense: Hyssop

9 Tuesday
Alphabet Day (South Korean)
Waning Moon
Moon phase: Fourth Quarter
Color: Red

Moon Sign: Cancer
Moon enters Leo 7:55 am
Incense: Ginger

10 Wednesday
Health Day (Japanese)
Waning Moon
Moon phase: Fourth Quarter
Color: Topaz

Moon Sign: Leo
Incense: Honeysuckle

11 Thursday
Medetrinalia (Roman)
Waning Moon
Moon phase: Fourth Quarter
Color: Green

Moon Sign: Leo
Moon enters Virgo 3:23 pm
Incense: Carnation

12 Friday
National Day (Spanish)
Waning Moon
Moon phase: Fourth Quarter
Color: Rose

Moon Sign: Virgo
Incense: Yarrow

13 Saturday
Fontinalia (Roman) begins
Waning Moon
Moon phase: Fourth Quarter
Color: Gray

Moon Sign: Virgo
Moon enters Libra 7:02 pm
Incense: Pine

14 Sunday
Battle Festival (Japanese)
Waning Moon
Moon phase: Fourth Quarter
Color: Orange

Moon Sign: Libra
Incense: Almond

🌑 **Monday**
The October Horse (Roman)
Waning Moon
Moon phase: New Moon 8:02 am
Color: White

Moon Sign: Libra
Moon enters Scorpio 8:06 pm
Incense: Clary sage

---

16 **Tuesday**
The Lion Sermon (British)
Waxing Moon
Moon phase: First Quarter
Color: Maroon

Moon Sign: Scorpio
Incense: Basil

---

17 **Wednesday**
Pilgrimage to Paray-le-Monial
Waxing Moon
Moon phase: First Quarter
Color: Topaz

Moon Sign: Scorpio
Moon enters Sagittarius 8:26 pm
Incense: Bay laurel

---

18 **Thursday**
Brooklyn Barbecue
Waxing Moon
Moon phase: First Quarter
Color: Turquoise

Moon Sign: Sagittarius
Incense: Apricot

---

19 **Friday**
Our Lord of Miracles Procession (Peruvian)
Waxing Moon
Moon phase: First Quarter
Color: White

Moon Sign: Sagittarius
Moon enters Capricorn 9:41 pm
Incense: Alder

---

20 **Saturday**
Colchester Oyster Feast
Waxing Moon
Moon phase: First Quarter
Color: Indigo

Moon Sign: Capricorn
Incense: Rue

🌓 **Sunday**
Feast of the Black Christ
Waxing Moon
Moon phase: Second Quarter 11:32 pm
Color: Yellow

Moon Sign: Capricorn
Incense: Marigold

October

22 **Monday**
Goddess of Mercy Day (Chinese)
Waxing Moon
Moon phase: Second Quarter
Color: Lavender

Moon Sign: Capricorn
Moon enters Aquarius 1:02 am
Incense: Neroli
Sun enters Scorpio 8:14 pm

23 **Tuesday**
Revolution Day (Hungarian)
Waxing Moon
Moon phase: Second Quarter
Color: Black

Moon Sign: Aquarius
Incense: Geranium

24 **Wednesday**
United Nations Day
Waxing Moon
Moon phase: Second Quarter
Color: Yellow

Moon Sign: Aquarius
Moon enters Pisces 7:00 am
Incense: Lavender

25 **Thursday**
St. Crispin's Day
Waxing Moon
Moon phase: Second Quarter
Color: White

Moon Sign: Pisces
Incense: Balsam

26 **Friday**
Quit Rent Ceremony (English)
Waxing Moon
Moon phase: Second Quarter
Color: Pink

Moon Sign: Pisces
Moon enters Aries 3:31 pm
Incense: Orchid

27 **Saturday**
Feast of the Holy Souls
Waxing Moon
Moon phase: Second Quarter
Color: Blue

Moon Sign: Aries
Incense: Magnolia

28 **Sunday**
Ochi Day (Greek)
Waxing Moon
Moon phase: Second Quarter
Color: Gold

Moon Sign: Aries
Incense: Eucalyptus

Monday

Iriquois Feast of the Dead
Waxing Moon
Moon phase: Full Moon 3:49 pm
Color: Gray

Moon Sign: Aries
Moon enters Taurus 2:15 am
Incense: Rosemary

---

30 Tuesday

Meiji Festival (Japanese)
Waning Moon
Moon phase: Third Quarter
Color: Red

Moon Sign: Taurus
Incense: Ylang-ylang

---

31 Wednesday

Halloween • Samhain
Waning Moon
Moon phase: Third Quarter
Color: White

Moon Sign: Taurus
Moon enters Gemini 2:40 pm
Incense: Bay laurel

October Birthstones

October's child is born for woe,
And life's vicissitudes must know;
But lay an Opal on her breast,
And hope will lull those foes to rest.

Modern: Opal or Tourmaline
Zodiac (Libra): Peridot

November ♏

1 Thursday
All Saints' Day
Waning Moon
Moon phase: Third Quarter
Color: White

Moon Sign: Gemini
Incense: Myrrh

---

2 Friday
All Souls' Day
Waning Moon
Moon phase: Third Quarter
Color: Rose

Moon Sign: Gemini
Incense: Rose

---

3 Saturday
Saint Hubert's Day (Belgian)
Waning Moon
Moon phase: Third Quarter
Color: Brown

Moon Sign: Gemini
Moon enters Cancer 3:43 am
Incense: Magnolia

---

4 Sunday
Daylight Saving Time ends
Waning Moon
Moon phase: Third Quarter
Color: Amber

Moon Sign: Cancer
Incense: Juniper

---

5 Monday
Guy Fawkes Night (British)
Waning Moon
Moon phase: Third Quarter
Color: Ivory

Moon Sign: Cancer
Moon enters Leo 2:39 pm
Incense: Clary sage

◖ Tuesday
Election Day (general)
Waning Moon
Moon phase: Fourth Quarter 7:36 pm
Color: Black

Moon Sign: Leo
Incense: Cedar

---

7 Wednesday
Mayan Day of the Dead
Waning Moon
Moon phase: Fourth Quarter
Color: Topaz

Moon Sign: Leo
Moon enters Virgo 11:35 pm
Incense: Lilac

November

8 Thursday
The Lord Mayor's Show (English)
Waning Moon
Moon phase: Fourth Quarter
Color: Purple

Moon Sign: Virgo
Incense: Mulberry

9 Friday
Lord Mayor's Day (British)
Waning Moon
Moon phase: Fourth Quarter
Color: Coral

Moon Sign: Virgo
Incense: Vanilla

10 Saturday
Martin Luther's Birthday
Waning Moon
Moon phase: Fourth Quarter
Color: Blue

Moon Sign: Virgo
Moon enters Libra 4:35 am
Incense: Sage

11 Sunday
Veterans Day
Waning Moon
Moon phase: Fourth Quarter
Color: Gold

Moon Sign: Libra
Incense: Marigold

12 Monday
Tesuque Feast Day (Native American)
Waning Moon
Moon phase: Fourth Quarter
Color: Lavender

Moon Sign: Libra
Moon enters Scorpio 6:10 am
Incense: Lily

Tuesday
Festival of Jupiter (Roman)
Waning Moon
Moon phase: New Moon 5:08 pm
Color: Red

Moon Sign: Scorpio
Incense: Ylang-ylang

14 Wednesday
The Little Carnival (Greek)
Waxing Moon
Moon phase: First Quarter
Color: Brown

Moon Sign: Scorpio
Moon enters Sagittarius 5:52 am
Incense: Lilac

November

---

15 **Thursday**
Islamic New Year
Waxing Moon
Moon phase: First Quarter
Color: Turquoise

Moon Sign: Sagittarius
Incense: Clove

---

16 **Friday**
St. Margaret of Scotland's Day
Waxing Moon
Moon phase: First Quarter
Color: Pink

Moon Sign: Sagittarius
Moon enters Capricorn 5:35 am
Incense: Vanilla

---

17 **Saturday**
Queen Elizabeth's Day
Waxing Moon
Moon phase: First Quarter
Color: Black

Moon Sign: Capricorn
Incense: Ivy

---

18 **Sunday**
St. Plato's Day
Waxing Moon
Moon phase: First Quarter
Color: Orange

Moon Sign: Capricorn
Moon enters Aquarius 7:10 am
Incense: Frankincense

---

19 **Monday**
Garifuna Day (Belizian)
Waxing Moon
Moon phase: First Quarter
Color: Gray

Moon Sign: Aquarius
Incense: Narcissus

◑ **Tuesday**
Revolution Day (Mexican)
Waxing Moon
Moon phase: Second Quarter 9:31 am
Color: Scarlet

Moon Sign: Aquarius
Moon enters Pisces 11:55 am
Incense: Cinnamon

---

21 **Wednesday**
Repentance Day (German)
Waxing Moon
Moon phase: Second Quarter
Color: White

Moon Sign: Pisces
Incense: Marjoram
Sun enters Sagittarius 4:50 pm

November

22 **Thursday**
Thanksgiving Day
Waxing Moon
Moon phase: Second Quarter
Color: Green

Moon Sign: Pisces
Moon enters Aries 8:12 pm
Incense: Nutmeg

23 **Friday**
St. Clement's Day
Waxing Moon
Moon phase: Second Quarter
Color: Purple

Moon Sign: Aries
Incense: Thyme

24 **Saturday**
Feast of the Burning Lamps (Egyptian)
Waxing Moon
Moon phase: Second Quarter
Color: Brown

Moon Sign: Aries
Incense: Pine

25 **Sunday**
St. Catherine of Alexandria's Day
Waxing Moon
Moon phase: Second Quarter
Color: Yellow

Moon Sign: Aries
Moon enters Taurus 7:18 am
Incense: Heliotrope

26 **Monday**
Festival of Lights (Tibetan)
Waxing Moon
Moon phase: Second Quarter
Color: Lavender

Moon Sign: Taurus
Incense: Hyssop

27 **Tuesday**
Saint Maximus' Day
Waxing Moon
Moon phase: Second Quarter
Color: Gray

Moon Sign: Taurus
Moon enters Gemini 7:58 pm
Incense: Bayberry

☺ **Wednesday**
Day of the New Dance (Tibetan)
Waxing Moon
Moon phase: Full Moon 9:46 am
Color: Yellow

Moon Sign: Gemini
Incense: Lavender

29 Thursday

Tubman's Birthday (Liberian)
Waning Moon
Moon phase: Third Quarter
Color: White

Moon Sign: Gemini
Incense: Jasmine

30 Friday

St. Andrew's Day
Waning Moon
Moon phase: Third Quarter
Color: White

Moon Sign: Gemini
Moon enters Cancer 8:55 am
Incense: Violet

November Birthstones

Who first come to this world below,
With drear November's fog, and snow,
Should prize the Topaz's amber hue,
Emblem of friends, and lovers true.

Modern: Topaz or Citrine
Zodiac (Scorpio): Beryl

December

1 Saturday
Big Tea Party (Japanese)
Waning Moon
Moon phase: Third Quarter
Color: Blue

Moon Sign: Cancer
Incense: Ivy

2 Sunday
Republic Day (Loatian)
Waning Moon
Moon phase: Third Quarter
Color: Yellow

Moon Sign: Cancer
Moon enters Leo 8:57 pm
Incense: Eucalyptus

3 Monday
St. Francis Xavier's Day
Waning Moon
Moon phase: Third Quarter
Color: Silver

Moon Sign: Leo
Incense: Clary sage

4 Tuesday
St. Barbara's Day
Waning Moon
Moon phase: Third Quarter
Color: Red

Moon Sign: Leo
Incense: Basil

5 Wednesday
Eve of St. Nicholas' Day
Waning Moon
Moon phase: Third Quarter
Color: Brown

Moon Sign: Leo
Moon enters Virgo 6:51 am
Incense: Marjoram

◐ Thursday
St. Nicholas' Day
Waning Moon
Moon phase: Fourth Quarter 10:31 am
Color: Green

Moon Sign: Virgo
Incense: Carnation

7 Friday
Burning the Devil (Guatemalan)
Waning Moon
Moon phase: Fourth Quarter
Color: Pink

Moon Sign: Virgo
Moon enters Libra 1:35 pm
Incense: Vanilla

December

8 **Saturday**
Feast of the Immaculate Conception
Waning Moon
Moon phase: Fourth Quarter
Color: Black

Moon Sign: Libra
Incense: Patchouli

9 **Sunday**
Hanukkah begins
Waning Moon
Moon phase: Fourth Quarter
Color: Gold

Moon Sign: Libra
Moon enters Scorpio 4:51 pm
Incense: Frankincense

10 **Monday**
Nobel Day
Waning Moon
Moon phase: Fourth Quarter
Color: Lavender

Moon Sign: Scorpio
Incense: Hyssop

11 **Tuesday**
Pilgrimage at Tortugas
Waning Moon
Moon phase: Fourth Quarter
Color: Red

Moon Sign: Scorpio
Moon enters Sagittarius 5:22 pm
Incense: Cinnamon

12 **Wednesday**
Fiesta of Our Lady of Guadalupe (Mexican)
Waning Moon
Moon phase: Fourth Quarter
Color: Yellow

Moon Sign: Sagittarius
Incense: Lavender

☽ **Thursday**
St. Lucy's Day (Swedish)
Waning Moon
Moon phase: New Moon 3:42 am
Color: Turquoise

Moon Sign: Sagittarius
Moon enters Capricorn 4:43 pm
Incense: Balsam

14 **Friday**
Warriors' Memorial (Japanese)
Waxing Moon
Moon phase: First Quarter
Color: Coral

Moon Sign: Capricorn
Incense: Orchid

December

15 **Saturday**
Consualia (Roman)
Waxing Moon
Moon phase: First Quarter
Color: Brown

Moon Sign: Capricorn
Moon enters Aquarius 4:53 pm
Incense: Pine

16 **Sunday**
Hanukkah ends
Waxing Moon
Moon phase: First Quarter
Color: Amber

Moon Sign: Aquarius
Incense: Hyacinth

17 **Monday**
Saturnalia (Roman)
Waxing Moon
Moon phase: First Quarter
Color: White

Moon Sign: Aquarius
Moon enters Pisces 7:48 pm
Incense: Rosemary

18 **Tuesday**
Feast of the Virgin Solitude
Waxing Moon
Moon phase: First Quarter
Color: Black

Moon Sign: Pisces
Incense: Ginger

19 **Wednesday**
Opalia (Roman)
Waxing Moon
Moon phase: First Quarter
Color: Topaz

Moon Sign: Pisces
Incense: Honeysuckle

◑ **Thursday**
Commerce God Festival (Japanese)
Waxing Moon
Moon phase: Second Quarter 12:19 am
Color: Green

Moon Sign: Pisces
Moon enters Aries 2:43 am
Incense: Apricot

21 **Friday**
Yule • Winter Solstice
Waxing Moon
Moon phase: Second Quarter
Color: Purple

Moon Sign: Aries
Incense: Yarrow
Sun enters Capricorn 6:12 am

December

22 Saturday
Saints Chaeremon and Ischyrion's Day
Waxing Moon
Moon phase: Second Quarter
Color: Blue

Moon Sign: Aries
Moon enters Taurus 1:25 pm
Incense: Sandalwood

23 Sunday
Larentalia (Roman)
Waxing Moon
Moon phase: Second Quarter
Color: Orange

Moon Sign: Taurus
Incense: Almond

24 Monday
Christmas Eve
Waxing Moon
Moon phase: Second Quarter
Color: Gray

Moon Sign: Taurus
Incense: Neroli

25 Tuesday
Christmas Day
Waxing Moon
Moon phase: Second Quarter
Color: Maroon

Moon Sign: Taurus
Moon enters Gemini 2:13 am
Incense: Ylang-ylang

26 Wednesday
Kwanzaa begins
Waxing Moon
Moon phase: Second Quarter
Color: Brown

Moon Sign: Gemini
Incense: Lilac

27 Thursday
Boar's Head Supper (English)
Waxing Moon
Moon phase: Second Quarter
Color: Crimson

Moon Sign: Gemini
Moon enters Cancer 3:06 pm
Incense: Nutmeg

☺ Friday
Holy Innocents' Day
Waxing Moon
Moon phase: Full Moon 5:21 am
Color: Pink

Moon Sign: Cancer
Incense: Cypress

December

29   **Saturday**
Feast of St. Thomas Becket
Waning Moon
Moon phase: Third Quarter
Color: Gray

Moon Sign: Cancer
Incense: Pine

30   **Sunday**
Republic Day (Madagascan)
Waning Moon
Moon phase: Third Quarter
Color: Orange

Moon Sign: Cancer
Moon enters Leo 2:45 am
Incense: Heliotrope

31   **Monday**
New Year's Eve
Waning Moon
Moon phase: Third Quarter
Color: Ivory

Moon Sign: Leo
Incense: Narcissus

December Birthstones

If cold December gives you birth,
The month of snow, and ice, and mirth,
Place in your hand a Turquoise blue;
Success will bless whate'er you do.

Modern: Turquoise or Blue Topaz
Zodiac (Sagittarius): Topaz

Fire Magic

Clashing of the Titans:
Mythology vs. Hollywood

by Laurel Reufner

How often does Hollywood get it right when it comes to history/mythology and the movies? Sometimes they do an excellent job—I know medievalists who truly appreciated *Henry V* and *Rob Roy*—and other times they get it so wrong that the only thing recognizable are the names. (*Braveheart* comes to mind.) In 2010, Warner Brother's released a new version of the 1981 cult classic, *Clash of the Titans*. The story of Perseus is the tale of one of Greece's earliest great heroes and a marvelous, epic adventure. Why don't we dissect the story alongside the two movies to see how they compare?

According to the classicists, Perseus is the son of Zeus and the mortal woman Danaë. Danaë was the only child of the king of Argos, Acrisius, who wished for a son. When an oracle informed him that not only would he have no sons, but that his grandson would be the one to kill him, he locked Danaë in an underground chamber that was accessible to the outside world only by a shaft leading to the open sky. Somehow Danaë drew the notice of Zeus, who was drawn to her beauty. He visited her as a golden shaft of sunlight, resulting in Perseus's birth.

When Acrisius learned of the babe's birth, he was terrified of the prophecy coming true. However, killing immediate family in the Greek world could bring the wrath of the gods and attract the attention of the Furies—all things best avoided. So, Acrisius locked Danaë and her infant in a chest, setting them adrift at sea and denying any responsibility for whatever fate they might meet.

After much travel, the chest came ashore on the Isle of Seriphos, where the pair was found by a fisherman named Dictys, who took the couple in and helped raise Perseus. There, Perseus grew to adulthood and became a fisherman with his foster father. Over time, they came to the attention of Polydectes, the brother of Dictys and king of Seriphos. The king fell in love with Danaë, but Perseus was always there to act as a buffer. Perseus had apparently grown into a strapping young man, as demigods and heroes are wont to do, and Polydectes knew that Perseus posed a very real obstacle in getting to Danaë. This is where our story becomes even more interesting, as our young fisherman is set on course to become one of Greece's earliest great heroes.

While Perseus isn't naïve enough to miss the looks Polydectes is giving his mother, he is naïve enough not to realize that the king may very well try to get rid of him. Polydectes throws a banquet where he demands gifts from all invited. And the gift must be a horse, which he will offer to Hippodamia for her hand in marriage. Of course, the scoundrel had no intention of marrying Hippodamia. He wanted Danaë, but he needed a ruse to throw Perseus off and get rid of the youth. As the son of a fisherman, Perseus had no horse to give Polydectes and so boldly offered to get him whatever else he might want. The king tells him to fetch the head of Medusa, whose gaze was so horrific it turned mortals into stone. Perseus promises to return with the head and off he goes.

However, Perseus doesn't just jump a ship and wander off. He seeks out some guidance first by consulting Athena. The goddess tells him to find the Hesperides, the nymphs who serve as caretakers of Hera's orchard, and request from them the necessary weapons to defeat Medusa. To find out where the Hesperides are located, Perseus first must find the Graeae, or, as they are referred to in the movies, the Stygian Witches.

The Graeae were three old women who were born ancient. They shared a single tooth and eye between them. Rumor also has it that they had a taste for human flesh. Perseus manages to snatch the eye as they are passing it back and forth. He holds it hostage until they tell him the location of the Hesperides. Both movies have a scene where Perseus interacts with the Stygian Witches in a similar fashion, although in the films he's seeking the location of Medusa.

The Hesperides are more than generous with Perseus, giving him a special knapsack in which to keep Medusa's head—her blood is toxic. His father, Zeus, gave him the use of an adamantine sword as well as a helmet of invisibility belonging to Hades. Hermes comes to our hero's aid by loaning a pair of his winged sandals, allowing Perseus to fly over great distances. Finally, Athena gives him a mirror-polished shield, explaining how to use it remove Medusa's head without looking at her directly.

Now, gentle reader, if you've been paying attention, you'll realize that this is not what happens in either movie. The 1981 film handles Perseus's birth pretty much according to the classical story line, although his mother has died by the time Thetis moves him across the lands to a place called Joppa. There is no mention of Polydectes lusting after his mother. Oh, and Zeus has the Kraken released to destroy Argos in retaliation for Acrisius's actions towards Danaë. This leaves no way for the Delphic oracle to come true, which is not the way Greek myth usually works. (Thetis is a goddess of the ocean and mother to a very spoiled demigod named Calibos.)

In the 2010 movie, the scriptwriters nearly toss the entire birth narrative out the window, making Danaë the wife of Acrisius. The gods in the 2010 movie are depicted as being petty and cruel tyrants and the overall tone of the movie is dark and grimy. Acrisius attempts to lay siege to Mount Olympus, the very home of the gods. In order to both humble Acrisius and teach him a lesson, Zeus disguises himself as the mortal king and spends the night with his wife. The movie actually starts with him launching the two of them into the sea in a casket-like chest. Danaë, being totally mortal, doesn't survive their ordeal, but the baby Perseus is made of hardier stuff. In this version, they are pulled out of the sea by a fisherman, Spryos, and his wife, and raised as their son.

Acrisius does return again later in the movie working in league with Hades. He has been altered by a lightning bolt from Zeus and now calls himself Calibos. The theme of man against the gods is revisited again and again as the story unfolds. Spryos appears to be a gods-fearing man until there is no more fish to gather. He then becomes bitter and angry. Perseus's happy little adopted family is killed by Hades (the favorite bad-boy of myth-inspired movies) when he is taking out a group of Argoan soldiers who have just toppled a statue of Zeus into the sea in open rebellion against worship of the gods. Perseus is pulled from the sea by the soldiers and taken to Argos where things continue to go downhill for him.

You may have noticed by now that neither movie has mentioned Dictys or his brother, King Polydectes. Medusa hasn't been mentioned yet either. Polydectes and Dictys never do show up in either movie, while Medusa still plays as important a role in both movies as she does in the classical myth. Needless to say, this completely changes the motivation of our hero, but you may have already guessed that. In the original 1981 film, our hero finds himself mysteriously transported across a great distance from Seriphos to Joppa. His mother is already deceased by this point and, already knowing that he's the heir to Argos, he feels no ties to his former home. What motivates him, aside from a desire to see more of the world and eventually regain his birthright? The answer, my dear friends, is love. And gifts from the gods.

Perseus wakes on his second morning in Joppa to find divine gifts strewn about the theater where he has been staying. Zeus had ordered several goddesses to give his son the tools needed to be a successful hero: a sword, a shield, and a helmet that leaves the wearer invisible. Wearing the helmet, Perseus sets off to explore the city, where he hears the sad tale of the Princess Andromeda. Pledged to marry Calibos before his horrific transformation, Thetis had decreed that she cannot marry at all unless potential suitors can solve a riddle. Each day, any suitor from anywhere could approach and ask for her hand. The beautiful princess would ask a riddle, which changed with the day. Those who failed to give the correct answer were to be burned alive. Thus far, no one had managed to succeed.

Intrigued, as well as taken with her beauty, Perseus uses the helmet to creep into Andromeda's bedchamber during the night, where he falls even more hopelessly in love with her. He also witnesses her spirit rise from her sleeping form and be carried off by a giant bird. A burning desire to find out where she goes at night leads to the capture of Pegasus, the last of Zeus's herd of winged horses. Calibos has killed the rest of the heard—part of what led to Zeus's harsh judgment against him. (Now is a good time to note that the mighty Pegasus doesn't appear in the classical myth until after Perseus kills Medusa. The winged horse was created spontaneously from her blood, along with the giant Chrysaor.)

Following Andromeda invisibly on Pegasus, Perseus learns the following day's riddle as well as its answer. After she has safely left, he battles with and defeats Calibos, leaving him alive but missing a hand. The next day he presents himself as her new suitor and successfully answers the riddle. Calibos whines to his mother about how he's been wronged, begging for her help. Thetis can't directly interfere with Perseus, but she can take vengeance on those he loves. She just needs the right opportunity, which soon presents itself.

Now is a good time to discuss why our heroes are after Medusa's head. It all has to do with an insult. In the classical mythology, Andromeda's mother, Cassiopeia compares her own beauty to that of the sea nymphs, or Nereids. Poseidon sends torrential flooding and releases a sea monster upon their land (Ethiopia). He demands Andromeda's sacrifice to the sea monster as an appeasement. Perseus happens to be flying back to Seriphos when he sees the beautiful maiden chained at the ocean's edge. Using Medusa's head, he defeats the monster and claims Andromeda for his bride. In the story, rescuing and marrying Andromeda is a side quest to the main story.

In the first movie, Cassiopeia is congratulating the happily betrothed couple when she thoughtlessly compares Andromeda's beauty to that of Thetis. The goddess sees her chance to get revenge for Calibos and seizes it, demanding Andromeda's sacrifice to the Kraken within the month. Deciding that the only way to defeat the Kraken is with Medusa's horrible, petrifying gaze, Perseus is off to save his beloved.

In the 2010 movie, Cassiopeia mocks the gods as their soldiers are being welcomed back from their mission. She deliberately compares Andromeda's beauty to that of Aphrodite, the goddess of love. Talk about hubris! Hades, awaiting his moment to threaten the mortals, swoops in to the throne room and chastises them for their disdain and insults to the gods. He ages Cassiopeia to death and then demands the sacrifice of Andromeda to the kraken. As he leaves, he comments on Perseus being a demigod, shattering our hero's concept of who he is—the son of a fisherman. Io, a woman who once spurned Ares' advances only to find herself cursed with being ageless, visits him in his dungeon cell, fills him in on his birth, and persuades him to go after Medusa as a means of thwarting the gods and saving an innocent Andromeda. Realizing that this will give him the means to get at Hades—the killer of his only known family—he reluctantly agrees.

The 2010 *Clash of the Titans* makes the insult even larger than that of the myth, but honestly they needn't have bothered. In the movie, Hades has already persuaded Zeus to let him terrify and punish the humans. All he needed was an excuse to trigger it into action. Apparently the gods need not only our worship to be strong and survive; they also need our love. Except for Hades, that is, who feeds on human fear. As the mortals' fear grows, so will his strength, until he is strong enough to overthrow Zeus and rule Olympus. While Cassandra's boast would no doubt have been punished in some fashion, it really just serves as the means for Hades to put things in motion.

Our Perseus in the newer movie isn't necessarily abandoned completely by his divine father. Zeus still finds a way to leave his son some important bits of equipment, including a special sword that Perseus finds while wandering in the forest. Still in denial of his divine nature, he insists on completing his quest as a man. Draco, the guards' captain, holds on to it for him. Continuing on, he comes across a herd of Pegasi, all white mares, as well as a black stallion. The beautiful steed comes to his aid later in the movie. In yet another scene, Zeus visits his son in person to offer him a safe spot on Olympus. When Perseus refuses, which his father expected, the god smiles and tosses his son a gold coin with which to pay Hades when he goes after Medusa.

In both movies, our heroes arrive in the nick of time to save our princess. In the first movie, Perseus gets to marry his beloved without further difficulties and they apparently live happily ever after. In the second movie, Perseus refuses to marry Andromeda and instead goes off with Io for his happily ever after. One gets the sense that Zeus is proud of his son, even if he does still refuse to live on Olympus.

In the classical story, Perseus returns to Seriphos in time to rescue his mother from Polydectes's amorous intentions, turning the ruler and his followers to stone. Dictys is made the new king and rules wisely with Danaë by his side. The young hero then returns his borrowed, divine equipment to its rightful owners. Athena is gifted with Medusa's head, which she places on her shield.

As for the Delphic oracle's prophecy, Perseus does indeed kill King Acrisius, while participating in some athletic games in the kingdom of Larissa. As he was demonstrating the use of quiot a burst of wind blew the weapon off-course, where it struck Acrisius, killing him. Out of shame, Perseus swaps kingdoms with a Megapenthes, becoming the ruler of Tiryns.

There are some other small differences between the films and the original, including the transformation of Medusa and the creation of some really big scorpions. And no commentary would be complete without mentioning the Kraken. A kraken isn't even a Greek creation. It's a Norwegian word for "sea monster." The classical myth refers to a cetus, which means "sea monster" in Greek. Poseidon unleashes a really big sea monster on the Ethiopians, but it's never given a name in the story.

While both movies are great fun to watch, it's probably the first version that gets the most right when compared to the myth. Remember, you can't trust Hollywood for lessons in classical mythology. Just look to them for entertainment—that's their business. Besides, it's always great fun to think back through a movie and see how much they changed things around and how much they got right.

For Further Study

Avery, Catherine B. ed. *The New Century Handbook of Greek Mythology and Legend.* New York: Appleton-Century Crofts, 1972.

Ovid, *Metamorphoses.*

Cutting Cords

by Calantirniel

If you spend any time at all pursuing spiritual knowledge to implement into your life, you may realize that while you are growing, some negative things keep popping up—often things that you had thought you ended or perhaps are having trouble ending properly. What is really happening here? It very well may be that you need to perform a "cord-cutting" ritual for yourself. While it sounds fluffy bunny and new-agey, the logic behind it is sound.

Very simply explained, we are spiritual beings with energetic bodies, as well as physical bodies. When we create relationships, two types of bonds, bridges, or ties that are also created. Connections, often called spiritual bonds or ties—are light, energetic cords based on balance, compassion, unconditional love, and respecting boundaries while allowing both parties to feel energized, happy, and uplifted. These cords are most often found in the upper charkas—the heart and above—and are more beneficial if they remain there. (Chakra resources listed at the end of this article.)

Attachments, however, are not based on unconditional love and equal exchange. Because we live in a world that is programmed to be in a constant state of conscious or subconscious fear, many ties of the "attachment" nature are imbalanced, unhealthy, and sometimes abusive—leaving one or both parties feeling drained, overwhelmed, and even controlled, suppressed, or violated. This can also be accompanied by a range of unpleasant emotions like guilt, shame,

repulsion, anger, abandonment, betrayal, or any act of self-devaluation. In nearly all cases, these attachments can feel like something that overly dominates your thoughts and even unduly influences your actions.

As you can imagine, ties with our sexual and romantic partners, as well as family members (especially as a parent-child) are among our strongest cords—these bonds remain even if both parties are not alive anymore. Other situations that can prove difficult are with friends, teachers, bosses, clients, students, employees—or even something more collective like a corporation, a community, a religion, a philosophy, an idea, or even any aspect of the law or military. It can also be a situation, event, experience, a memory, or a contract. And conscious or not, it even could have been from a past life that may not even apply to your life now.

In fact, we sometimes carry ancestral contracts that are not of our making (and often inapplicable), but if we don't take care of the issue, it could keep getting passed down in the family. It is not something you can run away from either, since attempting a drastic end to a relationship without cutting the cord (like moving across the country and ending contact) will probably attract a new person to live out the cord pattern instead.

Because attachments are based on levels of fear, it is natural to find most of these cords in the lower three chakras, with particular emphasis to the solar plexus. In fact, when an incident happens and the cord is still active, many people feel a sensation like being punched in the stomach. Our personal power is represented by the solar plexus chakra (yellow), while our nurturing and creative abilities are in our sacral chakra (orange), and our physical survival drive is in the root chakra (red). Sometimes attachment cords are in the higher charkas—as an example, cords of religious organizations tend to be located in the crown chakra (purple) and the third eye chakra (indigo). Or, cords of someone or something wanting you to keep your mouth shut may be on the throat chakra (blue). If the heart chakra has attachments, they are likely also in one of the lower chakras (think conditional love).

How do cords of attachment differ from cords of connection? The cords of connection are light, beautiful, and feel like nothing is wrong with them—they belong. Cords of attachment can appear or feel dark, murky, heavy, and even sticky. Some rather strong ones may appear to have a life of their own sometimes, since it has been described by some shamanic healers that upon removal, they can be like wrestling with an oversized worm with huge sharp teeth! This would particularly be the case for the rare conscious cord creator (including, but not limited to, using manipulative magic). However, most cords are made subconsciously, and as such, do not rise to that level. If you do not have third eye sight (clairvoyance), you can still tell the difference by how it "feels." Or, even better, take note of your actions (and the other party if you can), including unhealthy cravings and anything else you can observe.

How To Cut Cords of Attachment

You may wish to do this more than once, since cutting all cords of attachment can be very disconcerting—and may not even be safe. Your spiritual higher-self will know how much you can handle, so trust in your process. You may wish to obtain an object to help you focus your intention and be an energetic help to you—like a protective and repelling piece of black tourmaline! Smudge with sage before use.

It is best to schedule this during a waning or dark Moon on a Saturday or a Tuesday, which allows you to take advantage of the energies of Saturn (staying) and Mars (moving). It may be helpful to take a psychic cleansing bath before your cord-cutting ritual—bathe 15 to 30 minutes in water with two cups of vinegar in the bath water. You may wish to add baking soda, sea salt, Epsom salts, or even some purifying and spiritual essential oils.

Design and make your sacred space—intend and visualize through-and-through protection in the best way for you. Call in Spirit, your spirit guides, and any strong and fiercely protective deity(ies) you wish. As an example, some prefer the archangel Michael for his strength and warrior abilities. Some would ask for Buddha or Jesus; some would ask for Odin, Brighid, Hecate, Ogun, Isis, Ganesha; and still others rely on their spiritual higher-selves—all are acceptable, as long as it resonates strongly and empowers you.

Create your intention for cord-cutting that cuts all attachments, known and unknown, that you are spiritually ready to cut. Rest assured, you will not accidentally cut any cords that are to remain as connections or accidentally cancel a soul contract that is for your learning and highest good—these will remain intact.

Now, develop a cutting tool or device that you visualize yourself using to sever the cords. For instance, some visualize a blue flaming sword, while others may see a shining pair of golden scissors—be guided by what feels empowering to you. You can use a prop here like a kitchen knife if you so desire, but even your

fingers will work. It is the intention, focus, and visualization that matters.

Visualize a shield of a lightweight astral "armor" around your entire body that has a slippery surface that will cauterize anything that doesn't belong—this will prepare you for cutting the attachment cords so that they do not reattach. The healing will come later, as this is meant as a temporary measure to get you to the next stage in a smoother fashion than otherwise possible.

Now take your cutting device and visualize you cutting the cords—go to each chakra, starting at the crown and working down to the root—and if you desire, cut around your legs and feet, too. If you do not have clairvoyance, ask to be guided, or make a complete cutting gesture on each chakra with the intention of cutting and completely severing any attachment cords. Even if you don't see them, I bet you will feel something. However, even if you don't feel it, know without a doubt in your heart that they indeed are completely severed. If you so desire, throw each cord away from you, or ask the cut cord to dissolve and disintegrate. During this process, know that you are love and that you are loved! When cutting is complete and any other spiritual work is done, thank the energies present in a fashion that seems fit, and if needed, close down the spiritual sacred space in your usual way. You are emerging as a new person.

Healing Process

Now that you are free of attachments, you may wish to observe some things. First, notice if a person entirely disappears from your life—or the other extreme, calls or texts you twenty times in a row on your cell phone and then comes to your door. Believe it or not, both of these are signs that the cord-cutting was successful—both indicate a change in the relationship.

In the case of the latter, it is more difficult to avoid contact, but do your best to keep it utterly minimal. While it is often best if there is none, sometimes avoidance can make it worse—you be the judge. If communication must happen, you may notice that you are now being more assertive and feeling nonattached and nonmanipulated. Wrap up the business at hand in an empowering, loving way (loving to you first, then to them) and in a way that expresses healthy boundaries.

Do not engage in any fear-based behavior pattern that you cut away, or you may inadvertently reattach the cord, despite your temporary astral armor. If you find you still choose a fear-based way to handle a situation, perhaps you were not ready to cut that cord yet, and need to learn a lesson. You can ask Spirit for guidance in this area, and keep your observations open—you may be surprised.

If the person you cut a cord with still needs to remain in your life (i.e., a spouse, boss, employee), as long as you act from a space of love, you will see your relationship change—or either they will leave or you will leave. When you affirm that (for example) you get along with your boss, dynamics will reveal themselves so that your affirmation will manifest. So you will (a) begin to get along with your boss miraculously, (b) your boss will be removed and you will receive a new boss that you get along with, or (c) you will be removed—hopefully to a better place and right away—

and still receive a boss with which you get along. No one can say which option will happen, since your boss has free will. So allow Spirit to work for you and let go of the way everything will happen—just keep focused and clear on what you want, not how you will get it.

Eventually, when you arrive in a space and can express loving empowerment, the astral armor you made yourself becomes irrelevant. But it is useful when transitioning, since it can be pretty disconcerting when long-term, even lifetime, attachments are suddenly not there.

Repeat this ritual when you feel the need, or when you notice some symptoms that you had when doing your first ritual. While the cords you severed may not have reattached, others may have surfaced that are ready to be cut now. You will find that as you evolve spiritually and heal yourself, you will let go of more and more attachment cords, and create more and more connection cords! The more connection cords you have, without attachments, the more energy you have to live fully and purposefully. May you be free of attachment and connected to Spirit through love!

For Further Study

Mumford, Dr. Jonn. *A Chakra & Kundalini Workbook: Psycho-Spiritual Techniques for Health, Rejuvenation, Psychic Powers and Spiritual Realization.* St. Paul, MN, Llewellyn Publications, 2002.

Sherwood, Keith. *Chakra Healing and Karmic Awareness.* Woodbury, MN, Llewellyn Publications, 2005.

Croning the Maiden

by Sybil Fogg

Sometime in the 1980s, I heard about a Wiccan/Pagan store near my new home. When I went to check it out, I was surprised by the complete brush-off I received. At the time, I was heavily embroiled in the gothic subculture and spent many hours each morning creating the perfect facade for the world to embrace. This meant heavily painted eyes, blood-red lips, extremely pale skin, dyed black hair, dripping black lace, buckled boots, long skirt, and gloves. This was before the advent of "Goth in a box" down at the local Hot Topic. In fact, there were no stores selling gothic couture. This was an era of do-it-yourself. Perfecting my look meant sewing clothing, mixing cosmetic concoctions, and stocking up on geisha powder from the local Asian market.

I was used to being treated like an outcast, but I honestly expected to find kindred spirits at the "Witch" craft store. Somehow, I had convinced myself that everyone there would be Lestat wannabes like me. So, I was shocked when I was completely ignored and my hippie friend was embraced—and even allowed downstairs to check out the ritual rooms—while I was stuck wandering around the book collection because all of the fun stuff, athames, cauldrons, and wands were locked up in wooden cupboards.

Flash forward twenty-some years and the scenery has changed. Over the past few years, the color of the Pagan events I attend has turned from very bright to somber hues. As well, I have found that although black still dominates my wardrobe, the years have added other rich colors too. It is almost as if the trend and I have reversed sides. Again, I am finding myself in the minority, at least up here in Maine. I don't know if it is the mainstreaming of the gothic culture (since Gothic characters have started popping up everywhere, even kid's cartoons and *Country Living* sported a "Gothic Chic" bracelet for over two hundred dollars, the trend can hardly be referred to as a subculture anymore) or that Paganism is exploring its dark roots, but the change is permeating all aspects of the Pagan community.

At the same time that the Pagan community is seeing a boom in gothic culture, the vampire is on the rise again in media. From *Twilight* to *True Blood*, it has become apparent that Polidori's brooding vampire is popular again. The vampire represents youth trapped in immortality, a trend popular among goths. As "gothicness" spreads through the Pagan world, the Triple Goddess is being reinvented as the Crone and Maiden are embraced and entwined and the mother ignored.

This Crone isn't the dark grandmotherly figure (or Disney's Wicked Witch for that matter). This goddess is the maiden croned. Hecate, Kali, Lilith, Cerridwen, and the Morrigan are now eternally youthful with full dark locks, porcelain skin, and pouty mouths. It seems not only has the quest for ancient wisdom been replaced by physical attractiveness in our youth-obsessed culture, the mother is completely pushed aside as the Great Goddess is redefined as the ultimate representation of Gothic Beauty.

Tapping into the crone is an exceptional way to add self-confidence and to develop a healthy body image. But, is it possible to still accomplish this with the painted crone? Women have worked hard to present a healthy body image to their daughters and loving ourselves is integral to conveying this message. Our elders are to be revered for what they offer us in wisdom and what has come before. Wrinkles and gray hair are hallmarks of this knowledge. Covering it up will not make us stronger or create a mystical veneer. Peeling back the layers of makeup and hair dye will reveal the Crone Goddess in her former grandeur. The following ritual of the dark goddess is to pull on our grandmother's secrets and infuse her strength within us.

Invoking the Dark Goddess

Time: When the Moon is its darkest in Scorpio.

Tools:
• Quarter candles
• Small black candles
• One large black candle anointed with a combination of patchouli, sandalwood, and cedarwood oils
• Frankincense, myrrh, or vetivert incense. A mixture works well too.
• Chalice with red wine (or water)
• Round mirror that can be held
• Black cloth, cape, or veil that you can wrap around yourself
• Images of the Crone Goddess whose energy you would like to work with. It is important to find a youthful

and elder image. These are easy to find on the Internet. Google "Dark Goddess" and click on the "images" tab in the upper left hand corner of your browser screen. Print out the pictures you feel most comfortable meditating on.

• Any music you feel will assist in focusing. I am a fan of Shiva in Exile when I am working with the dark goddess.

Preparation:

Set up your sacred space by laying out the quarter candles and smaller black candles. Determine where your circle will be cast and place the mirror, chalice, working tools, images, and large black candle there. Turn on your music and light your incense.

A ritual bath is extremely helpful in setting the stage for this invocation. Mixing patchouli, rosemary, and sandalwood herbs into your bath crystals works well. Remember to bathe by candlelight in silence as you meditate on getting to know the dark goddess within you.

Before you bathe, it is important to remove all jewelry and makeup. If you are serious about getting in touch with the Crone, it would be helpful to strip any dye from your hair as well. The idea here is to see yourself as you truly are—and not only accept your physicality—but to embrace it.

The Ritual

Call the quarters and cast the circle as you normally would.

Light the smaller candles.

Cover yourself with the black fabric, leaving your face visible and an arm free to light the last candle.

Take a moment to focus your thoughts on the dark goddess. This ritual works best in silence, as you are taking the time to journey into your darkest self to tap crone energy.

Light the last candle and choose the croned maiden picture you have printed. Spend some time with this image.

Is this how you have always pictured the Morrigan (or Cerridwen, Kali, Hecate, etc.)? What would she look like if she were stripped of her maiden body? The crone has gone through the stage of mother. Whether or not she has had children of her own, her body will soften with age. She will curve; her breasts and hips will become full. Imagine your image with the appropriate added weight. With your mind's eye, peel back the smoothed out skin and find the wrinkles beneath. The crone will have these; she has earned them. Is her hair luxurious, full and pigmented? The crone will have gray or white hair. Give her this dignity back. She has earned it.

Call on the Crone Goddess in your mind. Ask her to show you her physical truth. Study the image in your hands until you feel the goddess moving through you and altering the lines on the page. Allow your vision to become blurry. Watch the paper you hold with hazy vision.

Trade out the paper with the mirror. Study your own face. Look for signs of the dark goddess there. Spend some time in communion with yourself.

Lay the mirror down and cover your face with your fabric. You are in the womb of the dark goddess. You are safe. You are loved. Spend as much time here as necessary. Picture yourself in all of the stages you have traveled through. Stop and spend time in each stage. We often travel so fast through life, we barely see ourselves. Even if we spend time in front of the mirror painting our face and styling our hair, we are only covering our true selves. Allow the guise to fall away.

Uncover your face and lift the mirror up again. This is the truth you infused with crone energy.

Uncover your hair and admire it.

Uncover your shoulders and chest. This is you.

Let the cloth completely fall away and study the body that you have. Look at your hands, feet, knees, ankles, and elbows. Appreciate the changes time has added to your body. Do you have stretch marks? You've earned them. Respect them.

Replace the youthful crone image with the grandmother crone image. Meditate on her and what you have learned during your time with the dark goddess. Allow the crone energy to flow through you. Talk to the crone. Make an offering through yourself to her and drink the wine, leaving some for your altar if you have one. (If not, you can pour it into the earth.) When you are satisfied, thank the crone and blow out the candle. Close the circle as you normally would and thank the quarters.

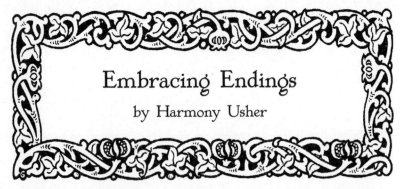

Embracing Endings
by Harmony Usher

A young child cries in protest that playtime at the park is over; she digs her heels into the sand, pulling against her mother's gentle tug on her arm. A mother dabs her eyes as the school bus picks up her son for his first day of school, stunned that her baby is now finding his way in the world without her. A man watches his elderly father climb stairs with great difficulty—stairs he once ran up two at a time. A woman feels a sense of unexplainable dread watching geese flying in a V over her head in late November. Her thoughts turn to her mother, who lives in a nursing home, and she wonders if they will see the spring together.

It is human condition, it seems, to resist—or even dread "endings."

Perhaps we are accustomed to the way things are and comfortable in the familiar. Sometimes we fear the unknown. At times, we simply resent being pulled away from something we are enjoying to do something less enjoyable. Sometimes endings remind us of our own mortality. Sometimes it seems life is just one ending after another, and we can experience a sense of uneasiness about it.

Why So Hard?

Urban life and our resulting disconnection from nature have much to do with our discomfort around endings.

Many of us living in cities go days without our feet coming in contact with the earth. Apartment dwellers have little opportunity to muck about in soil and often have little or no experience vegetable gardening or even tending to indoor plants. If we do garden, we often choose annuals in full bloom and simply discard them at the end of the season. This gives us little time to observe the ways nature allows for transformation—the sprouting, growth, going to seed, or seasonal "sleeping" of the perennial, which "dies back" each year, to return in the spring. If we never experience the magic of a hot compost pile that transforms garden and kitchen waste into beautiful, rich, dark soil, how do we learn to trust in nature's power? And how will we ever learn to challenge the very premise that what we don't immediately "need" is waste—as opposed to food for the future?

Because we live and work indoors and because our cities create so much light, we are also distanced from the most basic of nature's cycles—the rising and setting of the Sun, Moon, and stars. The majority of people, if you ask them, will not be able to tell you whether the Moon is in a waxing or waning state. We have lost touch with the seasonal cycles. Unless you are specifically celebrating the sabbats and esbats of the year, you likely wouldn't notice the changing length of days and night either, which connect us to nature's rhythms.

On the biggest ending of all—death itself—we are much more removed than we were even just two or three generations ago. Unless we are farmers, we have veterinarians who tend to the death of our pets. We often experience the death of loved ones separated from them by a medical professional who is not particularly committed to helping us understand what it is all about.

All of this disconnection from the natural cycles in nature has had a tremendous impact on how we see and experience endings, and ultimately, "deaths"—whether the death of dreams, times in our lives, or loved ones.

The Importance of Ritual

Because we spend so little time living in synchronicity with nature, we are also removed from rituals that help us understand and live in rhythm with the ebb and flow, the little and big "deaths" that occur in our lives.

Much of our uneasiness with endings comes from our distrust in natural processes. Having rituals that acknowledge and celebrate the earth's natural processes can go a long way to easing our discomfort and having us fully appreciate the paradox of endings.

Many articles could be devoted to ways in which we can celebrate endings through ritual, but for now, I will simply say that any ritual that celebrates the seasons, elements, or natural processes will help us to grow more deeply aware of the inherent beauty of endings. Consider that the sunniest day of the year wouldn't stand out if every day were just as sunny. Similarly, the bloom of a rose is special because we know its beauty cannot last forever. This sentiment is echoed in the words of a well-respected educator about dealing with grief in our modern secular society.

It's only when we truly know and understand that we have a limited time on earth—and that we have no way of knowing when our time is up—that we will begin to live each day to the fullest, as if it was the only one we had (Elisabeth Kübler-Ross).

Cultivating a deep appreciation of every moment—every pleasure we experience—can be a path that helps us embrace life's endings. Remaining conscious that the only moment that truly "exists" is the moment in which we currently live helps us appreciate that the passage of time, experiences, and our lives is simply an integral aspect of life itself.

Many of us are comfortable with a form of prayer or meditation that involves giving thanks. One way of becoming more comfortable with endings is to incorporate your awareness of the passage of time in these prayers. "Thank you for this beautiful day; this day that exists only in this moment, and will, with the arrival of another moment, be gone forever. Fill my heart with deep appreciation for the fleeting nature of life and all the gifts it brings."

Thinking in Circles

Contemporary society is built on linear thinking—things have a beginning, middle, and an end. This perspective has led to the growth of the idea that endings, particularly human deaths, are a "tragedy" and that death is to be seen a sad event, a loss to be dreaded.

The idea that life is constructed in circles is found in some cultures—but is particularly prevalent in Native American and other indigenous peoples. Teachings about the circular nature of life are particularly helpful in understanding the paradoxical nature of endings—that in nature's time, that which was an ending eventually becomes a beginning.

The Medicine Wheel

The medicine wheel or "sacred hoop" teaching is found in many native cultures. Although they differ from group to group, the basic principle is the same. The medicine wheel is a representation of a circle, which can be drawn on paper or in the sand, created out of stones, or created using plants and bushes. It is divided into sections; in some wheels it is divided into four, which represent the four directions (north, south, east, and west) as well as the four elements (fire, water, earth, and air). In most, totem animals are associated with a section and are considered to be guardians of that area of life and its qualities.

These wheels represent the sacred circle of life that all human beings travel, and which has no beginning, middle or end. Instead it represents a series of deaths and rebirths. To

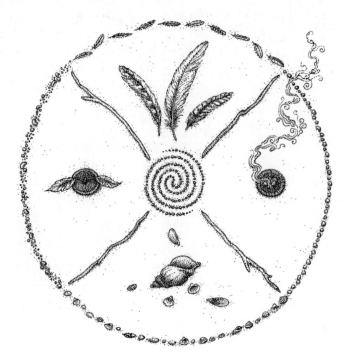

work with the wheel as a tool for meditation or contemplation, one can place symbols into the sections they feel need attention in their own life and use it during prayer, meditation, or contemplation.

This can be a very useful tool to help one become more conscious of the circular nature of life. A study of cross cultural use of circles in spiritual practices will surely lead you to other tools that, at their core, also teach the circular nature of life.

Beginnings

Every new beginning comes from some other beginning's end.

—Seneca

When we live with a growing awareness that our life experiences are circular in nature, we discover a whole new perspective that allows us to experience the richness that various "endings" have to offer. We begin to see both planned and unexpected endings are teeming with new opportunities that have the potential to carry us to new levels of understanding, insight, joy, and connectedness to others.

So it may be that the difficult death of a grandparent as a child later leads to an aspiring writer to author a book that helps thousands of people come to a new appreciation for the role of our elders in our society. An accident that causes a disability for a young man becomes the experience that opens the door to his development of an innovative new therapy that helps hundreds of thousands like him. A "mistake" made in a marriage leads to a deepening understanding of the selflessness of love, and strengthens a relationship.

Take time to learn about endings—and new beginnings—from nature. Spend time in the garden, following the sprouting, the growth, the seed production, and the decay of each plant's life cycle. Learn how to compost, watch the Sun both rise and set, and take time to fully appreciate and experience each moment with a deep awareness of its uniqueness. Remember that you too are an expression of nature and embrace each ending with a heart that is thankful for each new beginning.

Protection while Working Magic

by Graham Miller

I have read articles that suggest that there is no need for protections while working magic. That by engaging in magical work you will somehow be specially protected by angelic beings. Given that all the worlds are connected, it is far more likely that the numinous, magical worlds have a lot in common with the physical one. This physical world has its share of danger, but with sensible protection this fact shouldn't stop you from going about your business. So it is in the magical realms.

There are many ways to use magic to protect yourself while practicing your craft. These also offer a degree of security in the physical world and can be a useful part of a daily routine. For the purposes of this article, when I refer to magical work, it'll mean anything spiritual, Pagan, or psychic. So it could include tarot or other readings, candle or spellwork, and meditation, as well as more formal things like ceremonies. You might also want to clear the energy in a house or other place. This can include haunted places, but many places have picked up some emotional residue from the people who were there before. Common events like divorces, breakups, arguments, or depression can all leave their mark on a place and make it unhappy for the next people to move in.

Visualization

This is a good basic technique that has many useful applications. It can be used before any piece of magical work to establish a safe space. For an aura exercise, it can be used anywhere to improve your defenses and to clear an area. If you're living somewhere with disturbed energies, then the aura exercise will be of great benefit.

The simplest form of visualization is to imagine a circle of blue light surrounding the circle and your work area to be pure and clean and empty. This will be made stronger if you walk around or mark out the circle with your finger or an athame. This works best if you keep your thoughts positive. Imagine being safe inside strong walls instead of focusing on whatever you want to keep outside.

A more sophisticated form of this technique is the aura exercise. The aura is a field of energy that emanates a couple of feet from the physical body in a roughly spherical shape. It has a color, which frequently changes depending on your mood and physical health. Most people can't see other people's auras, but they can feel them subconsciously and react to them. If you walk into a room and you know there has been a quarrel or that you are interrupting a deep conversation, part of what you pick up will be the aura of the other people in the room. Your aura, as well as reflecting how you are feeling, also responds well to visualization. By using your imagination, you can affect it and make your response to the situation more positive.

Because the energies of others can be distracting, it's best to try this exercise at home where you feel safe and won't be disturbed. As you practice, you should find it easier, until eventually you can give your aura a boost when you need it while you're out and about.

If you know how to meditate, then use that technique to relax yourself. If not, clear you mind of thoughts and breathe a little more deeply, relaxing your muscles. When you feel calm and at ease, close your eyes and imagine a ball of bright white light above your head. Imagine it getting progressively larger until, starting at your shoulders, it slowly envelops your entire body. This ball of light should be spinning slowly clockwise and have flashes of light within it. Once you have your aura visualized, then you can imagine that it is turning bright blue. When you have this clear in your head, make the aura turn slightly darker toward the outside, and give it a hard edge, as if you were sitting in the center of a glass ball. When you have this image firm in your mind, you can open your eyes. You should feel calm and protected. If you feel a little lightheaded or disoriented, have something to eat or drink.

Once you are happy with this it can easily become part of your daily routine. I would definitely recommend taking a moment or two to do this when waking up, before leaving the house, and before going to sleep at night. Also, you can use this exercise when you know you are going into a stressful or difficult situation.

Sympathetic Magic

This is a very good technique to establish a working area in your home or a place you have good access to—a room you use for magical work, a special part of your garden, or somewhere outdoors. It can work equally well as a temporary measure or you could make it a permanent fixture, if that is appropriate.

Sympathetic magic is magic by imitation. This means that you are using the correspondences between elements to work magic. By using symbols you can draw things into your life. For example, a spell would use green and gold cloth to draw in more money. Because those colors are associated with, or sympathetic to, the concept of wealth and growth, then the spell should work.

The most powerful set of correspondences are the classical four elements—earth, water, fire, and air. Everything is composed of one of these four elements, so harnessing all of them will mean that your defenses keep out everything that could do you harm. It is worth noting that the traditional Pagan symbol is the pentagram. This has four points to represent the four elements, and a fifth point, which is spirit, that traditionally rises above the other four. So if you use elemental defenses, then your spirit will still be above them—which means you shouldn't be blocking yourself off from any psychic input.

Looking at traditional folklore surrounding Witches and fairies gives insight into elemental protections. Salt and iron both repel magic and represent the element of earth. Traditionally, Witches won't cross flowing water and it can be used for cleansing as well. Fire was also seen as a way of getting rid of Witches, although this is primarily folklore. Far more women were hanged as Witches than were burned at the stake. Words, spoken prayers, and using smoke and incense are also seen as a valid defense against witchcraft, and these are attributed to the element of air.

Before you place your elemental protections, mark out the area you want to protect. This could be as simple as visualizing a ring of light around it. Or, if you are outside, you could draw a line in the earth with your finger or an athame or sweep clockwise around the area with a besom or traditional Witches broom. Some people use a line of salt to mark a circle to work in. If you are working in a large area or trying to protect a house or property, you might wish to walk around the boundary. While doing any of these, it is good to physically tidy up the area of any rubbish. View this in your head as ritually purifying the area. All this activity should be carried out in a clockwise direction.

One of the simplest ways to establish a safe space for working is to have a representative of each element in the correct quarter. If you wish, you could use the ace from each suit in a deck of tarot cards. Many Pagans keep their artifacts in cupboards, or even out on shelves when they are not working. Out of context, to the casual observer, they simply appear to be ornaments. This makes it easy to turn what looks like an ordinary home into a safe magical working space in a matter of minutes. Below is a table of basic correspondences to each of the four elements. If you wish, you can research this and make up your own far larger list.

Quarter	Element	Symbol	Artifact	Tarot Suit
North	Earth	Pentagram	Rock, bowl of salt	Discs
West	Water	Cup, chalice	Bowl or cup of water	Cups
South	Fire	Athame	Candle	Wands
East	Air	Wand	Feather, incense	Swords

While putting your items out in a clockwise fashion, acknowledge in your mind that you are doing so as part of a ritual to clear a space ready to do some magic. And likewise, when you've finished, take them down in reverse order, starting with the last one that was put out.

Crystals

Using crystals for protective work is very similar to sympathetic magic. It works best as a technique for permanently protecting a space and for restoring balance to energies where there has been a disturbance.

The best crystals to use are unpolished, plain white quartz. You will need four crystals, one for each point of the compass. They should be cleaned first. You can do this by leaving them out in the Sun on a windowsill for a few days, putting them in a glass and leaving them in running water for ten minutes, or by smudging.

When you have your cleansed crystals, you need to charge them up to be protective. Find a safe space to sit down where you won't be disturbed. You might like to use some of the other techniques to ensure the space is clear—the aura exercise works particularly well in this case. Or you could charge your crystals away from the area you want to protect.

When you are settled and relaxed, hold the crystals cupped in your hands. As you breathe in, imagine you are breathing in golden energy. This energy, once you've breathed it in, flows out down your arms and into your hands. Here it surrounds the crystals in golden light. While you're visualizing this, imagine feelings of safety and security. It's important to keep your thoughts positive—focus on cleanliness and purity, not on the negativity that you want to keep out. After a couple of minutes, very gently lay the crystals aside, let your breathing

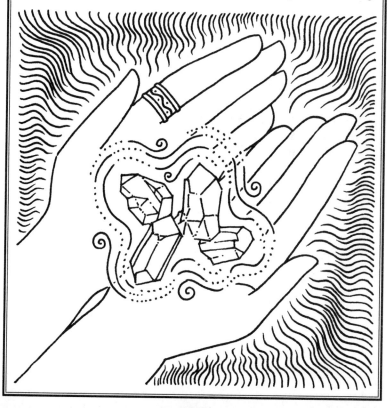

return to normal, and repeat the aura exercise. Have something to eat and drink, and keep the crystals in a bag made of natural material until you need to use them.

When in use, they should be hidden, either just underground, under a lifted carpet, or behind a cupboard, as near the four cardinal compass points around the edge of the area as you can. As with all protections, work in a clockwise direction with knowledge and intent of what you are doing.

Smudging

Smudging started off as a Native American shamanistic technique. Commonly known as a very good way to clear a house, garden, or place, it can also be used to cleanse crystals or other objects used in sympathetic magic.

In order to change the atmosphere, bundles of herbs are bound and dried into a smudge stick. When it was needed, the end would be lit and fanned until it smoldered. Then it would be used either to mark out an area or to purify a specific object or person by passing it through the smoke.

Again, correspondences come into play here—the choice of herbs in the stick makes a big difference to the overall outcome. The traditional herb to use is sage. Although the Native American white sage is a different member of the sage family than the common kitchen herb, all sages are regarded as protective plants. Lavender is also commonly used to bring in a positive atmosphere. Other commonly used protective herbs are mugwort and sweetgrass.

Smudge sticks are available commercially, and although fiddly, can be made at home. Once you have chosen the herbs you wish to use, tie them up into a bundle with pure cotton thread. Take the end of the thread and wind it diagonally around the bunch of herbs to the end and then back down to the base where it is tied off. It can then be rolled in a sushi mat to make sure it is nice and tight. Once it is dry, it is ready to use.

There are several warnings about smudging. First of all, always remember that you are waving around a burning bunch of herbs! Be very careful around curtains, sofas, carpets, and other fabrics, as embers can fall off the end. An ashtray or saucer of sand or earth is essential so you have somewhere to set the smudge stick down or extinguish it. Do experiment with your own mix of herbs, but remember that burning the herbs has a powerful effect, especially indoors. If you're not sure what you're doing, start off with commercially bought sticks. And check that anyone who's going to be present is all right with smoke, especially in confined spaces. Sage in particular has been known to trigger asthma.

Bearing all that in mind, it's best to light the stick in a candle flame. To smudge a place, walk about it clockwise, making sure the smoke gets into all the corners. The smoke will attract the negativity to itself and carry it away. To smudge an object, pass it through the smoke, or hold the stick below it so that the smoke covers the object. Likewise, with a person, waft the smoke toward and around them—carefully!

Lesser Banishing Ritual of the Pentagram

The top end of the scale of defensive work is full ritual defenses. Probably the most famous of these is the Lesser Banishing Ritual of the Pentagram. This was first recorded by members of the Hermetic Order of the Golden Dawn, and now thanks to the Internet, instructions can easily be found, complete with videos and sound. Here, I'll use it as an example to show how it is an extension of the elemental system of protecting yourself and your home. Because it was recorded by the Golden Dawn, it is quite male-centric and Judeo-Christian, dealing with god names and male archangels. Some Pagans are quite uncomfortable with this, but I hope this discussion highlights the principles behind it so people can adapt it and find what works for them. I won't go into detail as to exactly what each stage is because it is well documented in books and on the Internet. The internet is particularly useful as it can show the actions needed clearly and gives examples of the vibration of the god names—this last point is much easier to learn if you can see and hear the lesson.

The ritual starts with the Qabalistic Cross. This is a short procedure to center the worker in the ritual. This is similar to the Catholic practice of crossing yourself, and the words in Hebrew are also in the Lord's Prayer.

Then the circular space to be made sacred and protected is marked out. This is done with an athame or dagger, or with

the worker's hand or fingers. It should be visualized in blue or white light. If working outdoors, a line could be drawn in the earth with a staff or wand.

Next, each of the four quarters are banished with a pentagram ritual and a resounded god name.

Once the space has been marked and cleared, the archangels are called in to guard each of the cardinal points. Again, this is done with the traditional attributions to the elements.

Finally the pentagrams are named and a six-rayed star visualized, before a second Qabbalistic Cross is performed.

The first thing to note about this ritual is that there is balance and symmetry. All four quarters are banished and all four quarters are guarded by archangels. The ritual starts and ends the same way—with a personal centering. However you change things to fit in with your tradition, there should always be this balance, which is pleasing to the eye. Secondly, the overall system is the same. The space is cleared out, and the elements are attributed to the quarters.

The important thing to remember about protection is that like everything else, it starts off as thought. Everything that mankind has achieved starts off as a thought in some-one's mind. Like all magical work, protection can be viewed through the lens of the four classical elements. First you have the idea, the thought—air. Then you imbue it with passion and will—fire. Then you create some protections—water. Finally you have a physical manifestation, a safe space around you—earth. While these steps will always work it is worth noting that when necessary they can be done entirely in the head with equally good results.

Conversely, but similarly, other people's thoughts can cause trouble. For example, if you are looking for another job then it may be wise not to mention it to your co-workers. While they may wish you well, they may be thinking that if you get a new job, they will be left in the lurch. They may start to worry about finding a replacement for you and if they will like them. All these negative thoughts will have an effect on your job search. And this could well be happening on a subconscious level, with your colleagues believing that they are wishing you well.

~

So, sometimes the best form of defense is to be a bit circum-spect about your hopes and dreams. See them as delicate flowers that need nurturing, and before you reveal them to anyone consider if that person will also nurture or if they may have reason not to.

Inner Demons:
When You are the Bump
in the Night

by Diana Rajchel

The signs of haunting are all present: bumps in the night, inexplicable power surges that fry your brand-new light bulbs, items disappearing and then reappearing in places you know you did not leave them. Along with these peculiarities comes a claustrophobic sense that something lies in wait. As an experienced practitioner, you reach into your bag of energy-management 101 tricks: smudging, blessing, and prayer. You leave offerings to protective deities and perhaps burn a seven-day candle to settle a disturbed condition. Despite it all, the feeling remains. Worse yet, this energy starts to follow you everywhere. Then, it spreads—your lover refuses to let you sleep over because of lingering weirdness above the bed at night. Your workplace looks to you like it hosts a perpetual storm cloud above it, and even your favorite coffee shop feels uncomfortable.

Because of this persistent atmosphere, you may experience disrupted sleep. The deprivation can lead to signs of paranoia. A twitching of legs and arms that wakes you up may make you think someone is shaking you or some entity is trying to possess you.

After an incident where a nearby object defies the laws of physics in order to break, you get out the asafetida. You take your protection work to level two: you shield, perform protection spells, and even try nontraditional exorcisms. The clouds clear for a little while, right after you work, but the next morning the oppressive atmosphere has returned.

Fear not! You are not living in a Japanese horror movie. Most likely, you experienced or are experiencing a spectacularly stressful period in your life such as the loss of a loved one, foreclosure, or divorce. What you're experiencing is a manageable, if unusual, byproduct of that freight train of change coming at you.

During stressful periods, your body purges itself; when the stress reaches crisis levels, the purge intensifies, too. This is most recognizable on the physical level: you catch the flu and spend a day vomiting, or a fever causes you to sweat out toxins. Sometimes, however, your body/spirit (aura) may take a metaphorical route on its way to a purge. What affects the body affects the spirit, and a spirit releasing poison from its wounds can make itself physically known, especially when the undirected outgoing energy involves releasing massive amounts of negativity. We often compartmentalize the physical, such as touch from the abstract like emotions, and we forget that the objects we touch resonate with all our energies—moods included. The computer you use regularly carries your imprint, as does the bed you sleep on, the utensils you eat with, and the clothing you wear. Each of these absorb detritus from your auric body regardless of your intentions.

The stress built up in your body is also built up in your auric field. This means you need a few changes to your daily energy-management techniques. While the approach sounds painfully prosaic, a few simple acts of accounting will set you on the road to a happier space.

First, carefully evaluate your situation. Make a list of recent stressful events going back two years. Stress can also include positive events like weddings and job promotions, so include those along with the more easy-to-identify negative events. Check your emotional response to your list of events, and check it against the phenomena you experience. Look for ways that the energy or its associations match. If you think of a funeral, and you experience a certain mood, check the texture of that mood against the texture of the energy hovering in spaces you often inhabit. Take special note where you feel fear and discomfort. You may want to use a pendulum or dowsing rod to look for any spots where the energy is especially thick. Bless and cleanse those areas. You can add a small "kick" to a smudge bundle or smudge spray by adding a pinch of dragon's blood; this will increase the herb's ability to alter the energy it contacts.

If you still feel discomfort after a cleansing, burning a black or dark-green candle can absorb any remaining undirected energies.

The principles of magical energy follow the same basic rules of bacteria management—you want to cultivate the right energy. Too much wrong stimuli can throw your ecosphere out of balance. Extremely long periods of worry, depression, and fear leave distinctive marks. Those marks make us vulnerable, and this vulnerability manifests most strongly while you sleep.

As you resolve difficult life situations through dreams, your body also releases the emotions you process. You may not even realize that your body is shedding excess energy. If the energy release wakes you, you may initially interpret the instance as something attempting to enter you instead of something leaving. This jettisoned energy still requires direction. Just like a Wiccan circle after ritual, this energy needs release, direction, or banishing. The first "instinct" of undirected energy is to try to stay close to its source—over time creating a toxic atmosphere if unmanaged.

If it's just me, why didn't my initial cleansings work?

Smudging ceremonies typically address energies that did not originate from the person performing the ceremony. Unless you consciously banish your own energy or include it in your banishing, it will remain. On a subconscious level, you still recognize the hovering energy as an extension of yourself. Becoming conscious of your own energy and how it meshes with your environment is a skill that develops over time. While you may not like the impact of that energy extension, on some level you may choose to keep it until you consciously realize what it does to you.

Entities

Your high-level haunting of yourself may also cause low-level haunting in your home. Intense psychological states attract astral entities, enough that you might mistake a minor attachment for a major attack. Stress can cause tunnel vision, and you end up missing the big picture. When you perform a banishing, you may banish a few of the astral creepy crawlies that came in as a response to the energy that your body jettisons at night. When you sense their departure, you naturally assume you're all done—and then surprise! The next night you feel the same crowded foreboding. Understandably, you then assume you're under psychic attack. While technically the minor entities are attacking you, they bear you no more malice than do mosquitoes seeking food.

No matter how strange the night phenomena, never rule out medical problems until you see a doctor. If you are experiencing sleep disruption such as "night hag" visitations more than once in six months, you must see a doctor in order to rule out sleep apnea, asthma, or any other physical problems that can affect your psychic life. Lack of sleep can result in hallucinations, as well, so some of the phenomenon you might see might also be an unfortunate side effect of your brain trying to compensate for your conscious sanity.

If meditating, banishing, and aligning your chakras doesn't control your energy/space runoff, you may need to seek outside spiritual help. Be realistic. Just as your metaphysical situation did not happen overnight, you will need to spend a few weeks and even months cleaning it up. Most spiritual practitioners can see and solve the problems of others, but are unable to do so for themselves. And just as doctors make the worst patients, practitioners can be the most difficult and silly spiritual petitioners. This is especially true when under stress—practitioners do a lot more to their brains than average, which means that the runoff from the physical and auric body gets strange. If you are yourself an experienced practitioner, it is okay to admit you don't fully understand what's happening. Second opinions happen among spiritual practitioners just as much as they do among medical practitioners. Getting second opinions keeps us grounded; only someone of low self-confidence puts more concern on losing face.

Since it can take a while to find a fellow practitioner to help, you can take steps toward resolution on your own. First, keep a journal at hand. Check your emotional states daily—record what you eat, how long you sleep, your dreams, and your daily stressors. Revisit all your basics: grounding, shielding, meditation, and coming in and out of altered states. Note what triggers strong emotions as well as times your energy seems "off." If you don't already, add some physical exercise to your regimen. You need not go for full on fitness nut, but even twenty minutes of simple yoga stretches can align and release energy from your body safely and cleanly. Clearing your own energy fields will do much to clear the energy of places you frequent.

Whenever uncomfortable energies persist, it's most important not to control your fear, but to manage it. Just as fear can rule you, it can be a trusted adviser. Using this time to befriend and command your fear will greatly enhance your skills at reading energies. All people have instinctive strategies for dealing with the unfamiliar—fight or flight. Chances are, if you've practiced for a long time, you don't choose avoidance and can end up using time you need to sleep and be well to struggle with an energy or entity that's coming out of you in the first place. You must find a way of starting a conversation with yourself about whatever's happening to you. This conversation must be constant. Any confluence of massive events is a sign of major, pow-

erful life-changing developments ahead. Much of the time you might not realize this comes from a resistance to change. While fearing and resisting change is understandable, especially after a lot has happened, you can make some aspects of it pleasant by continuing to deal with the energy you set off within it in a conscious and deliberate way. Fear less! You are the source of that stubborn haunting. So look deep—what's haunting you, and what do you need to do to be at peace?

Magickal Moving and Relocating

by Blake Octavian Blair

Moving can be quite the stressful life experience. For many of us, the occasion will arise at least a handful of times. With all the planning, packing, and coordinating that needs to be done even before you get to your new destination, it can fast become an overwhelming experience. The need to relocate might simply be a deliberate personal choice, but a move often coincides with a transition in life: college, job transfers, family concerns, relationships ending, and relationships beginning. The ideal scenario would include a comfortable amount of advanced notice. In the worst-case scenario, receiving notice means you need to move immediately. The good news is that the stress can be considerably lessened by taking a spiritual approach and adding a little magic into the relocating process.

Chances are that if you know that you will be moving in the near future you are probably thinking about, and putting a lot of energy toward, finding a home. Whether you're single and looking for a small apartment or have a sizable family and are in the market for a large house, finding an affordable home that meets your needs can seem increasingly difficult in hard economic times. Fortunately, you can use some simple magic to assist in your search. Make a list on a sheet of paper outlining the qualities you require your new home to possess: number of bedrooms, number of bathrooms, square footage, how many levels, or in the case of an apartment, do you require a ground-floor unit or would upper floor do just fine? Be sure to also indicate the desired area or location you'd prefer for your new home. If you are moving within your current city or you are familiar with your future city you can specify the area of town or neighborhood you desire. If you are unfamiliar with your new locale, simply list the qualities that you will require (or desire) such as a safe neighborhood, close to your work, near public transit, and so on. Finally, be sure to list the price range you can afford to spend for the home. Anoint the list with an oil associated with attraction or prosperity such as cinnamon or clove. Place the list under a brown candle (brown being associated with matters of the home) and light the candle while focusing on the intent of finding your ideal new home. The candle can be extinguished and relit, burning a down a small amount each day until your new home is secured.

When packing up your home in preparation to move, in addition to plenty of padding and packing material (bubble wrap is your friend), don't forget to use your witchy skills to enchant a bit of ethereal protection and intent for safe travel on the boxes. To guard goods against damage during transport, sprinkle a small amount of comfrey in the bottom of boxes containing fragile items. Mercurial charms are also especially effective when implemented in relocation matters, as the Roman god Mercury has long been associated with travel. You can invoke him to watch over your cargo as you travel simply by drawing the astrological symbol for Mercury with a marker of an associated color (orange is often associated with Mercury) on the side of boxes.

This now seems to be an appropriate time to discuss spirits of place. People often speak of how cities seem to possess individual characters and energies. This is likely in no small part due to the spirits of the place. These spirits, also called *genius loci* in ancient Rome, can be seen as the guardian spirits or elementals of that city or area of land. As you are finishing packing and are preparing to depart for your new location, you should honor the spirits of the place you are leaving behind. Thank them for the learning experiences and life lessons (both pleasant and otherwise) that the location has provided. You can leave offerings for the city's spirits at a location that you find fitting: perhaps at a prominent landmark or monument, a building with sentimental meaning for you, a park you visited regularly, a city limits or welcome sign, or another spot that calls to you where you can feel the presence of the local spirits. Food and drink are appropriate offerings and will also biodegrade or be consumed by wildlife. However, feel free to be creative in your offerings so long as they are mindful to the land. Similarly, upon arrival at your new location, you can address and leave offerings to the spirits of place presiding there as well. Appeal to them and ask for protection and guidance so that you may experience growth and happiness during your tenure there.

Arriving at a new home that lacks any comforting familiarity can be a bit disconcerting. Even the perfect home can feel a bit uninviting until you settle in and mesh with the new energies. However, here are a few simple ideas to help you feel more at ease and make the first days in your new home a bit more welcoming. First, you can actually send yourself a housewarming card, including a written charm or blessing, to your new address. Try to mail it so that it will arrive around the time you plan to move in. Include on both the card and envelope symbols of blessing and protection such as the pentacle, Om, or a rune such as algiz (ᛉ). This type of simple spell can be custom designed to work for you on several levels. Not only does it begin your blessing and protection magic on your new home even before you arrive, it also sets into motion the law of attraction to bring forth blessings from other sources (friends, family, new neighbors)! If you choose to perform this spell, do not be surprised to have a well-attended housewarming party or to receive seemingly random gestures of goodwill from your new neighbors!

On a related note, I've even heard of a few thoughtful Witches who moved within the same town who, before moving anything else into the new home, went in and set up an altar in the main room to greet them when they and their family arrived. If you have the ability to do the same, I can imagine it would be wonderful to experience upon entry—to be greeted by sacred space of your own creation.

Another tip is to take a couple of boxes small enough to fit in the trunk or backseat of your car, and pack them with extra-special items you can unpack immediately upon arriving at your new home. Perhaps include your altar tools, a favorite tarot deck, a statue of your patron deity, a favorite piece of art to hang on the wall, crystals with comforting energy, protection charms to hang over the doors, or a favorite quilt that makes any room feel cozy.

When my partner and I moved to our current location, this tip helped immensely. Even in a strange and unfamiliar place, our apartment had an instant touch of familiarity once my metal Ganesha mask was hung over the outside of our bedroom door, our favorite woven Indian blankets were draped over the back of the sofa, and a few of our favorite crystal clusters and statuary were set out. Even if you have piles of other boxes surrounding you from the moving truck, you will have these comforting magickal touches help your new living quarters have that touch of familiarity, making it truly feel like home.

Other items you'll want to have readily available on move-in day include house cleansing and blessing tools. Most magickal practitioners often already have small kits assembled with such materials as sage or other smudge, a censor, incense, sea salt, a bell, and/or any other particular cleansing and blessing items that may be called for in their tradition. Upon your arrival, make a sweep through the new dwelling and do a thorough house cleansing. If possible, do this before the moving truck is even unloaded. If time is short, at least do a initial sweep through the home with sage or other smudge, and save the longer and deeper house blessing and cleansing to do with family, friends, and loved ones; perhaps at a housewarming party. Starting off with fresh and clean energy is a propitious start to your new beginning.

At some point, a friend or family member will almost certainly ask you to help with their change of abode. The support you can provide your loved ones physically, emotionally, and spiritually can provide a great sense of stability and grounding for them during a time of transition. In addition to mundane types of assistance such as an extra set of hands to pack, move, and unpack boxes, you can serve as an outlet for them to express some of the myriad emotions that can be stirred and summoned by what is often a significant life event. If you are trained in spiritual counseling or an energy healing modality (such as Reiki), these too can be offered and provide great benefit.

Housewarming parties can be one of the more enjoyable parts of relocation. Whether you have a small intimate gathering or a big bash with dozens of attendees, a housewarming can serve as the celebratory ritual marking the culmination of the moving process. Whether you are the one who has moved or you are organizing such a party for a loved one, such events are an old custom that can be pulled off with magickal flair! In addition to the standard socializing, tours of the new home, and requisite finger and party foods ("No! Not another jelly mold!"), you can include magickal elements such as a group

candle-lighting ritual, house cleansing and blessing ceremony, and gifting circle.

If you plan to have a large number of attendees, a group candle-lighting ritual or spell is a stunningly beautiful and touching sight. Purchase at least as many tealight candles as you plan to have attendees and obtain an equal amount of glass holders (empty glass jars are a thrifty option) and set up a large table to put all of the jars on. Have each attendee infuse and light a candle to place on the table with their intent of blessings for the party's guest(s) of honor. The glow and energy created by such a display will result in a wonderful energetic vibration in the new home and will be a cherished memory for years to come.

Performing a group house cleansing and blessing ceremony is a great way to involve your loved ones in the celebration of the new home. In many traditions, the standard format is to make respective rounds around the home using implements to represent the elements such as salt water (water/earth), incense (air), a lit candle (fire), sage (spirit), and finishing with a bell or rattle to cleanse through sound.

Attendees can break into groups and each group can perform a different elemental round of the ceremony. A great deal of merriment almost always ensues during such a ceremony. Don't be afraid to alter and personalize the ceremony to be your own. Once everybody has completed his or her round and reassembled in the main space, a great deal of merriment is usually buzzing amongst all involved and presents the perfect time for forming a circle for gifting.

A gift-giving circle can serve as a continuation of the previous blessing ritual, and by using the circle format it creates an intimate setting to present gifts to the guests of honor. As each gift is presented and opened by the home's new resident(s), the giver can say a blessing, words of wisdom, or gratitude of friendship to the recipient. While simple in format, this can be wonderfully powerful and emotionally intense circle for all involved and finishing off the circle with a round of cakes and ale is an advisable idea for grounding. Alternatively, make sure there are still plenty of finger foods available.

Magical folk tend to rank among the most creative of gift-givers. Thus, it is no surprise that there are many options for magickal housewarming gifts that can allow you to utilize your creative juices. While traditionally requested housewarming gifts like toasters, dishes, and other household goods are often useful, don't forget to recognize the metaphysical and spiritual realms. For example, a traditional favorite for the Witch is a decorative broom with embellishments, such as dried herbs for protection, health, and happiness, to hang near the home's entryway. A few other possibilities that are often received well are cleansing and blessing kits like described above as well as homemade quilts infused by stitchery magic. There is an old anonymous quote that he who sleeps under a homemade quilt sleeps under a blanket of love. Good friends gifted my partner and I with a lovely large wooden sofa table to serve as our household altar after our last move. Brainstorm and think about what the perfect magickal gift would be for the individual receiving it. Be creative and don't be afraid to go with an original idea or a one-of-a-kind kind item you've created!

~

After settling into your new location, you will surely want to connect with others of a like mind. The Internet is a useful tool in this search as many community groups, covens, and metaphysical shops have websites with postings about community events such as workshops, social outings, and public rituals (and don't forget to visit the online mega-resource Witch-Vox.com!). If your area has a brick and mortar metaphysical shop, I highly recommend making a visit in person and making yourself familiar with the staff, as they generally have the details on the metaphysical scene in the area and receive notifications of all manner of events.

We can use our magickal skills and resources to reduce and manage the stresses involved with moving. Perhaps energy that would have manifested as stress can instead be transformed and focused on the transformative and celebratory energy that can be a part of the relocation experience. Next time the need for relocating presents itself in your life or that of a loved one, may you feel empowered and inspired in the power of change!

Down the Rabbit Hole:
A Meditation on Alice's
Descent into the Underworld.

by Sybil Fogg

Alice's Adventures in Wonderland and *Through the Looking Glass* have fascinated children for decades. Scholars have argued Lewis Carroll's tale from mathematic standpoints to the more philosophical theory of it being an allegory for coming of age. Alice's story has been near to my heart since I was a child and my father first read it to me. I have often thought of Alice's descent in terms of my own search for myself during my tumultuous teen rebellion years and premature mother phase and most consistently throughout my early years as a Wiccan practitioner. Now I find it not only illuminating, but also soothing to use this story as a guided meditation into a personal spiral into the underworld and back again.

Alice is educated on herself throughout the text. Each character she meets in her journey is a representation of an aspect of her personality. Each challenge teaches her to grow. After all, it is our ability to change that assists our development in this lifetime. Without it, we would grow stagnant and our greatest potential would be wasted. (I have found this particular meditation to be an excellent means to discovering aspects of myself that need honing or must be overcome, just as Alice is forced to accept her shortcomings, rejoice in her strengths, and correct her weaknesses.)

It is necessary to have a working knowledge of the text to fully realize this meditation, so I recommend reviewing a copy of the book. I would purchase a copy because it is not only disrespectful, but also fruitless to jot notes on a borrowed book. Before beginning this self-guided meditation, read the book and get to know the characters, spending some time reflecting on how each might represent aspects of your personality.

Here is a list of the characters that will be encountered in order of appearance:

Before the Descent:

Alice's sister: She is a symbol of what we are to become if we play by the rules.

The White Rabbit: He is a clear contrast to Alice's sister. This is who we follow because we are not sure yet if conformity is where we belong.

After the Descent:

The Mouse: This is Alice's first attempt at socializing in Wonderland and she does a horrific job with it. The mouse represents those awkward moments when our belief systems are put to the test. This is a good time to slow down and spend time considering both sides to an argument.

The variety of animals present at the Caucus Race: How we react in group settings tells us much about our inner workings. Are you a leader or a follower? Which role do you wish you were in? Are you changeable?

Little Bill: He symbolizes when we are put upon to complete tasks we do not wish to. As my mother used to say, "We all have to do things we don't want to do." Then again, my father used to tell me that we don't have to do anything we really don't want to do. How's that for growing up in Wonderland?

The Caterpillar: He gives Alice what she needs regarding the ability to grow or shrink to the necessary sizes in Wonderland. He also gives her the best advice, "Keep your temper." As he has the ability to change his physical self, he represents change, which is the only constant in Alice's or our world.

The Duchess and the Cook represent the ugliness that we carry within ourselves.

The Baby who turns into a pig showed Alice that things are not always as they appear.

The Cheshire Cat: This is our ability to transcend.

The Mad Hatter, the March Hare, and the Doormouse: Often depicted as the most important character in Carroll's story, the Mad Hatter resonates in most fan's minds, but he wasn't even present in the original tale. The perpetual tea party signifies our constant battle with time. We want it to move faster, slow down, stop, etc.

The King and Queen of Hearts: Power without reason.

With these brief descriptions, we can get down to the task of putting together a self-guided meditation. It is possible to have someone read the mediation out loud, but this specific one works well alone. In fact, I prefer to do this kind of work by myself, as it is me that I am spending time getting to know and others present can be distracting.

Although we can meditate at any time, I find spiral work best done at the Spring or Fall Equinox as these are times of balance, and this meditation is an inward spiral with the goal of achieving balance of our different natures and selves. I have had the most success with this particular meditation around Mabon.

Meditation: Alice's Descent to the Underworld

Tools needed:
- Blanket, pillows, anything that you would normally use for comfort

- Black and white candles
- Any relaxing incense that you prefer. I am a fan of HEM incenses for meditation. Nag champa, forest, and Moon are favorites.
- Music. Instrumental is the best choice, though diehard fans of Jefferson Airplane's "White Rabbit" can get away with that too, but I would find it distracting. I tend to meditate best to Eastern melodies, particularly Indian carnatic music. Even chants similar to what one would hear at a Kirtan would be helpful because the words are repetitive and do not string together to form sentences that would require listening.
- Tools for casting the circle as you normally would.
- A copy of the meditation. This saves you from having to memorize, but that is acceptable as well.
- Quarter candles

Before meditating, I find it centering to take a ritual bath. For this purpose, I would use bath salts mixed with apple for goddess energy and clove for driving away negativity.

The Ritual

Set up your space. Put out the quarter candles. Lay out your resting spot and then organize the black and white candles around where you will be lying in a spiral formation, starting near the quarter candles and ending in the center where your makeshift bed lies. Use a clockwise pattern. Make sure to leave enough space to walk through the candles, as you will be lighting them as you work your way to your resting spot. Always use caution and common sense when using fire. A warm glow surrounding you is mood setting. Burning fabric or hair is not, so be safe!

Leave the words to the self-guided meditation on your pillow.
Turn on your music if you haven't already.
Light the incense.
Call the quarters.
Cast the circle.

Visualize a crossroad. Alice's sister is moving down one road and the White Rabbit is running along the other. This road is dark and mysterious. The other road is bright and orderly. You choose to follow the white rabbit down the mysterious path.

Begin lighting the spiral candles, working your way inward. Remain silent through this part. Allow your focus to center on Alice's descent. As she fell, she drifted past everyday objects. These are the tangible qualities of your normal life, your table and chairs, cupboards, all of the things we use and encounter in our "ordinary lives." Say goodbye to each. I like to create mental images of the objects that represent stale parts of my life. My computer for instance that tethers me to work.

When you reach the center, lie down and get comfortable. You have landed in Wonderland.

Self-Guided Meditation

The first thing you notice when you open your eyes is that the gilded walls surrounding you depict images of the different Wonderland characters. Each one is similar to a family member or friend. Spend some time walking the length and width of the room getting familiar with these characters. Is your mother the door mouse? Perhaps you find your sister's face on the Queen of Hearts? Remember each of the personalities described above and ascribe a pertinent person in your life to each image before you.

The arches leading out of the room curve upward into crown shapes. There are curtains through each and when you throw them open, you are met with fine sandalwood carvings of vines creeping in all directions. Slowly, you work your way around the room in a clockwise manner until the last curtain reveals a door no taller than your knee.

Crouching, you peer through the keyhole and spy a garden filled with color. There are blues representing the Triple Goddess, whites for the Maiden, reds for the Mother, and blacks for the Crone. You see yellows and greens for the god. The image is so vibrant it feels like a blue-screen rendition for a movie. You want to be in that garden.

The door opens easily and you slip in, but you are suddenly in a vast pool of salt water. Everything is black and the liquid is warm and encloses you. You can breathe and you feel warm. The gentle lull of the undulating water relaxes you and a rhythmic beat washes over you. You are safe here. Spend some time exploring without sight. You are at the core. This is the beginning, your center, the Mother.

Eventually, your feet touch ground and you walk. There are others waiting on the sandy beach. Everyone is wet, and everyone is jubilant, as they have all experienced the same rebirth. You can spend time here getting to know some of these creatures or you can continue onward in your journey. Either way, before you move on, you must give of yourself to each of them. Look through your pockets for items that represent treasure to you and pass them around.

A path appears in front of you and at the end you can just make out the white rabbit's house. It is important to catch up with him as he represents the direction you want your life to move in. As you get closer, you notice his obsession with his pocket watch. He is late, are you late? Spend some time filtering through the things that you desire to obtain or do that always seem to elude you. If any of these goals seem unnecessary now, drop them on

the path, and they will be swallowed by the brown earth and returned to the mother.

The path turns sharply as you near the rabbit and a new scene unfolds. Suddenly you feel a house grow around your body, your arms stretch out the windows, and your feet through the doorway. Your neck bends at an uncomfortable angle and you feel trapped. What is holding you back in your life? Drop these fetters and the house will fall away freeing you to continue your journey.

A mushroom that looks like a tasty cupcake appears in your path. A caterpillar decorates the top. This is where you learn that you are in control of your destiny. Change is all right, in fact, sometimes it takes a few tries to get it right. Think about your goals. Is there only one path? Look around you and you will notice the path you are on has splintered and grown many heads like a hydra.

Above all floats the Chesire Cat. He represents that voice inside of all of us that we discuss our options with. He points out where each path leads—there is the duchess, cook, and baby where we could go to work out the ugliness that resides in all of us. There is the Mad Hatter's Tea Party where we might want to spend some time figuring out time. Or perhaps we want to meet with the Queen of Hearts and work out our issues with power and control.

You choose one path and follow it to its destination. Once you have finished you find yourself back in the middle and will spiral out again until you have fulfilled your goal of finding out a little bit more about yourself. Your final destination will be the garden where you will spend time with the flowers. This is the part of you that is the most vibrant. Here, colors dance and the wind sings. You will feel fulfillment because you have reached your goal. You will spend much time here, and when you have completed your journey in Wonderland, you will find yourself back in the ocean of tears, then back in the room with the gilded walls. Open your eyes when you are ready, retrace your steps out of the rabbit hole by blowing out each candle. Open the circle. Thank the quarters and spend some time reflecting on what you have learned about yourself.

Water Magic

Four Seasons of Water Magic

by James Kambos

Water is the most versatile of the elements and can be used in spellcrafting in all of its forms throughout the wheel of the year. In liquid form, it can be used as simply water from the tap or from a lake, river, ocean, and naturally as rain. In its solid state, water can be utilized as snow or ice. And when combined with the element air, water is transformed into vapor, mist, or fog.

Whether it's a day at the beach, making a snowman, or jumping in puddles after a summer storm, most of us have joyful memories of experiences we've had with water. My own love affair with water began as a boy on my grandparents' farm. My first chore each morning was to bring a pail of water in from the well to the kitchen. The water was crystal clear and cool, and the well was a place of mystery for me. It was deep and dark, but not frightening. To me it was like an entrance to a secret realm within the earth. And when I'd drop a coin into it, I could never hear it hit the bottom. Where did it go? Was there a bottom?

Needless to say, that old well sparked my imagination, and so began my interest in the magic of water.

What follows is a collection of magical lore and spells using water combined with the natural energies of each season. They're organized in the natural order of the year, spring through winter. For some of the magical work I've described, you needn't use water in its physical form, instead you'll only need to visualize it.

Water Magic for Spring

Now the streams and rivers begin to flow and spring rains turn the countryside green. The keywords for spring water magic are cleansing, growth, and renewal.

The rains of spring provide us with a chance to cleanse ourselves of any bad habits we've lived with through the winter, and here is one spell to help with that. For this spell, you'll need garden soil and a terra cotta saucer from a flowerpot. Pack the soil into the saucer. Using a twig or your finger, write a few words expressing the negative quality you wish to rid yourself of—it could be something like "quit smoking," or "reduce stress." When rain is predicted, place the saucer outside where it won't be disturbed. As the rain dissolves your words, your habit will begin to diminish. Now you must begin to take steps to rid yourself of the habit you're concerned with.

Spring water magic can also be used to bring growth into your life, and here is an example. Cut some tall grasses or flower stems and bind them with green garden twine; concentrate on growth. If you wish, shape your bundle into a human form, which will honor the Green Man. Take your grass bundle to a stream or river and gently place it at the water's edge. Let the current carry it downstream. Your wish is now being carried into the life force contained in all flowing bodies of water.

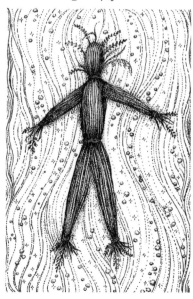

Traditionally, spring was thought to be the perfect time to perform magic involving wells or springs. Wells are considered to be portals to the Otherside and as such, they are frequently used for scrying. To do this, simply relax your mind and gaze into the well. To bring a wish into your life, drop an item symbolizing your wish into the well. This could be a coin for abundance or a seed for fertility. Then walk around the well three times, speak a charm, or think of your desire. Before you leave, if possible, take a sip of water from the well.

If you feel that the flow of positive energy coming into your life is blocked, this meditation performed in springtime will help get things moving again. Visualize a stream in the early spring. See the water, icy and clear trickling over rocks, and smell the air—fresh and earthy, as it can only be in the spring. As you visualize this scene, feel the earth stirring with new life. In your meditation, see yourself walking along the stream until you see a waterfall. Now the water is rushing over boulders. Feel your own energy quickening, and sense your goals being met. Breathe slowly; return to your normal frame of mind. Your energy is now flowing, just like the water you've "seen" during your meditation.

Water Magic for Summer

During summer there is a sense of abundance and energy. Flowers, herbs, and vegetables reach their peak, and on warm afternoons thunderstorms rumble, releasing their power. Water magic during the summer should focus on prosperity and strength, as well as love and pleasure.

To draw prosperity and protection to you and your home, try this water magic spell while fresh herbs are available. You'll need a half cup of fresh basil leaves and about a cup of water. Use rainwater or bottled spring water. Place the basil and water in a saucepan, bring to a boil, and simmer for fifteen minutes. Let this mixture cool, and then strain the water into a clean jar and discard the basil. You can use this magically charged water in prosperity and protection spells. If you can't use it immediately, store this infusion in the refrigerator for up to a week.

If you take a trip to the shore during summer, gather some seashells to aid you later in fertility, love, and prosperity magic. To perform a love spell using seashells and water, try this. Gather some shells you find attractive, especially those colored pink or any containing a hole. Before you perform a love spell, wash your shells in sea salt and water. Then rinse them in bottled rose water, which you can purchase. Dab some of the rose water over your heart and place the shells on your altar. As you proceed with a love spell of your choice, visualize the goddess Aphrodite rising from the sea, being carried by a seashell. Shells are gifts of the sea, respect them and when done store your shells in a special place. You may draw upon their power at anytime.

A summer thunderstorm is a good time to energize any magical tool. As the sky darkens, place any magical tool you wish to charge outside in a safe location, secure it if necessary. Let the rain, thunder and lightning do the work for you. When the storm is over, bring in your tool, and dry it with a clean cloth. Your tool has been charged by the forces of nature and is ready to use.

Water Magic for Autumn

The wheel of the year begins to make its final turn and now we enter the twilight of the year. The spirit world is closer to us now. Autumn water magic includes working with spiritual energies, contacting ancestors, scrying, and harvest blessings.

Since ancient times, it has been believed that spirits of the deceased make their journey to the Otherside by water. So it would be appropriate to use water to contact a deceased loved one. Begin by writing a letter to your loved one, using white paper and black ink. Either in the early morning or at dusk, go to a quiet body of water such as a pond—if it's foggy or misty that's even better. Kneel at the water's edge, fold your letter, and let it float away. If there are any fallen leaves upon the water, you may place your letter on them instead. Your message has been received.

Scrying at this time of year by using water can be very effective. Fill your cauldron or a dark colored bowl with water, drop a silver coin into the water, and gaze at the ripples. Allow your eyes to focus on the coin and begin to gaze at the water. If you wish, perform this ritual after dark outside during a Full Moon. Using the water and the Moon together will aid your psychic powers.

Since colonial times, as the harvest season came to a close, water was used to anoint the last stand of grain to ensure a bountiful crop the following year. You can do this in your own garden. Simply leave one plant standing in your garden. This could be one herb, tomato plant, or a flower. Before a killing frost, sprinkle this plant with water you've blessed. Don't remove this plant until next spring.

Water Magic for Winter

A new cycle of time begins. The cold deepens and water is transformed into its solid states—snow and ice. Winter has been a period of wonder and questioning since first woman and man walked our planet. And why not? To our early ancestors, the appearance of snow and ice must have been magical. In cold climates, snow and ice still create a feeling of magic and mystery. Water magic for winter should deal with transformation, getting rid of negativity, and healing. If you live in warm climates, substitute crushed ice for snow to perform the following rituals.

To transform a difficult situation into a positive one, write the problem on a piece of paper and place it in a bowl. On top place some fresh clean snow and a drop of honey. Let the snow melt. Pour the melted snow down the drain and discard the paper.

To rid yourself of any habit or problem, try this. Write the problem on a piece of paper and rub the paper with cool ashes or soot. Crumple the paper, go outside, and make a snowball with the paper in the center. Place the snowball on the ground. If possible, trace a circle around the snowball using an icicle, crush the snowball with your foot, and then walk away.

Winter water magic doesn't mean you only need to use snow or ice. This is also a good time to take a healing bath. Run a warm bath and use your favorite bubble bath. As the water is running, pour in a quarter cup of orange flower water. Orange flower water is a fragrant water made by distilling water through orange flower petals.

You may purchase bottles of it at Middle Eastern food stores, or at health food stores. The scent of your bath should be heavenly, and the orange fragrance should give you a sense of well-being. Immerse yourself in this healing bath. Feel all tension and stress leaving your body.

~

Our urge to enjoy the wonders and magic of water is as ancient as the human race. Water is always the same, but forever changing. The water you see today in a river will be different tomorrow, because water is always flowing, always moving. And, water magic is ours to enjoy at anytime of the year.

Dreamwork,
Your Secret World

by Mickie Mueller

I learned about the power of the dreamworld very early in life. As an adolescent haunted by nightmares and night terrors, I had to figure out a way to control what was happening in my dreaming mind because I wasn't getting any sleep, and my grades were suffering. I worked hard and learned much from my own sleep exploration and hitting the books. Eventually, I learned to control my dreams, have lucid dreams, and had even helped some friends avoid nightmares. Later on in life, I discovered that I could use the control I had gained over my dreams to work magic, solve problems, and even communicate with otherworldly spirits.

Magical Dream Journaling

The first thing that you need to do if you want to do any kind of dreamwork at all is to start a dream journal. It can be a beautiful journal with fancy pages and a lock on it or a plain spiral notebook. What is of the utmost importance is that you keep it right next to your bed. It should be somewhere that you can grab it easily without having to get up. You'll also need to keep a pen or pencil with it at all times.

Dreams have a way of fading quickly, especially once you get up. Have you ever woken up and had your head full of impressions that seemed really important, only to lose them like petals in the wind once you are out of bed? That's why the dream journal is so important. The first thing you need to do upon waking, while you're still in bed, is to write down any impressions you might have from your dreams—the more detail the better. Sometimes you'll remember a lot, other times it might only be feelings, colors, and smells. Write the date at the top of each entry, so that you can always reference when your dreams occurred. You can find dream dictionaries online, and there are several good books on the topic, so that you can look up what elements of your dreams mean and make sure to write those down as well. Remember, not all interpretations ring true for all people; if one interpretation of a symbol doesn't ring true for you, then search out other meanings. If you watched an upsetting news story or movie the night before and you think that it influenced your dreams, make a note of that too.

Here are a few common themes of dreams and what they mean:

Flying: Freedom and the ability to rise above limitations, successful endeavors

Losing teeth: Fears of loss, losing power, lack of confidence or inability to communicate, or money problems

Being naked in public: If you're embarrassed in the dream, it can reflect a fear of being unprepared for a situation, or being caught off guard. If you're not embarrassed, it represents a free spirit and confidence.

Being chased: Stress and anxiety, as well as trying to avoid facing an issue having to do with someone else or yourself.

Cars: Cars are often symbolic of where we are going in life, are you driving, or a passenger? Is your car driving safely or veering out of control?

Sometimes dreams are merely our brain working to reorganize thoughts, feelings, and other input. When we're dreaming, we're more open to possibilities, the part of our mind that believes in limitations quiets down and allows other parts of our brain to wake up and play. Dreaming is a great place to discover what your psychic mind has learned throughout the day. So if you consistently keep a good dream journal, when something surprising happens, you'll be able to go back and see if you've dreamt it before it happened. Then watch for patterns to develop, what kinds of dreams are prophetic for you, what kinds of dreams are problem solving dreams? You'll learn the secrets of your own mind and how to read them properly by the exercise of a dream journal. This is also a great tool to help you develop your lucid dreaming skills.

Pinch Me, Am I Dreaming?

The act of keeping a dream journal sends a magical message to your brain that dreams are important and that you want to be aware of them and remember them. Once you're used to writing in your dream journal and it's become a habit, you're ready to try lucid dreaming. A lucid dream is a dream in which you're aware that you're dreaming, everything from the moment that you say to yourself, "This is a dream" becomes a lucid dream. Why are lucid dreams useful? If you are doing magical dreamwork, you can do powerful things in your dreams that you can't do in the waking world due to the laws of physics. But what you do in dreamstate can still be directed and sent into the astral in the same way you do it in a magical circle. Anyone can have lucid dreams with some practice. Most people can't do it on the first try, but it's well worth a little time and effort to be able to access all the power and information that your dreaming mind can provide.

Carlos Castaneda first introduced this technique in his book, *The Lessons of Don Juan.* In order to become aware that you're dreaming in the midst of a dream, the first thing you need to do is to consciously teach yourself the difference between dreaming and waking experiences. You may say, "Well, I know when I'm awake!" And that's true—your conscious mind knows when it's awake—what you're teaching your subconscious mind is the difference. That part of your mind doesn't know, that's why a crazy dream seems so real while you're having it. Throughout the day, tell your subconscious mind, "I'm awake right now." It'll feel silly, but do it anyway. Doing something that feels silly catches your subconscious mind's attention.

Now that you've reminded your subconscious what feeling awake is like, get ready for bed. Look down at your hands and study them, telling yourself again, "I'm awake." Now you will send your subconscious a very important message, "When I'm dreaming tonight, I'll remember to look at my hands and I'll know that I'm dreaming." Do this right before you fall asleep. It might take a few tries, but eventually, you'll be dreaming and you'll look at your hands, and they won't look exactly the same as they do when you're awake. Your subconscious mind that you've been teaching to recognize the waking state will realize that you're dreaming. You've done it! Now you can experiment, make something appear out of mid air, shoot lightening out of your hand, and yes, you should be able to fly. This is the first exciting step to being able to perform powerful magic in your dreams. People have done life-changing things while lucid dreaming—overcoming emotional problems and blockages. When in a lucid dream, you can face a difficult issue from the waking world and by conquering it in the dream, you can create powerful change and healing in your life.

What a Nightmare!

Everyone dreams, it's a scientific fact. If you didn't dream, you'd go bonkers. There have been many studies of sleep deprivation and dream deprivation. When subjects were woken up as soon as they started to dream, even though they got to sleep, they became restless, unfocused, and began to hallucinate. We need to dream. Those who think they don't dream, really do, they just don't remember their dreams. In the case of nightmares, that could be a lucky thing. Sometimes nightmares are a warning system, letting us know something is wrong in our life that we need to deal with. They can become too much, however, and rob the dreamer of much needed sleep or leave you feeling horrible all day, and when that happens, you need to take action. Some people have such vivid nightmares that they seem to have been directed by the greatest horror movie directors of our time. I'll share some tools for your magical tool belt to fend off these horrible haunting dreams.

The movie reference I used was a nod to my favorite childhood tool, and the first one I used to get rid of my nightmares. I call it directing technique, here's how it works. First, use the above techniques for lucid dreaming. The key here is to recognize that you're in a dream. It's best if you can use directing technique before things in the dream start to turn really bad. Through your dream journal, you'll begin to see a pattern like, "My nightmares always begin after I see that big stone wall," or something like that. So as soon as you see the big stone wall, you realize that it's a nightmare coming up. At this point, simply yell out something like, "Cut! Cut! People, this is the wrong scene!" You can even produce a movie clapperboard and click it. Don't be shy, because you're the director of this dream. You're Kevin Costner, man, you wrote it, you're the director and the star, and it's your mind, your movie, your dream! So yell at the guy in the monster suit around the corner to get out of the shadows, take that ridiculous low-budget costume off and get back to wardrobe for a costume change, and tell him his part, whatever you want it to be (Ed McMahon with a big check, or whatever you want). Call in the set people and tell them to get rid of that stupid stone wall and the graveyard around the corner, too, and bring in the birthday scenery, or the sunny meadow location, etc. This is a technique that really works; I've used it and taught it to others with great success.

There are also things that you can do in the physical world to help program your mind to reject nightmares in the first place. A stone with a naturally occurring hole is supposed to prevent nightmares when hung on your bedpost. Hanging a dreamcatcher over your bed snags nightmares in its net like structure and the good dreams pass through the hole in the middle. You can make your own, either of a simple star shape, or the traditional web-shaped

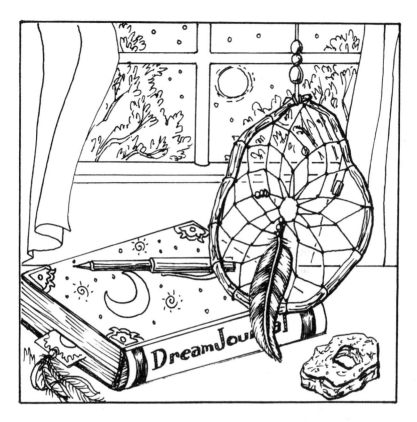

Ojibwe style. It is easy to find instructions for making both on the Internet. If you're not crafty, you can purchase one. Make sure you pass it through sage smoke or some good incense smoke to clear it before you use it. If you begin to have nightmares again, taking the dreamcatcher outside and passing it through sage smoke will destroy any nightmares trapped in its web.

What's on the Program Tonight?

So far, we've explored ways to control dreams that you're already experiencing. What about consciously deciding what you want to dream about? This is a great way to use dreams for problem solving. Once you've begun your journey into dreamwork, you can begin programming your dreams before you go to sleep. Similar to the method for lucid dreaming, you can teach your subconscious mind to dream about a topic that you decide upon. The simplest method for this is as follows. Fill a glass with water and place it by your bedside. As you wave your hand over the water state aloud what you wish to dream of, or state a question you want the answer to. For instance, "I'll dream of the best course of action for my job." Drink the water, and go to sleep. By doing this, you have sent your intention into the water and then made it part of yourself by drinking it, sending it to your subconscious mind. The more you practice, the easier it will become.

You can use this technique to discover solutions to all kinds of problems. Ask questions that need an answer, and gain insight into any situation. Your subconscious mind already has the answers, and programming yourself to dream about it can help you locate those answers.

A Temple of Your Dreams

This is where you get to take it to the next level! By using both the techniques for programming a dream and lucid dreaming, you can use your dream realm to perform rituals and magic. Why would you want to do that? For one thing, you're closer to the astral when you're dreaming. Sending magical energy toward a purpose from the realm of dreams can be a very dramatic experi-

ence. Spellwork focusing on problem solving and self-empowerment can be especially moving and effective when performed in you dream temple. It can also be a sanctuary for your soul in difficult times you can visit and recharge your mind, body, and spirit.

The first step is deciding what your dream temple would look like. It doesn't have to look like a temple per say, it should be simply the best place you can imagine to do magic. It can be Stonehenge, a meadow, a stone palace, or even Lothlorien from *The Lord of the Rings*. It can be a place in the physical world, or a place of pure imagination. No matter what kind of location speaks to you, it should be one that makes you feel safe, comfortable, and magical. If you don't have a physical place in mind, you can sketch it out, or look for elements of your location in magazines and make a scrapbook page. Feel free to include whatever you want to be there: an altar with tools on it, quarter candles, a big cauldron, that ritual sword you've always wanted, a cabinet full of every herb imaginable, whatever you want. Remember, it's your dream temple, and you get to decide. Study the images, fill your mind with every detail, and look it over again before you go to sleep. Then use the looking at your hands method, and program yourself to dream of your dream temple.

You'll have to practice. The more you visit your dream temple, the more real and solid it will become, and the more details will become noticeable. Use your dream temple to meet with spirit guides, recharge your spirit, and perform magic. Cast your circle, and call in the elements and deities the way you normally do, but because this is a dream, these beings may manifest in a more interactive way. Don't be surprised if they show up in a physical form. Raise and channel energy the way you usually do, and send it into the realm of spirit to manifest. You may wish to repeat the ritual on the physical realm as well, although you don't have to.

Working with your dreams can be a positive and fulfilling way to bring new and advanced forms of magic into your practice. It can help you become more self aware, creative, and bring a feeling of magic into your everyday life.

For Further Study

Waggoner, Robert. *Lucid Dreaming: Gateway to the Inner Self.* Needham, MA: Moment Point, 2009.

Lennox, Michael. *Dream Sight: A Dictionary and Guide for Interpreting Any Dream.* Woodbury, MN. Llewellyn Publications, 2011.

Castaneda, Carlos. *The Lessons of Don Juan: A Yaqui Way of Knowledge.* Berkely, CA: University of California Press, 1968.

Spells for the Bathtub

by Calantirniel

When I was starting off in the area of spellwork years ago, I loved gathering tools that helped me focus my conscious mind. I realized early on that this mechanism would allow my subconscious (or superconscious) to do the real work of fully releasing clear intention to Spirit. This, in turn, brought forth nearly instant physical manifestation.

I enjoyed working with representations of the elements: fire, air, water, and earth. I could see that everything is made of these elements, so translating an idea into physical being had to go through this elemental process first. The tools I had collected were candles of all colors for fire, music and incense for air, a beautiful blue bowl for placing water, and a wonderful flat stone from a nearby river for earth. Later, I created a wonderful wand from a tree branch that I loved, and have found that I like using a wand better than an athame. I sometimes used tarot cards to help me tap into the right energies for intention as well.

When I discovered another ritual tool, a cauldron, I instantly saw a connection between it and the universe, with the four elements placed inside, according to a "recipe" of intention. But, what could I use as a cauldron until I could get one? In looking around my home, I didn't see much in the kitchen that worked. However, when I concluded the bathtub would work perfectly, I also realized it had an advantage. I could have the four elements along with my body itself inside of the perceived center of creation! Bathtub spellwork was born!

You can easily adapt any existing spells you may have to include the bathtub. Again, concentrating on having the four elements well-represented is often the key. The bathtub itself may be seen as the universe, or if you like, Cerridwen's Cauldron. It is the "womb" or the vessel in which your spellwork, or "recipe of intention" will take place.

You can still use candles to represent fire. I always use votives in votive holders. You can write or draw symbols on the candle, and oil before lighting, if desired. I only use one candle for safety reasons, and keep it in the inner corner, away from my head. The right votive holder ensures smoke resin will not stick to the tiles. If you are not allowed to burn things or cause smoke in your space, a picture of a roaring fireplace flame or a battery-operated tealight may suffice. Perhaps have some cinnamon, cloves, cayenne, or other warming spice nearby as well.

If music for the air element is desired (soothing music works best), keep your electronics away from the water. If incense or sage smudge is used, you can burn a small amount and snuff it before it gets overwhelming. If smoke is not allowed, try a purifying essential oil like lavender or eucalyptus mixed in a mister with distilled water and a tiny amount of vodka or brandy to preserve it, if needed. A feather can also be used for air and kept on the tub ledge or designated small table by the tub. If you don't have a table, get two inexpen-

sive cement blocks from a home improvement store (the type used for retaining walls), stack them in the driest place near the tub on a towel (to to protect the tub and the floor), and try not to get them wet.

The water element is taken care of when adding hot water to the bathtub. If you create bath salts, the earth element will also be handled. Here's a recipe that's worked for me: one-third cup Epsom salts, one-third cup baking soda, and one-third cup sea salt or table salt. Then after thoroughly mixing: Add ten to twenty drops of favorite essential oil or blend. However, I also like to have my river rock and several crystals that are attuned to my spellwork handy, and I often put them in the water with me.

If you decide to implement tarot cards into your spellwork (a great idea since you can more easily grasp energies to direct toward your final goal), consider having a deck dedicated for spellcasting. And make an effort to protect the cards used from getting wet—even if this means putting each card in a plastic sandwich bag! Smudge with sage or incense after each use before putting away. You can use old CDs instead of mirrors for reflecting or shielding purposes (the hole in the center can inspire an escape route for good energy if desired, similar to how a dreamcatcher is said to work). And if you have a wand or athame, keep it close!

If healing is a part of your work, try adding drops of flower essences to your bathwater as well. You can also prepare a cup of tea with safe herbs that relate to your bathtub spellwork. If you prefer an all-purpose mix, try this mild seven-planetary blend: chamomile (Sun), mallow (Moon), red clover (Mercury), alfalfa (Venus), nettle (Mars), dandelion (Jupiter), and mullein (Saturn). Substitutions can be made if you are aware of the planetary rulers of those herbs. If you usually place herbs into your water when working, consider making a cup of tea and adding the tea to the bath water instead—it makes for fewer plumbing issues, and cleanup is much easier.

Once you are all set, you can cast your directions and any deity energies while seated in the bath water, and bathe in your spell for at least twenty to thirty minutes while feeling how powerful you are, and then funneling this power into your intended creation. You can imagine you are surrounded by white light while visualizing your intentions made manifest. Or, if it makes more sense for your work, feel enveloped in the loving comfortable darkness of the womb and creative potential. If you are doing any banishing work, when draining the water, see everything not needed any more easily draining away with the water.

You may wish to keep a journal of your bathtub spells to see what works and what could be improved or streamlined. And, once you do indeed obtain a cauldron, you may still prefer working in your bathtub. Besides, it is relaxing! I often use my cauldron for my candle-burning instead of the bathtub corner since it is that much safer, and I can fit more candles if I wish! May your bathtub be a source of healing, inspiration, and manifestation for you!

For Further Study

Beyerl, Paul, *The Master Book of Herbalism*, Blaine, WA, Phoenix Publishing Inc., 1984.

Cunningham, Scott, *Cunningham's Encyclopedia of Magical Herbs*, St. Paul, MN, Llewellyn Publications, 1985, 2nd edition 2005.

Cunningham, Scott, *Magical Aromatherapy*, St. Paul, MN, Llewellyn Publications, 1989.

Renée, Janina, *Tarot Spells*, St. Paul, MN, Llewellyn Publications, 1998.

Tyson, Donald, *Portable Magic*, St. Paul, MN, Llewellyn Publications, 2006.

Magical Places

by Suzanne Ress

Many people have had the experience of sensing the energy of a particular house or building. These are often old, well-used homes that seem to want to tell us stories if we are able to listen. Or they might even present us with ghosts or visions, regardless of our desires. Occasionally new homes or buildings are infused with overwhelming and inexplicable sensations—perhaps left over from the people who built them or from the earth they were built upon.

Sometimes the plants and animals living in a particular place have formed a community with a unique energy that sets it apart from the surrounding areas, effectively imparting it with an enchanted air.

Just as individual human beings, animals, and plants generate different energies we can pick up on and respond to, there are certain places that hold and emanate a positive energy especially conducive to magic. Due to physical, spatial, sensual, and other indefinable qualities, these are places where people are easily lulled into a relaxed twilight, or threshold, state of consciousness. It is when you are in such a state that both unexplained and desired magical things are likely to happen, and magical spells can more effectively be worked and begin to take shape.

Thresholds, both natural and manmade, have long been considered to possess magical energy. Traditionally, the most well known magical places are forests, groves, grottoes, caves, crossroads, cemeteries, burial grounds, springs, wells, riverbanks, shorelines, and mountaintops. The one thing all of these magical places have in common is that each of them represents a threshold, or a doorway, which can lead into one's unconscious mind, and to change.

Forests and Groves

Think about it: The forest, typically outside of or surrounding the land space inhabited by human beings, represents unknown territory, and entering into this uncharted space is like entering the natural wild world of your own self. In the forest, human beings are not the dominant species, and we do not make or even fully understand the rules, if there are any. The forest is a seemingly unruly place inhabited by other beings—birds, squirrels, foxes, wolves, owls, bears, wildcats, and possibly elves, ogres, and fairies.

Inside an enchanted forest, you might find a special grove of trees. Although groves are usually situated in a forest, pasture, or field, they can also occasionally be found within human settlements, such as towns or cities. Of all magical places, the magical or sacred grove is the most ancient. This comes from a time way back in our collective history when trees were worshipped, and special groves of a single species of tree were considered powerfully sacred by the many polytheistic or Pagan cultures, including Greeks, Romans, Eastern Europeans, Germans, and Celts, as well as in India, West Africa, and Japan.

Only very recently have studies[1] done by medical scientists revealed that the airborne chemicals released by trees called phytoncides greatly enhance the human immune system by raising the number of white blood cells by as much as fifty percent after two hours of exposure. Modern Japanese city dwellers practice *shin rin yoku,* or "forest bathing," for its health benefits, which include lower heart rate, lower blood pressure, and lower levels of cortisol.

We would do well to find the time to spend a few hours each day, or at least each week, thanking and worshipping trees for the important part they play in the complexly interconnected and dynamic relationship we share with all other living things here on earth. For without them we could not survive! Ancient peoples knew this. Forests and groves are magical places because they truly put us into a more relaxed, concentrated, and healthier state of mind. The more time you spend in a forest or grove, the clearer your inner vision will be, and natural magic will flow easily through your life in surprising and enchanting ways.

The magic, or sacredness, of a grove of trees often directly corresponds to how old the trees are. I recently visited an ancient grove of wild olive trees on the Italian island of Sardinia. The central tree, the oldest and largest of the group, was nearly four thousand years old! This wise old tree, matriarch of the other impressively sized and gnarly trees in the grove, emanated a strong sense of peace and permanence that was impossible not to feel. We walked around and under her huge heavy branches, leaned against her solid trunk, and felt her being and the related fleeting small beings of all the various long dead shepherds, sheep, goats, dogs, mules, wolves, and nomadic humans who had rested thankfully in her shade. I felt the very strong sense of community among this special group of olive trees, and knew that they would outlast us. I certainly would call that a sacred grove, but it was also magical!

When I sit in the much younger birch tree grove near my house, I get a different type of sensation than when among the olive trees, but it is also magical. I like to visit this grove especially on moonlit nights when the whiteness of the trees' trunks makes

---

1. Effect of phytoncide from trees on human natural killer cell function. *International Journal of Immunopathology and Pharmacology.* 2009. Oct-Dec; 22 (4): 951-9.

them glow softly in the dark like spirits. Because of its brightness and light, and the protective, quiet community feeling the trees convey, the birch tree grove seems enchanted. It is in this grove that my friends and I have performed much magic work with excellent results.

Grottoes, Caverns, and Caves

Grottoes and caves represent the womb of the earth, and so, a retreat to one's subconscious. The atmosphere inside grottoes and caverns is especially magical because they are comfortable year-round. These natural shelters, which consistently have a temperatures of about 57 degrees Fahrenheit in both summer and winter, have been well used over the millennia by both humans and animals. With the strange beauty of their interiors, along with the way sounds echo off their inner walls and the way natural sunlight and moonlight enter them at various times of day, when you are lucky enough to be able to make use of them, grottoes, caverns, and caves are extremely potent magical places. They are especially good places for working fertility magic, or communicating with the dead, for they also represent a threshold between the world and the underworld, or afterworld.

Cemeteries and Burial Grounds

Even modern cemeteries can be magical places because they are areas set aside from the hubbub of daily human activity, meant for quiet reflection, and slow, considerate movement. Cemeteries have individual human stories to tell us, but, taken as whole environments, they offer a remarkably peaceful atmosphere where all kinds of magic, but most particularly love magic, can be worked to great effect.

When you are in a cemetery or burial ground, pay special attention to the way natural light, during both day and night, plays upon the landscape and various stone structures. Notice the coolness and heavy permanence of the stone, and the layout of the graves or tombs. Be aware that, although you walk among the dead, cemeteries and burial grounds are created and meant for the living—to make us more aware of death, and hence, of our own aliveness and the life cycle. Once again, these are threshold places, and help us get in touch with our deeper consciousness, putting us into a quiet mind state where magic can happen and flow freely.

Crossroads

Crossroads are interesting magical places, for in order to understand their significance and power, you need to get outside of yourself and imagine looking at them from above, as if you are hovering over them in the air. The most magical crossroads of all are five roads that come together to make a star shape. Admittedly, these are somewhat rare, and if you do find one that is not too heavily trafficked and built up, by all means make use of it.

There is a five-pointed star crossroads near my home here in Italy, made up of unpaved country roads, with an eleventh-century chapel and cemetery on one corner—a very powerful magical place, indeed, for working all kinds of magic.

Simple crossroads, which form a cross, are good places for protective magic.

Always be certain that you can work your spells undisturbed by possibly negative outside influences. To this end, look for very quiet crossroads where few, if any, cars pass, and preferably away from human habitation. Special old or unusually shaped trees, cemeteries, wells, bodies of water, rock formations, or even a statue or monument on one or more of the corners will increase the crossroad's power.

The meeting of three roads in a T or Y shape is also powerful, as these shapes signify the meeting of male and female energies. All crossroads signify, and actually offer, a choice of paths to take, and magic worked at the point where various paths of lines intersect will generate energy that goes in the direction of your chosen path.

Incidentally, crossroads are also the best places to dispose of leftover, used, or finished spellcasting or magically charged objects such as burnt-down candle stubs, used mojo bags, bits of cloth, cords, dried herbs, flowers, berries, and other biodegradable items. You can take these things to a special crossroads at night and bury them, or safely burn them. Any remaining magic powers in them will discharge, becoming available for future use at that same crossroad intersection.

Mountaintops

Mountaintops are where heaven and earth meet, and are typically considered to be highly spiritually charged masculine places. If you happen to be on a mountaintop it would be well worth your while to perform some magical spellworking, particularly for spiritual clarity, or in matters regarding the men in your life.

Riverbanks and Shorelines

Riverbanks and shorelines are prime examples of magical threshold places, for they represent the wavering dividing line between life and death, consciousness and unconsciousness, as well as the convergence of three elements (earth, water, and air).

Since the beginning of time water has been sacred and magical to human beings, for it is the giver of all life, ruled by the Moon. Realizing how much we do not know about how nature works makes our life on earth and our interconnection with all other living things and elements ever more mysterious. Sometimes the best way to understand that which we cannot make logical sense of is to hand it over to our unconscious mind, which, not surprisingly, is represented by water—the life giver.

Riverbanks and shorelines are excellent places to practice magic that involves life changes or transformations, or simply, magic for inner clarity, which can often lead to desired transformations.

Wells and Springs

Wells and springs seem to defy gravity by making water move up and out of the earth, rather than down and in. This in itself is a magical gift, especially since the water they issue forth is usually sweet and fresh. Symbolically, wells and springs are considered to be entrances to mother earth's womb, and so, another threshold.

Wells have long been known as places where wishes are made and granted. Thus, they are also very effective places for magic work, particularly spells involving healing, love, fertility, and money. Spells worked near wells and springs are equally effective whether done in daylight or at night, but because they involve water they should always be worked during the fortnight of the waxing Moon, unless they are diminishing spells (for example, for someone's illness to go into remission, or for unwanted amorous attention to wane).

Take the time to be aware of your natural surroundings and of the energy inherent in all places. Try to notice or seek out the magical places close to you for more effective spell work. Even city dwellers should manage to find at least a small grove of trees in a park or green space, a quiet crossroads, or perhaps a powerful old well hidden in a surprising place.

Sekhmet:
Goddess of Medicine

by Tabitha Bradley

Sekhmet has become an icon for women's spirituality and power in the Southwest over the last twenty years. Since 1993, a temple dedicated to the goddess has stood in the desert outside of Indian Springs, Nevada. The temple, built by Genevieve Vaughan, has been staffed continuously since then by a succession of priestesses whose job it is to maintain the temple and minister to those who come to commune with Sekhmet. The temple welcomes anyone who honors the goddess in all her forms, and is dedicated to Sekhmet to honor a promise the founder made to the goddess while in Egypt.

It was at the Sekhmet Temple that I, a dedicated priestess of the goddess Bast, first really met Sekhmet and got to know a side of this goddess that is extremely important, but rarely discussed.

Like Bast, Sekhmet is considered a dark lady, one of those types that tend to get cast in the "honor at arm's length" category by many Pagans. There is a sizable contingent of people who ignore warnings like that and proceed full bore into learning everything there is to know about dark goddesses like Sekhmet—and it is these people that Sekhmet tends to draw into dedicated service. You will find many people who work with dark gods and goddesses in the mainstream health care industry as well as in alternative medicine and the healing arts. It's from these people that we learn the most about Sekhmet's amazing association with medicine and healing.

Sekhmet, as a goddess, has been popularly associated with her most prominent story, the Eye of Ra, in which Ra charges Sekhmet with the punishment of the people of Egypt, a task she performs with such relish that she has to be drugged with beer-laced blood to stop a wholesale genocide. This is how we get the epithet: "Lady of the Bloodbath," one of the 100 Names of Sekhmet, which anthropologist Robert Masters compiled and is used today by Sekhmet's followers to invoke her presence during ritual and meditation.

Some might think it quite odd that a goddess who is rightly associated with death and distraction, plagues and disease would also have been one of the primary goddesses invoked by doctors in ancient Egypt. However, this is exactly the case. Along with Thoth, the god of physicians, Sekhmet was invoked in the healer's profession as goddess of medicine with very good reason. As a goddess of disease, the ancients reasoned, Sekhmet would then logically understand the workings of disease ,and thus, be able to heal it accordingly. So Sekhmet and Thoth were a doctor's companions when he went to call on the sick, the injured, and the dying.

Medicine in ancient Egypt was extremely advanced for the ancient world. Egyptian physicians led the field for centuries, pioneering advances in medical practices that are still used today. Although their methods might seem strange and barbaric to our modern eyes, when put into perspective during the classical era, it's clear that the Egyptian doctor was one of the most accomplished medical specialists in the world.

Although modern doctors no longer rely on invocations and prayers to gods to help treat their patients, holistic and pagan healers as well as Witches will do exactly this when treating their own and others' physical, emotional, and spiritual disorders.

Sekhmet is a wonderful goddess to invoke when you are ill or injured. She will not turn her back on you, as she has never turned her back on anyone whose request for help was sincere.

Like Bast, her fellow Eye of Ra, Sekhmet is a tough lady to deal with, and like any good physical therapist, may make you hurt so that you can heal correctly. Her answer may be something you don't like at first, but you will later realize was the best thing for you. When you ask for help, you're opening yourself up to Sekhmet's diagnosis, which may in fact, be quite different from your own.

Sekhmet won't be offended if you feel the need to get a second opinion or double-check the answers you have been given, particularly if it seems contradictory to your current course of treatment. (For instance, if you're on a medication and are told to stop taking it.)

She's a good clinician and will cooperate with any other medical, spiritual, or magical caregiver you are working with. Eventually, you will find yourself following the Sekhmet prescription, even if the path to getting there was completely chaotic.

As a goddess of destruction, Sekhmet is particularly good at helping you combat disease—dis-ease and any condition that breaks down your health and well-being. This can include physical as well as mental disorders such as depression and grief. Sekhmet will direct you to those who can help you in the mundane world, while she works with you to heal you in the spiritual.

In cases where a complete return to health is not the goal, or not possible, you can still ask Sekhmet to help with pain management and improving the quality of life of the person who is ill. She can comfort and strengthen those who need it, which is at the core of what she is really about. This is at odds with her frightening reputation that can be intimidating and make her hard to get to know and understand, but once you do, people realize Sekhmet is not a scary lady, she's just intense.

Once you ask for her help, she's not easily (if ever) blown off. She can be strict—not going to kiss your boo-boo and make it all better—goddesses like her rarely behave that way (Bast is very similar). If she's hard on you, it's because you need her to be, not because she likes torturing you. On the contrary, when you need comfort, or when you need the scary questions answered, she is there with a bedside manner that surpasses all others and she will see that you get the help you need.

Of course, no illness or injury is too insignificant to her, no matter how minor you might think it is. She doesn't mind being asked to help your body heal from

a cold or flu, to bless your medications, or to help you recover from surgery. She only asks that you do your part in facilitating the healing process. If that means visiting your doctor for a checkup, taking your prescribed medications, or exercising, then you'd best do it, or she will step in to make sure you're taking proper care of yourself. Recall that she not only works in the magical, but also in the mundane world. If you need to see a doctor, she'll ensure that you will end up in his office.

~

Here's a simple, quiet, and kind of fun spell to bless and charge your medicine, herbal remedies, prescriptions, or assistive equipment (things like canes, braces, crutches, wheelchair, etc.). You can use it as written or use it as a basis for something more specialized. Just keep in mind that it should be easy for you to do if you're ill or injured, so add and subtract ingredients accordingly.

For instance, if you have a cold or allergy, you may want to substitute something for incense.

It is something that you can do in silence if you like, since I'm designing this to be easy to do for people who are injured, ill, or in situations where a spell or ritual might attract unwanted attention (such as a hospital or extended care facility).

Note: This spell is easily adjusted to fit your personal practice or tradition, nothing is a must-do or must-have, besides the red items, which are associated with Sekhmet herself.

Sekhmet Medicine Spell

Supplies:
- Red altar cloth
- The item or items you wish to bless
- A small container of clear water

Optional items:
- 1 Red and 1 white candle
- Figurine or picture of Sekhmet or a lioness
- Incense: cinnamon, dragon's blood, or something mildly astringent like frankincense
- Red stones like jasper, garnet, or fire agate
- Clear quartz crystal
- Flowers or any other items that you like and associate with healing, cleansing, and Sekhmet.

Think about what you ultimately need from the item and develop your goal accordingly. We are cleansing your medicines or related equipment of any residual energies—negative or positive—that may have collected within or around the item when it was made, from where it was stored, or from people who handled it before it came to you. As when we cleanse our magical tools, we are making the item ours before we charge it with a purpose. With medications, you may be charging it to help you manage pain from an illness, or to help your body combat an infection. With an assistive device, you might want to strengthen it and charge it to help you in your recovery process or to become part of your life, helping you to return to more normal activities.

Write this down if you feel you might need a reminder.

Cover your altar or working area with the red cloth and if you have an image of Sekhmet, place it at the top of your working area. Place the red and white candles to either side of Sekhmet, preferably with the red candle in the south or southwest area as this is traditionally associated with her. Set the bowl of water to the west side of the altar (or the direction your tradition associates with the water element or purification). Place your medicine bottles in the middle of the altar, or if the item is larger, like a cane, put it to the side of the working area, where it can be easily reached.

Add your incense, flowers, and any additional items you like, such as crystals and stones. Make the altar as comforting and pretty as you like.

When you're ready to cast the spell, light your candles and incense; get comfortable; ground and center, and meditate a couple of moments on your goal. When you feel focused, invoke Sekhmet with a simple prayer, perhaps chant some or all of the 100 Names list.

Picking up or touching the water in the dish, cleanse it either by visualizing the water being cleared with a pure, white light, or use your own water cleansing ritual. When the water is ready, anoint your item with the water. You may trace a pentacle or an ankh on it if there's enough surface area, or simply touch a little water to it, envisioning the water's energy clearing the item of any impurities.

As you do this, ask Sekhmet to bless your item and empower it to help you achieve your goal.

When you have finished, thank Sekhmet for her help and conclude your spell the way you usually would.

You can add elements to the spell, like tying spell ribbons on your item or using stones and crystals, herbs or magical oils, or you can use it just as written and it will be very effective. If you're unable to have any kind of altar set up at all, you can perform the spell in your head, with just your energy and Sekhmet's help to bless and charge your item. Regardless of how simple or how elaborate the spell is, the important part is asking Sekhmet to help you achieve your wellness goal and your focus on that goal.

~

Enjoy getting to know Sekhmet. She's really a very interesting and complex goddess and I think you will find her a valuable companion in your healing work.

For Further Study

Cannon Reed, Ellen. *Circle of Isis: Ancient Egyptian Magic for Modern Witches*, Franklin Lakes, NJ: Career Press, 2002.

Masters, Robert. *The Goddess Sekhmet: The Way of the Five Bodies.* New York: Amity House, 1988.

The Temple of Goddess Spirituality Dedicated to Sekhmet, Cactus Springs, Nevada: www.sekhmet-temple.com

Vaughan, Genevieve. "My Journey with Sekhmet Goddess of Power and Change," www.sekhmet-temple.com/Herstorypage.htm

Psychic Fitness

by Abby Willowroot

All psychics and spellcasters want to be skilled and powerful. Those doing psychic work of any kind—from beginners to skilled practitioners of the magical arts—have a great deal of control over the growth of their skills, powers, and the effectiveness of their psychic or magical work.

Any great musician, artist, athlete, or dancer acquired their skills by combining their natural gifts with insight, practice, and repetition. It is no different with psychic skills or magical work. To shine, they also require work, practice, attention to detail, and a commitment to excellence.

Some of us have an obvious natural gift for the psychic and magical arts, while some of us have to dig deeper to connect with those gifts within ourselves. It isn't always the most gifted and magical person who is the best at the magical arts, sometimes it is the most devoted, prepared, and balanced practitioners who excel. A person may be a gifted natural runner, but if they only run for fun when they feel like it and never challenge themselves, they will soon be overtaken by runners with less talent, but more passion and commitment. Psychic work and magic are no different. There is no wand, tarot deck, or magical amulets that can give you the powers that must be acquired through practice.

Psychic fitness is a way to ensure that you make the most of your natural gifts through necessary basic training. Practicing psychic fitness brings challenges, pleasures, and surprises—it is a lifelong adventure.

Let's begin this journey toward powerful and effective psychic and magical work with some basics. If you sincerely want to learn to use your gifts well, you will quickly progress with this holistic approach toward mastery of your natural gifts.

Mental Health and Your Overall Well-Being

Practice clearing your mind of mundane things, which creates space for visions and visualizations to form freely and present themselves to you. With a little time and practice, you will master this. It is important to ground and center yourself before beginning any type of psychic or magical work

Breathing is something we all do every moment, but effective breathing is a learned skill, and a basic skill in harnessing your power. Taking several minutes to breathe in deeply and exhale deeply before any psychic or magical work will clear out mental and physical debris, focus your energy, and create a beneficial environment for clear communication with other realms. Practice breathing this way every day until it becomes natural for you, and all your skills will automatically sharpen.

Water is the fluid of life, the sea within that births all mastery. Nothing is more important to psychic work than being properly hydrated. Our bodies are 98 percent water, so it is important to add enough fresh water daily to keep our cells free of toxins and free radicals, which slow down our psychic signals. Drinking eight glasses of water a day, and one large glass of water just before doing psychic or magical work will amplify the signals and result in more powerful magical spells and psychic connections.

Magical foods are a way to maximize your vitality and psychic sharpness. Dark berries, leafy greens, and nuts all carry enormous positive energy. Best eaten raw, these foods are favorites of the faerie folk, since they all occur ready to eat in nature. The enzymes in these foods strengthen the pathways and electrical connections in your brain as well as the rest of your body. Of course, if you have allergies, they should be avoided, since they will only unbalance you. These foods should be eaten slowly, mindfully, and with positive intent at least several days a week, and especially on days when you will be doing psychic and magical work.

Onions, garlic, radishes, and cabbage are also powerful foods for enhancing magical work. They have a long tradition among healers and sages. Adding them to your daily diet will help

improve connections to your natural magical gifts and strengthen your life force.

Fast foods, gooey foods, and heavy food should be avoided on days you will be doing psychic work, as they make you sluggish and slow down the electrical vibrations and psychic connects. Allow at least eight hours between eating these kinds of foods and doing important magical work.

Sugar, best taken in the form of honey, can enhance psychic work if it is taken in moderation an hour before you begin. One spoonful of honey in a glass of water and apple cider vinegar will sharpen your psychic connections significantly. Use one spoon of honey, one-third cup apple cider vinegar, and two-thirds cup of water.

Physical energy is essential for doing anything well. Your mind and your psychic skills will only work well if you have enough energy to power them. That means having enough sleep, exercise, sunshine, healthy foods, and positive thoughts.

Physical exercise is essential to good psychic and magical work. It doesn't have to be a drag, exercise can be dancing, skipping, running, doing cartwheels, swimming, or anything else that moves your muscles. Moving the body clears out the cobwebs, stimulates the immune system, circulates oxygen, carries away debris, and feeds your brain and the psychic pathways. If you really hate any kind of exercise, try twirling around and dancing as if you are a fairy.

Draw strength from the energy around you. We all have experienced being around people, places, and things that either make us feel energized, or sap our energy. Surround yourself as often as you can with things that inspire you and feed your spirit. Avoid people that drag you down, and gravitate toward people that uplift you, it will benefit your psychic work.

Mental clarity and sharpness are essential. It is easy to get sloppy in your thinking; we all do from time to time. Practice keeping your thoughts clear of unnecessary and unrelated mundane distractions. Let inspiration and related thoughts in, but practice staying with a thought all the way through to completion. This can be tricky in our multitasking world, so we all need to practice honing our mental sharpness and clarity on a regular basis. If your magical skills are to flourish, it is essential to be able to focus on a single thought.

Visualization and holding an image is essential to all magical work. This is a skill that improves very quickly when you focus on it. The stronger, the brighter, and the clearer an image is in your mind, the more effective your spells will be. The ability to hold a clear, strong image will also enhance psychic work greatly and will enable you to receive psychic visions and impressions more clearly. NLP (Neuro-Linguistic Programming) is an excellent technique for training you to visualize effectively, Google it.

Focusing energy and directing it well is an art that takes some practice, but it is essential to transmitting your visualizations and spells. The act of gathering energy and focusing it sharply is a part of all magical work. Laughter and enthusiasm amplify energy. The brighter you keep your spirit, the more powerful you will be. Your life force controls all psychic and magical work, and laughter, joy, music, and an expansive spirit feed that essential life force.

Sharpen Your Senses

Psychic expansion comes more easily when we sharpen all our senses. When we integrate our five senses with incoming perceptions more vibrant and easily understood pictures or perceptions are created. If our five senses are dull, the images we receive will be fuzzy and dull, too.

Color communicates many things. You can easily experience pure color by visiting a hardware store and gazing at paint chips. Choose a range of shades in the same color. Look at the subtle differences between the different shades; notice how gradual changes lead to major changes in color, intensity, and luminosity. Look at all the variations in a single color range. Don't rush, take your time and really look and absorb the vibrations of the colors. In a few days, return and do it again with a different color. Continue doing this until you have mentally absorbed all the colors and their subtle distinctions feel familiar.

Touch is another sense that can be expanded easily at a hardware store. Touch a variety of surfaces: hard, soft, squishy, rough, smooth, wood, metal, paper, tile, carpet, cement, screening, and tools. Take time to form an impression of each item you touch, feel what is unique about it, what is unusual, and notice how it makes you feel.

Move on to shapes and get a strong sense of them as well. Touch flat, curved, regular, irregular (like keys), thick, thin, flexible, etc., paying attention to what is unique about each one. Feel moldings, two-by-fours, plywood, fencing, doors, etc., and get a sense of all different kinds of substances, paying attention to their density, their flexibility, and their essence.

Sound is experienced by most people every day, but how much attention do we really pay to the sounds around us? Practice listening, really listening to daily sounds: clocks, wind in the trees, people walking, paper tearing, a car going by, etc. There is no end to the sounds we barely hear. Learning to be mindful of sounds is important, and we should be able to easily identify the sounds that fill our lives. Take half an hour each day and concentrate on really hearing the sounds of life around you.

Smell is the sense most closely linked to memory. Practice smelling things, as almost everything has a scent. Paper, wood, plastic, fire, saltwater, wool, carpet, all have unique smells, as do flowers, trees, and garden soil. The world around you is made up of a variety of smells and aromas. Take some time to learn to identify different smells because they are often clues in psychic visions. Begin with food smells since they are fairly easy to rec-

ognize. Try to identify all the different smells in a food item like soup or baked goods.

Taste is also important and is closely linked to the sense of smell. The basics of taste are salt, sweet, sour, bitter, and umami (umami is the response to salts of glutamic acid). Everything we taste is a combination of these five things in different proportions. Pay attention to what things actually taste like, and see if you can identify when one or another taste is present or absent in a certain food. When we experience panic, we often taste a bitterness in our mouths—that bitterness is adrenalin that fuels our fight or flight reaction to a dangerous situation. Adrenalin bitterness may be present in a psychic vision, as other physical reactions can occur.

Your entire body can be involved in a psychic experience. There may be physical symptoms when viewing an illness, or a sense of exhaustion, or a flush or rush of energy. It is important to be aware that these "reactions" can be let go of once they are recognized. The point is that your entire body and your five senses are often vehicles for the expression and interpretation of psychic experiences. The sharper your awareness of your senses, the better able you will be to interpret psychic events.

Exercise your psychic muscles daily. Nothing improves psychic skills as much as using them regularly. Each day, practice listening to the signals you get from the universe. Pay attention and write down any impressions you get that appear to be "outside your own experience," read tarot daily, etc. You will soon begin to recognize patterns in the things that come to you. Practice sending psychic messages to a friend—the more you practice, the better you will get.

Working with others is a great way to exercise and expand your skills. Your natural gifts are a loan to you from the universe, so use them well and share what you learn with others. Never be afraid to admit when you need help to sharpen these gifts. Learning is something we all have to continue to do if we want to reach our highest potential skill level. Sharing and working with others is an excellent way to both give and receive magical skill.

Never make developing skills into a competition with others. Focusing on being "better than" only calls up a whole host of potentially dangerous, negative emotions that will not serve you well. These negative emotions will only make you weak and interfere with the power of your magical work. Compete with yourself as you work alongside others. Strive for your personal best and you will grow quickly in skill and positive, empowering emotions.

Motives are important. The reasons you do psychic work and use magical skills are very important. If your goal is simple self-interest, your skills will be greatly hampered in their development. Larger purposes always inspire us and fuel the growth of our skills. If you harbor such desires as revenge, one-upsmanship, and other less-than-lovely motives for practicing magic, I suggest you change course now before you do yourself real harm. Magical work born of fear, resentment, envy, or other negative emotions is always reactive, and in the end, such magic is always doomed to failure. Why? Because it has grown out of weakness and petty concerns. Positive magic is always more powerful and more effective because it draws on strength and natural balance.

You are what you do, and you attract what you are. The more you apply these simple suggestions, the more effective your psychic and magical work will be, and the more highly skilled people and positive experiences will be attracted to you. As you find your way, your skills will expand and your options will increase. I wish you many blessings on your own magical journey of exploration and discovery.

Magical Muscle Testing

by Dallas Jennifer Cobb

There are many divination tools to use—pendulums, runes, rods, crystal balls, cards, and others. These tools enable us to magnify and make visible the subtler energies at work in our lives, giving guidance to our inner selves, our magical work, and our practice. While many divination tools rely on using a separate device, muscle testing is an accurate divination tool that uses only your body as a tool for magnifying and making visible the subtle energies at work.

Muscle testing is also called kinesiology, applied kinesiology, and energy testing. Muscle testing is used by many alternative and holistic practitioners such as chiropractors, osteopaths, and physiotherapists. It is also a tool used in the practice of energy medicine. And, muscle testing is simple. Anyone can do it.

What is Muscle Testing

Muscle testing is a technique that taps into your body's electrical system and your muscles to determine if something has a positive or negative effect on you.

The body has its own electrical system. Our brain and nervous system function electrically, sending messages out to the muscles. The field of kinesiology holds that the body is an electrical system that continually communicates with the hundreds of muscles in the body. If something negatively affects your electrical system, it causes a short circuit, and your muscles will be negatively affected and will be unable to hold their strength. Things that affect our electrical system positively have a positive effect on the muscles and enable them to remain strong, balanced, and fully functioning.

If a muscle is electrically in balance, it remains strong. If a muscle is electrically out of balance, it will become weak. When the muscle is asked to perform a task, such as resisting pressure applied against it, it reacts according to its electrical balance—either strong or weakened.

Why Muscle Test?

Like in the old saying "you are what you eat," you are also what you experience and consume in other ways. Muscle testing is a tool that enables us to tune into the subtle signals of body, mind, and soul. These signals tell us what has a positive or negative effect, literally what weakens the systems and what strengthens them.

For example, perhaps you experience symptoms that seem to indicate a food allergy, but can't pinpoint what food or foods are causing the problems. You could use muscle testing to clearly determine which food weakens your system. You wouldn't even have to eat the substance, because just holding it, taking it within your own personal "environment," will be enough for its effect to register on your electrical system. What challenges the balance of your electrical system also challenges the homeostasis of your personal environment, and these positive and negative effects can be discerned through muscle testing.

Muscle testing can be used for much more than determining what foods you are sensitive to. You can test yourself for other substances that cause an allergic reaction, chemicals and additives that produce a negative response, what supplements or remedies your body needs, what healing modalities could support you, and even what (or who) is blocking or disrupting your energy.

Just remember, muscle testing helps answer yes/no questions, and can indicate positive or negative energy and effect. So take care to phrase questions so they can be easily answered. Muscle testing is a dependable decision making tool and can help you get information that your body "knows" versus what you might "think."

Because it doesn't require any special equipment, muscle testing can be taught and used very quickly.

Muscle Testing Methods

There are several methods of muscle testing. Muscle testing can be done on yourself, on a friend or partner, or in a group setting.

Testing Alone

Using your nondominant hand, make a circle by touching the tip of your little finger to the tip of your thumb. Think of this circle as a simple circuit.

Using your dominant hand (the one you write with), make a simply U shape with the index finger and thumb. Place that U gently inside the circle of the nondominant hand.

Now ask yourself a "determining" question phrased so it can be answered with a simple "yes" or "no." A determining question is one that you know the answer to, and the answer is "yes." A good determining question is "Is my name ……..?"

After asking the question, focus on pressing your "circuit" fingers together, tip to tip. At the same time, gently use your dominant hand U to try to separate the "closed" circuit. With a "yes" answer, the circuit fingers should hold, and will not easily separate. They will feel strong and connected.

To become familiar with the feel of the circuit, and its strength, ask yourself a series of questions whose answers are "yes." Sure, you already know the answer, but the point here is to get a feel for what a strong, closed circuit feels like.

When you have a feeling of the closed circuit strength, experiment with a negative response question. You will find that the electrical circuit will feel weaker and it may be easier to separate the finger tips. The muscles have less strength to hold the circuit.

Take some time to experience what a negative response feels like. You may even find that your fingers don't separate, but you are aware of their weakness. Or, there may be a big difference in what a positive response verses a negative response feels like. Get used to knowing that difference.

Before finishing a session, always return to a positive answer question, so that you restore positive energy within your own electrical system. Leave your body with a positive charge so that your cells will vibrate happily, and your synapses will fire effectively.

Take time to learn your own technique, and practice, practice, practice.

With a Friend

Have your friend stand in front of you, facing away from you. Ask your friend to choose an arm, raise it straight out to the side of the body, hold it at shoulder height, and to gently resist your pressure.

Ask a determining question, with a positive answer, such as "Is your name ………?" Use both of your hands to gently push down on the raised arm, which should feel firm and strong. Again, ask several positive determining questions in order to get a feel for what "yes" feels like before you move on to negative determining questions. And, the cardinal rule, always return to a positive answered question before you finish the session to restore the body energy to a positive level.

With a Group

Group muscle testing is a great way to introduce many people to the technique, and secondarily, to help them understand how powerful thoughts are in creating reality.

First, establish an agreement with the group that when you turn your thumbs up they will think good thoughts about the person you are testing, and when you turn your thumbs down, they will think negative thoughts. Don't let the person you are testing know what the agreement is.

Get the person to be tested to stand in front of you, with their back to you, facing the group. Use the thumbs-up or thumbs-down signal to instruct the group what sort of thoughts to project at your test subject. Using the arm technique described above, ask

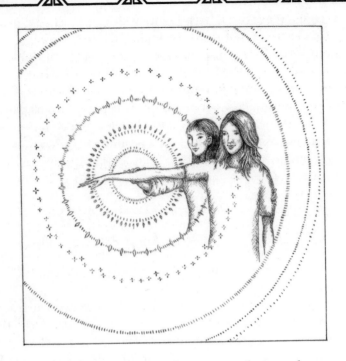

them to resist your pressure, and as you gently press down on the test arm, see the physical effects of thoughts (both negative and positive) upon a person.

Again, don't forget to end the session with lots of positive thoughts flowing to your participant from the group.

Magical Muscle Testing

With a bit of practice, you will develop a feel for your own positive and negative response energy, and you will be better able to interpret the energetic responses of others. As you develop the skill, you will be able to use muscle testing to understand your responses to people, places, and things (especially foods and supplements).

You can use the technique to help family and friends determine what foods, supplements, situations, and people don't agree with them. As I always say, pay attention to how you feel, and with magical muscle testing you have a finite tool for divining how you feel at an energetic level, tapping into your truest self, and magnifying the electrical energy that flows through your body.

Even if you have a hard time believing what you don't see, magical muscle testing will enable you to clearly see the effects of positive and negative energy on your body. Armed with this fabulous tool, you can make concise choices to reduce negativity and accentuate positivity in your life, and that, is magical.

For Further Study

Eden, Donna. *Energy Medicine.* New York: Tarcher/Penguin, 1998.

Levy, Susan, and Carol Lehr. Your Body Can Talk: How to Use Simple Muscle Testing to Learn What Your Body Knows and Needs. Prescott AZ: HOHM Press, 1996.

Thomas, Linnie. *The Encyclopedia of Energy Medicine.* Minneapolis, MN: Fairview Press, 2010.

Alternative Casting Patterns

by Elizabeth Barrette

Pagans customarily cast a circle to contain the energy for a spell or ritual, often invoking the four quarters. This is a simple and versatile casting that works well for most purposes. However, other options exist, depending on how many people you have and what you want to do with the energy you raise.

Energy and Geometry

Sacred geometry plays an important role in energy work. The people in a casting, the points they invoke, and the shape they create will all influence the flow of energy. The number of casters will determine which options are available, although you have some flexibility because you can use fewer people in the casting than the total number of participants. The shapes created by the casters' arms and bodies can then draw on established symbolism for geometric shapes as the energy flows through them.

Note that some castings include specific powers to be invoked at the points, while others are versatile and let you define your own points if you wish. There are castings with open spaces in the middle for charging items, and castings that create a denser weave. Some have different options you can customize according to your needs, such as whether to place your body at the point or the middle of a line. All of these things also affect the energy you direct.

Patterns for Three People

With only three people, you can't cast a circle in the usual way, with a different caller for each of the four quarters. It is

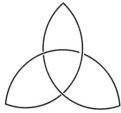

possible to have a single person call all four quarters, but if you're not careful, some of the distinction can get lost. A better approach is to step down to a casting that only needs three people. Note that three is a feminine number, useful in Goddess work, and the triangle shape relates to the element of fire, useful for romance or power raising.

The Three Realms casting comes from Celtic tradition. It invokes the realms of Land, Sea, and Sky. Land corresponds to earth. Sea corresponds to water. Sky corresponds to air. Together they make up the habitats of life, arranged in a triad because the number 3 is sacred in Celtic culture.

For a Three Realms casting, the callers should stand in a triangle. First Land is called, then Sea, then Sky. The invocations often include animals, or occasionally plants that are native to each habitat. For example, "I call on the Realm of Land and the creatures that dwell within: the swift horses of the field and the steady badgers of the burrow..."

The Triquetra casting is inspired by Celtic knotwork. It combines not only the sacred number 3 but also the weaving of energy through a looped pattern instead of a simple circuit. This allows the energy of each person, or point, to remain more distinct.

As before, the participants should stand in a triangle. The first person reaches out with right hand palm-down; the second person takes hold with left hand palm-up. (Most people project energy from the right and receive from the left.) The second person reaches in the same manner to the third person, who then reconnects to the first. The right arms cross over the left arms, creating the knotwork effect. This casting is ideal for Celtic rituals, but also for directing energy to an item or person placed within the center, though with only three people it's a small space.

Patterns for Four People

A square casting with four people symbolizes the stability of earth and the material plane. This makes it good for prosperity or security rituals. Note that four is a masculine number, useful in god work. If you have more than four people,  you can add extras to the square casting, as long as you add them in fours—eight will give you a bigger square, etc. Unlike some of the other castings, the square gives you a lot of room in the middle, without a tangle of arms: a good choice for working with an altar table.

The square can be created in two different ways. For the first, each person holds their arms out straight to the sides, clasping hands to form the corners of the square. This version allows each person's energy to remain more distinct. For the second, each person reaches forward with both arms at an angle to clasp hands; the body forms the corner and the joined arms form the sides. This version allows the energies to merge more at the corners. Both versions can be created with or without a set of principles, such as four seasons.

The Quaternary Knot represents polarities. You need two pairs of people, preferably a male pair and a female pair. You also need to choose two dualities, such as north/south and east/west or Sun/Moon and sky/earth. Pick dualities that relate to your ritual if possible, or ones with a broader focus. This casting facilitates work with balance or with any kind of opposites.

For a Quaternary Knot casting, begin with the callers standing in a cross shape. The first caller reaches across the center to the second caller, with right hand palm-down and left hand palm-up, naming the first half of a duality: "As the golden Sun represents the God..." The second caller takes both hands at once, right hand palm-down and left hand palm-up, naming the second half of the duality: "...so the silver Moon represents the Goddess." To make the weave, the third caller reaches across the loop, passing right hand palm-down above the joined arms and left hand palm-up below the joined arms, naming the first half of a duality—"As above, in the sky..." The fourth caller then grasps both hands at once, passing right hand palm-down above the joined arms and left hand palm-up below the joined arms, naming the second half of a duality: "...so below, on the earth." This creates a dense weave, using the center as a pivot rather than a receptacle. For best results, the rest of the ritual should be designed to match this approach, so that each pair continues to work together.

Patterns for Five People

With five people you can create a pentagon or a pentacle

pattern. In numerology, five is the number of expansion, opportunity, and mystical vision. These patterns are good for many types of magical work, but especially divination or other psychic practices.

The Eastern Five Elements casting involves the magical elements as framed in Asian culture: fire, earth, wood, water, and metal. This casting therefore suits any kind of Asian ritual or magic. It's also heavy on material aspects (Earth, Wood, and Metal) but missing a direct correlation to Air. This gives the pattern a lot of grounding energy.

For the Eastern Five Elements casting, begin with people standing in a loose pentagon. Call the elements one at a time, going around the outside of the pentagon. In positive or summoning work, use the constructive cycle of elements: water, wood, fire, earth, metal. In negative or banishing work, use the destructive cycle of elements: water, fire, metal, wood, earth. Choose correspondences for the invocations that relate to the topic of your spell or ritual. For instance, you might invoke water like this: "I welcome the conservative power of water, which rules over the dormant season in winter, carried hence by the sacred black tortoise." Each caller should then hold out a hand to the next caller, who takes it and invokes their own element, and so on around the pentagon.

The pentacle casting weaves together five people in a knotwork pattern. This is another casting that works well with an extra person or object contained in the center. It is well suited to protective or defensive magic due to the geometric symbolism of the pentacle. This can be done with or without a set of five principles to be invoked. Also, if you have a bunch of extra people, you can actually make a second, circular casting outside the pentacle weave.

For the pentacle casting, begin with the participants standing in a loose pentagon. Imagine numbering them one through five, beginning at the top point. This casting "draws" the pentacle with people's arms, rather than going around the outside of the pentagon in numeric order. If you're invoking principles, such as the Western Elements (earth, air, fire, water, spirit) then call those as part of the weave. Caller 1 reaches to caller 4, right hand palm-down, with an invocation such as, "Earth to Air." Caller 4 takes hold of caller 1 with left hand palm-up. Then caller 4 reaches to caller 2, right hand palm-down, saying, "Air to Fire." Caller 2 takes hold of caller 4 with left hand palm-up. Then caller 2 reaches to caller 5, right hand palm-down, saying, "Fire to Water." Caller 5 takes hold of caller 2 with left hand palm-up (passing that left arm under caller 1's right arm). Then caller 5 reaches to caller 3, right hand palm-down (passing that right arm over caller 4's left arm), saying, "Water to Spirit." Caller 3 takes hold of caller 5 with left hand palm-up (passing that left arm under caller 4's right arm). Caller 3 reaches to caller 1, right hand palm-down (passing that right arm over caller 2's left arm), saying, "Spirit to Earth." Finally, caller 1 takes hold of caller 3 with left hand palm-up (passing that left arm under caller 2's right arm), which completes the weave.

Patterns for Six People

Six people can create a variety of hexagon or hexagram figures. In numerology, the number six stands for nurturing, intuition, and community. These castings are useful for family or coven work, and also for healing or regrowth.

The hexagon casting may be produced in two different ways. First, each person may hold out both arms in a straight line, clasping hands to form the points of the hexagon. This  allows the personal energy to stay individual. Alternatively, each person may hold out both arms at an angle, clasping hands to form the straight sides of the hexagon, with the body forming the point. This tends to merge the energies more. Both of these approaches form a large, open space, which is helpful around an altar table or even a small fire pit. Because the hexagon also appears in honeycombs, this shape is beneficial in rituals that relate to bees or industrious work.

The Magical Hexagram casting creates a six-pointed star from a single woven line. Also called the Wizard's Hexagram, this geometric shape is used in enchantment, summoning, protection, and other magical workings. Note that it has bilateral symmetry both vertically and horizontally, but not full radial symmetry like the other patterns. Instead it has a tight cluster of four points at the middle with the top and bottom points separated more widely. It also lacks the central gap common to several other designs. This creates a very snug weave of energy, along with two "teams" of callers—the middle four and the outer two. You can use this to distinguish groups of people for other activities in the ritual after you finish the casting.

For the Magical Hexagram casting, begin with the callers in an oval. Starting at the top, number the callers 1 through 6. This one is trickier because it doesn't maintain identical hand positions or right-to-left grasps. Caller 1 reaches with right hand palm-down to caller 5. Caller 5 takes hold of caller 1, left hand palm-up. Caller 5 reaches with right hand sideways to caller 2. Caller 2 takes hold of caller 5, right hand sideways, forming a handshake. Caller 2 reaches with left hand palm-up to caller 4. Caller 4 takes hold of caller 2, right hand palm-down. Caller 4 reaches with left hand palm-up to caller 6 (passing that left arm under caller 5's right arm). Caller 6 takes hold of caller 4, right hand palm-down (passing that right arm above caller 5's left arm). Caller 6 reaches with left hand sideways to caller 3 (passing that left arm under caller 1's right arm). Caller 3 takes hold of caller 6, left hand sideways (passing that left arm under caller 4's right arm), forming a handshake above the right handshake of caller 5 and caller 2. Caller 3 reaches with right hand palm-down to caller 1 (passing that right arm over cCaller 2's left arm). Caller 1 takes hold of caller 3, left hand palm-up (passing that left arm under caller 2's right arm), thus closing the weave.

Conclusions

Now that you've seen examples of different castings for magical/sacred space, consider trying a few of them to discover which ones you like. It's easier to start with the simple shapes before trying the weaves, and work through the Triquetra,

Woven Cross, and Pentacle before attempting the Magical Hexagram. Once your coven learns which patterns work, then you can choose a casting that suits your ritual, rather than always casting the same basic circle.

For Further Study

Dominguez, Ivo. *Castings: The Creation Of Sacred Space.* Georgetown, DE: SapFire Productions, 1996.

Edwards, Ian. "Casting an Effective Sphere." Bella Online. www.bellaonline.org/articles/art65841.asp (accessed August 19, 2010).

K, Amber and Azrael Arynn K. *RitualCraft: Creating Rites for Transformation and Celebration.* Woodbury, MN: Llewellyn Publications, 2006.

Venefica, Avia. "Celtic Knots and Celtic Knots Meaning." What's Your Sign? www.whats-your-sign.com/celtic-knots.html. (accessed August 19, 2010).

Zell-Ravenheart, Oberon and Morning Glory Zell-Ravenheart. *Creating Circles & Ceremonies: Rituals for All Seasons And Reasons.* Pompton Plains, NJ: New Page Books, 2006.

The Magic of Your Cup

by Janina Renée

The cup is one of the most basic magical implements, and many of us enjoy choosing an elegant or novel cup to suit our personalities, for ritual work and magic. Because the cup is such a beautiful and versatile magical tool, we can also do some creative ritual working with different types of cups, and different arrangements of cups when we want to engage the emotional and spiritual qualities of elemental water. Working with the receptive, unifying qualities of water and cups also suggests the Cups cards of the tarot deck, which in turn suggests possibilities for little rites and spells inspired by those cards. The following are some tarot-inspired exercises that you can do when you have some of those cards come up in a reading—or just because it's pleasurable to work with their symbolism.

Ace of Cups

The Ace of Cups typically features a single, ornate cup, but whether fancy or simple, a single cup can be an object to meditation upon.

Cup of Blessing: We all have to drink, to take in fluid, and we have to do it throughout the day. For many of us, a cup of coffee, tea, or what-have-you taken at a certain time each day, in a certain place, and often with a certain cup is a ritual to look forward to. So, as long as you're going to be sitting down with a hot mug of cheer or a cold glass of refreshment, why not dedicate it as a special purpose ritual? For example, you might fill your cup with something good, then gaze at it for a moment, reflecting on its quality of fullness and what it means to develop fullness of spirit. Then, drink your beverage while mentally repeating affirmations about the sort of good energies you want to take inside you, including such spiritually nurturing Ace of Cups qualities as comfort, contentment, ebullience, open-heartedness, and spiritual healing. With every sip, you could think, "As I empty this cup, I fill my being with blessings."

Cup of Emptiness: If you have drawn the Ace of Cups reversed, or if you feel emotionally overwhelmed, try exploring

the sensation of emptiness. In Asian philosophy, this is a desirable state, though in Western life, we tend to be uncomfortable with emptiness, and fill our lives with mental and emotional clutter in order to avoid it. There are many ways of cultivating emptiness, but one technique you might try is to sit holding an empty cup, while you gradually empty your mind. (Or, you could start with a full cup of water, which you slowly empty into a basin.) When you are able to achieve a degree of calm and hold your mind empty, even if only for a few seconds, you can discover how peaceful it feels.

Two of Cups

The Twos concern our relationship with others, and the Two of Cups is especially concerned with meeting the emotional needs of loved ones.

Vessels of Communication: For symbolic as well as physical reasons, including the fact that our bodies are primarily made up of water, water is "the medium of emotional communication," according to *Slavic Sorcery: Shamanic Journey of Initiation* by Kenneth Johnson, and can be used to send blessings to loved ones. For example, if you are concerned about someone's well-being, you can fill a cup with water or other fluid, then utter a prayer or other blessing words over it (with your breath vibrating across the water). You can also visualize your loved one's image in the water, imaging him or her in a state of perfect health and happiness. It is all the better if you can use your loved one's favorite cup for this purpose.

Vessels of Healing: For purposes of healing, the body imagery is redoubled by the fact that containers have physical body symbolism, as cups have lips and ears (in Greece and Poland, cup handles are called "ears"), and bottles have necks, mouths, and lips. To promote healing wishes, you could store medicinal herbs in a bottle or brew a cup of herbal tea, while thinking about the cup or bottle as your loved one's body and visualizing the healing factors going to work. (Of course, you can also do this for yourself.)

Three of Cups

The Three of Cups can stand for creativity, community, and celebration, which suggests finding creative ways to come together in a community of celebration.

Calling the Graces: The three maidens featured in many illustrations of this card relate to the Three Graces. (Actually, different regions honored different numbers of Graces, with different names, but the trio are the best known.) The mystery cult of the Graces was very ancient, and in some places, such as at the Acropolis, it was conducted with secret rites. People sought the Graces' blessings not just for artistic endeavors and social celebrations, but in all areas of life. (For example, when young Athenian men entered military service, they took an oath by the Graces as they received their swords and shields.) Even the gods poured libations for the Graces and called on them to inspire their work, whether it was Athena's crafts or statesmanship, Aphrodite's lovemaking, or Hermes's trickery or words of persuasion. If you are starting an art project or any other sort of enterprise, you could invite the Graces into your work by setting out three elegant goblets filled with fine wine or other liquid. (An altar arrangement to honor the Graces could feature shining, beautiful gemstones, ornaments, and other things that reflect your desire to create beauty and harmony.) Toast the Graces with the three cups, incanting their names "Aglaiea! Thaleia! Euphrosyne!" (which forms the mantra, "Radiant Overflowing Delight"), and then pour the cups as libations or set the cups out as altar offerings. Better yet—invite your two most creative friends over to help you with the libations, (if they can bring their own favorite cups, this adds to the symbolism); afterward, you can exchange creative ideas over a celebratory meal, finished off with a fancifully decorated cake.

Four of Cups

The Four of Cups sometimes denotes phases when your life may seem secure, but emotionally flat. When this card is accompanied by cards of frustration, you may feel that you are locked into a situation where you are unable to change your circumstances (at least not quickly).

Blessing Ways: Something that you can always do, even when you can't do anything else, is perform gestures of blessing. One way to do this is to extend Lovingkindness to the four directions by turning to the east and reciting, "I greet the beings of the east. May all beings find happiness!" while projecting a mind suffused with Lovingkindness. Proceed with the other three directions. You could also salute the quarters with a libation cup.

House Blessing: Because the Fours often pertain to one's house and home life, you could direct the Lovingkindness meditation above toward the four quarters of your house and land— for example, saying or thinking, "As I salute the eastern quarter, I greet the spirits of my house and land. May we live and thrive in harmony!" To extend the symbolism, you could set out a water-filled offering cup in each quadrant of your house or garden (picking out cups that suggest the colors and qualities of the different quarters). For an additional ritual activity, perhaps as part of a new house dedication, you could adapt the old Netherlands practice of burying a pot in an important location to attract luck to the house—bury four cups or pots, which can be filled with potpourri with luck-attracting ingredients (such as cinnamon, bergamot, allspice, bay, ginger, lemon, or orange) at the corners of your house.

Five of Cups

Because the Fives can denote the loss that comes with risk and change, Five of Cups illustrations often portray a scene of regret. However, negative responses can be mitigated by learning to accept and adapt.

Ritual for Regrets: While we all know that it is a waste of time to dwell on recriminations and regrets, it can be very difficult to stop obsessing about them. To help accept the wisdom of the old adage that "there is no use crying over spilt milk," make a libation of milk at a spot that is associated with your personal loss. If this is not possible, you can just go outdoors and perform this action as a general offering to the forces that be, by saying:

> *I spill this milk*
> *as an offering to the Past,*
> *as an offering to the Present,*
> *as an offering to the Future,*
> *as an offering to Wisdom,*
> *and as an offering to the Universe.*
> *here is no use crying over spilt milk,*
> *so let this libation be a blessing*
> *to all of the Living.*

You could play up the tarot symbolism by using five libation cups, one for each statement of offering.

Six of Cups

The Sixes represent times when things are going fairly smoothly. In the case of the Six of Cups, this is a good time to look back on childhood pleasures, which is why this card often shows a scene of children in a garden.

Child Blessing: To engage this card's image of an idealized childhood, you could find a miniature tea service with six cups and give it to a child you know, or you could arrange a tea party for the important children in your life (with delicacies including finger sandwiches and miniature cupcakes), and also provide settings for their dolls and teddy bears. Of course, there's no reason

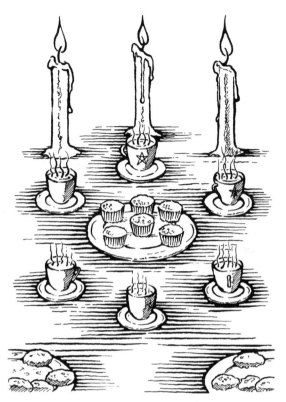

you can't also do these things for your inner child of the past, or for your friends' inner children, or as a way of reconnecting with childhood friends.

Seven of Cups

The visionary, forward-looking quality of the Sevens working on the fluid, emotional nature of the Cups sometimes evokes a multiplicity of dreams and fantasies.

Divining Choices: If the Seven of Cups indicates that your ability to focus on a goal is complicated by too many choices, you could try a little divination—identify seven alternatives and write them on slips of paper. Then roll them up, and have a friend put each in a separate cup (or under an overturned cup), while you are not looking. Then, pick up the cup you are most drawn to, and consider whatever alternative is suggested as a potential course of action.

Delusions: If you are concerned that you have been chasing illusions, you could make a carnie game of it by shattering them: name seven delusions that you want to be rid of, write them on slips of paper, roll or fold them, and then put them into seven old, cracked, cups, bowls, or other vessels. Set them on a fence or other high place, and throw rocks or balls at them until you have broken them or knocked them all over.

Eight of Cups

The Eights are about organized patterns of behavior, but sometimes the Eight of Cups can indicate a problem with certain habits of mind or habits of emotion.

Changing Patterns: When you feel locked into an unrewarding emotional situation or overall life situation, you could try making an arrangement of eight cups, and then daily change the arrangement, which makes a statement that you can change your patterns. You could use different shapes, sizes, and colors of cups, and then also change the individual cups to affirm that you can bring variety into your life. You can even move some of the cups outside of the original grouping, or add or subtract cups to change the number as a way of symbolically changing your reality.

Nine of Cups

In magical numerology, Nine is the number of self-replication. Combined with the Cups, this can denote a rich emotional life, which is why the Nine of Cups is often interpreted as wishes fulfilled.

Wishing Rite: To boost the power of your wishes, inscribe nine candles with hearts and put them in votive cups. Then write different wishes on nine slips of paper, put them under the candles, and recite:

Nine cups, nine hearts, nine candles.
By the power of $9 \times 9 \times 9$,
my wishes are granted,
and happiness multiplied!

Ten of Cups

Ten is the number of completion, as well as the start of a new cycle, which is why an illustration of a happy family is often used to portray the emotional fulfillment suggested by the Ten of Cups.

Family Harmony: You can start some family rituals inspired by the Ten of Cups. For example, if you have the wall space, mount a shelf or rack to hold a cup for each member of your family. (It is not necessary to have exactly 10 cups.) Here, it is important that each person choose a favorite mug or cup that will represent him or her—so don't force a selection based on what looks good with your decor. The daily sight of this shelf or rack is a visual affirmation of both unity and diversity, and the regular use of the cups keeps it energized. Sometimes you could insert a loving message into each cup, and for special occasions, you could put little presents or treats in the cups. When a family member is absent, you could burn a candle in the cup as a wish for his or her well-being, or simply kiss the cup to convey a blessing. Also, an absent person's cup could be filled with whatever the rest of you are drinking, whether you are having a family breakfast, dinner, nightcap, or some kind of get-together, and then later poured as a libation to the living universe with a wish for that person's safety and happiness. Friends who regularly get together at a certain place could do something similar.

For Further Study

Johnson, Kenneth. *Slavic Sorcery: Shamanic Journey of Initiation.* St. Paul: Llewellyn, 1998. p. 2, (citing Vadim Polyakov).

A DIY Guide for Healthy and Natural Living

Spice up your favorite barbeque dishes. Chase away illness with delicious soup. There are hundreds of ways to benefit from nature's most versatile plants inside *Llewellyn's 2012 Herbal Almanac*.

Featuring thirty articles, this treasury of innovative herbal ideas spans five categories: gardening, cooking, crafts, health/beauty, and myth/lore. In this edition, you'll discover how to keep bees and make herbal honey, put together an autumn luck bag, whip up Presto Pesto Pasta and other quick meals, open your energy, create stunning crafts with sunflowers, control pests in your garden, and much more.

From the carnivorous bog violet to innovative urban gardening to nasturtium's role in myth and literature, this practical almanac is your gateway to the herbal kingdom.

LLEWELLYN'S 2012 HERBAL ALMANAC
312 pp. • 5¼ × 8
ISBN 978-0-7387-1205-5 • U.S. $10.99 Can. $12.50
To order call 1-877-NEW-WRLD
or visit www.llewellyn.com

Shadowscapes Tarot

Renowned fantasy artist Stephanie Pui-Mun Law has created a hypnotic world of colorful dragons, armored knights, looming castles, and willowy fairies dancing on air—a world of imagination and dreams.

Lovingly crafted over six years, this long-awaited deck will delight all tarot enthusiasts with its wondrous blend of fairy tales, myth, and folklore from diverse cultures around the world. Featuring breathtaking watercolor artwork that fuses Asian, Celtic, and fantasy elements within the Rider-Waite structure, each exquisitely wrought card draws upon universally recognized symbols and imagery. A companion guide also presents evocative stories and insightful interpretations for each card.